Documents in Modern History

The American Civil Rights Movement

A documentary history

Edited by
Robert P. Green, Jr.
and Harold E. Cheatham

Manchester University Press

Published by Manchester University Press
Altrincham Street, Manchester M1 7JA, UK
www.manchesteruniversitypress.co.uk

British Library Cataloguing-in-Publication Data is available

Library of Congress Cataloging-in-Publication Data is available

ISBN 978 0 7190 7013 6 paperback

First published by Manchester University Press in 2009

First reprinted 2014

Printed by Lightning Source

To Martha Lancaster Green and V. Arlene Cheatham

Contents

List of illustrations   *page* ix
Acknowledgments   xi
List of abbreviations   xvi
Introduction   1

1   'Nobody knows the trouble I've seen': dimensions of Jim
    Crow   3

2   'Walk together children': elements of resistance   24

3   'We are soldiers in the army': emergence of the Movement   49

4   'I'm a rollin': the Movement gains momentum   78

5   'Up above my head': Albany to the Civil Rights Act
    of 1964   102

6   'I shall not be moved': Freedom Summer, Selma, and
    the Voting Rights Act of 1965   126

7   'We'll soon be free': Northern efforts, Black Power, legal
    endorsements   148

8   'Oh, freedom': contemporary expressions   183

Chronology   211
Guide to further reading   215
Index   219

List of illustrations

1 Sandy Run Store. The ugliness of Jim Crow was not
  hidden. Cecil J. Williams   *page* 4
2 Racial separation ranged from water fountains to
  cemeteries. Elliott Erwin/Magnum Photos   17
3 Lynching: the ultimate terrorist tactic. AP IMAGES   20
4 Septima Clark and Rosa Parks at the Highlander Folk
  Center. Highlander Folk Center   41
5 Congregants sing 'We shall overcome' at a mass meeting.
  Leonard Freed/Magnum Photos   52
6 Elizabeth Eckford braves hateful Whites outside Central
  High. Courtesy of Arkansas Democrat-Gazette   62
7 Student activists stage a sit-in at Woolworth's in Atlanta.
  AP IMAGES/Horace Cort   86
8 Freedom Riders' bus bombed outside Anniston, Alabama,
  May 14, 1961. Copyright, The Birmingham News, 2006.
  All rights reserved. Reprinted with permission   93
9 Charles Sherrod canvasses outside Albany, Georgia.
  Danny Lyon/Magnum Photos   108
10 Police brutality in Birmingham contributed to national
  support for civil rights. AP IMAGES/Bill Hudson   116
11 FBI flyer: Goodman, Chaney, and Schwerner were
  murdered in Mississippi in June, 1964. Courtesy of
  the FBI   132
12 Bloody Sunday at the Edmund Pettus Bridge, Selma.
  Library of Congress, Washington, DC   139
13 The Selma to Montgomery voting rights march.
  Courtesy of the Estate of James Karales   142

14 Malcolm X addresses a rally in Harlem. AP IMAGES   165

15 Stokely Carmichael addresses a rally in Berkeley, California. AP IMAGES   167

Acknowledgments

As with any endeavor such as this, many people played a role. We extend our thanks to Lawrence R. Allen, Dean of the College of Health, Education, and Human Development at Clemson University; Michael J. Padilla, Director of the Eugene T. Moore School of Education; and William R. Fisk, Chair of Teacher Education, for various forms of administrative support. Student assistants played key roles throughout the project, and for their efforts on our behalf we thank Lisa Richberg, Yashica Jenkins, Alison Little, and, especially, Whitney Welcome. Whitney served as the 'right hand' of Pamela Ulosevich, who orchestrated, organized, and managed permissions, editing, correspondence, and a myriad of other chores, and without whom we would truly have floundered. To Pamela we extend most sincere thanks. Thanks also to graduate student Amy Montalbano, who assisted during the final stages of the project.

Among colleagues, we especially appreciate the support and advice of Suzanne N. Rosenblith, who reacted to early drafts of the manuscript; University Librarian Priscilla G. Munson, who is always willing to help in whatever way she can, including finding obscure documents; and Thomas G. Poole and James B. Stewart, both at Pennsylvania State University, for timely advice on resources.

Among our colleagues in the United Kingdom, we extend special thanks to series editor Harry Bennett, who suggested the project and provided feedback during the process. Emma Brennan and the staff at MUP were patient, helpful, and supportive as we brought this project to conclusion.

On the personal level, Bob Green notes that it has been a special pleasure to work with his mentor, friend, and former boss, Harold E.

Cheatham, Dean Emeritus of the College of Health, Education, and Human Development at Clemson. Harold brought significant skills to the project and, more important, personal experience with – and insight into – the issues of race and civil rights explored herein. And Harold notes that Bob Green both flattered and honored him with his invitation to join in the project. 'His openness and confidence in me provided an affirmation that I succeeded in being the "boss" whom I envision. Bob also extended the horizon of my life as an academic.'

Finally, our deepest gratitude goes to our most thorough critics and unselfish supporters, our respective life partners, Martha Lancaster Green and V. Arlene Cheatham, to whom we dedicate this volume.

The editors and publisher gratefully acknowledge permission for the use of the following material:

1.3: Copyright © 1941 Richard Wright. Reprinted by permission of John Hawkins Associates, Inc.

1.4 and 1.5: © 2001 by the Center for Documentary Studies for the Behind the Veil Project. These excerpts are taken from *Remembering Jim Crow: African Americans Tell about Life in the Segregated South* edited by William H. Chafe, Raymond Gavins, and Robert Korstad with Paul Ortiz, Robert Parrish, Jennifer Ritterhouse, Keisha Roberts, and Nicole Waligora-Davis. Reprinted with the permission of The New Press. www.thenewpress.com.

1.6: Clark Foreman Papers, Cambridge, Mass., by permission of Shelagh Foreman.

1.7: From *Notes of a Native Son* by James Baldwin Copyright © 1955, renewed 1983, by James Baldwin. Reprinted by permission of Beacon Press, Boston.

2.1, 2.6, 5.2, 6.1, 6.2: 'Joseph Lowery,' 'James Farmer,' 'Laurie Pritchett,' 'Lawrence Guyot,' and 'Dave Dennis' from *My Soul Is Rested* by Howell Raines, copyright © 1977 by Howell Raines. Used by permission of G. P. Putnam's Sons, a division of Penguin Group (USA) Inc.

2.2, 3.12: Reprinted by permission of the University of Tennessee Press.

Acknowledgments

2.3: Reprinted by permission of the A. Philip Randolph Institute.

2.5, 3.15, 4.1: From *Time on Two Crosses; The Collected Writings of Bayard Rustin*, edited by Devon W. Carbado and Donald Weise. Published by Cleis Press of San Francisco, 2003.

2.7: Reprinted by permission of Africa World Press, Inc. and The Red Sea Press, Inc., Trenton, NJ, www.africaworldpressbooks.com.

2.12: Reprinted by permission of *Louisiana Weekly*, Renette Dejoie Hall, Executive Editor, New Orleans, La.

3.2: *Prejudice and Your Child* ©1988 by Kenneth B. Clark and reprinted by permission of Wesleyan University Press.

3.8, 3.10: Daisy Bates, excerpts from *The Long Shadow of Little Rock: A Memoir*. Copyright © 1986 by Daisy Bates. Reprinted with the permission of the University of Arkansas Press, www.uapress.com.

3.17: Reprinted by permission of *The Journal of Negro Education*.

4.2, 5.3, 5.6: From *Voices of Freedom* by Henry Hampton and Steve Fayer, copyright © 1990 by Blackside, Inc. Used by Permission of Bantam Books, a division of Random House, Inc.

4.3, 4.8: Abridged from *Walking with the Wind: A Memoir of the Movement* by John Lewis with Michael D'Orso. Copyright © 1998 by John Lewis. Used by permission of Simon & Schuster Adult Publishing Group.

4.4: Reprinted by permission of Rev. James Lawson.

4.5: Reprinted by permission of The Estate of Ella J. Baker by Dr. Carolyn Brockington.

4.10: Reprinted by permission of the Robert F. Williams Memorial Fund.

5.1: Reprinted by permission of University of Washington Press.

5.8: Alabama Department of Archives and History, Montgomery, Ala.

6.3, 6.4, 6.5: Excerpts from *Letters from Mississippi*, edited by Elizabeth Sutherland Martinez. Original edition copyright © 1965 and renewed 1993 by Elizabeth Sutherland Martinez. New edition copyright © 2002 by Elizabeth Sutherland Martinez. Reprinted with permission of Zephyr Press, www.zephyrpress.org.

6.6: Used by permission of Arybie Rose, Fannie Lou Hamer Living Memorial Charitable Trust Fund and the Hamer Family.

7.4: Reprinted with the permission of Simon & Schuster Adult Publishing Group, from *Institutional Racism in America*, edited by Lois L. Knowles and Kenneth Prewitt. Copyright © 1969 by Prentice Hall, Inc. All rights reserved.

7.5: From *Alternatives to Despair* by Leon H. Sullivan (Valley Forge, Pa.: Judson Press, 1972), pp. 88–102. Reprinted by permission of the publisher. 1–800–4–JUDSON. www.judsonpress.com.

7.7: Copyright©1971 by Merlin House,Inc./Seaver Books.Reprinted from the *The End of White World Supremacy: Four Speeches by Malcolm X*, edited by Imam Benjamin Karim. Published by Seaver Books, New York, New York.

7.8: From *Black Power: The Politics of Liberation in America* by Stokely Carmichael and Charles Hamilton, copyright © 1967 by Stokely Carmichael and Charles Hamilton. Used by permission of Random House, Inc.

7.9: From *Think Black*, copyright 1969, by Haki R. Madhubuti, reprinted by permission of Haki R. Madhubuti, publisher of Third World Press Inc., Chicago, Illinois.

7.10: 'Soul Food' (pp. 101–104) from *Home: Social Essays* by Leroi Jones, Copyright © 1963, 1966 by Leroi Jones. Reprinted by permission of HarperColllins Publishers, William Morrow; in UK and Commonwealth, reprinted by permission of SLL/Sterling Lord Literistic, Inc., Copyright 1998 by Amiri Baraka.

8.2, 8.5, 8.7: These excerpts are from articles first published in the November–December, 2005, September–October, 2007, and July–August, 2006 issues of *Focus* magazine, published by the Joint Center for Political and Economic Studies. Reprinted with permission.

8.3: *Harvard Law Review*. Copyright 1986 by Harvard Law Review Association. Reproduced with permission of Harvard Law Review Association in the format Textbook via Copyright Clearance Center.

8.4: Reprinted from *Gotham Gazette* (www.gothamgazette.com), an on-line publication about New York City.

8.6: Reprinted by permission of Harvard Health Care Society.

Acknowledgments

8.8: Reprinted by permission of Manning Marable, Professor of Public Affairs, History, and African-American Studies, Director of the Center for Contemporary Black History at Columbia University.

While every reasonable effort has been made to trace owners of copyright for the material quoted herein, in a few cases that has not been possible. The editors offer their apologies to the copyright owners and will be happy to receive information, through the publisher, leading to more complete acknowledgments in any future edition.

Robert P. Green, Jr.
Harold E. Cheatham

List of abbreviations

AAE	Adult Armchair Education
ACMHR	Alabama Christian Movement for Human Rights
BSCP	Brotherhood of Sleeping Car Porters
CBC	Congressional Black Caucus
CIO	Congress of Industrial Organizations
COFO	Council of Federated Organizations
CORE	Congress (originally Committee) of Racial Equality
EOA	Economic Opportunity Act
FBI	Federal Bureau of Investigation
FEPC	Fair Employment Practices Committee
FOR	Fellowship of Reconciliation
GOP	Grand Old Party (Republican Party)
ICC	Interstate Commerce Commission
KKK	Ku Klux Klan
MFDP	Mississippi Freedom Democratic Party
MIA	Montgomery Improvement Association
NAACP	National Association for the Advancement of Colored People
NOI	Nation of Islam
OIC	Opportunities Industrialization Centers
SCLC	Southern Christian Leadership Conference
SNCC	Student Nonviolent Coordinating Committee
VRA	Voting Rights Act
WCC	White Citizens Council
WPC	Women's Political Council

Introduction

Most students own a mental, capsule history of the modern Civil Rights Movement. Such a capsule history may include the December 1955 date when, in a rare public display of courage, Mrs. Rosa Parks with quiet dignity defied a bus driver's command that she accommodate a White man by relinquishing to him her seat in the section reserved for 'colored passengers.' Fewer know that in the preceding summer Mrs. Parks's appetite for full equality had been whetted through her participation in a United Nations workshop at the Highlander Folk School in Monteagle, Tennessee. Most know also that her courageous act gave rise to a charismatic, energetic, and eloquent young minister who, though reluctant when first summoned, answered the call to provide leadership for the boycott that was to presage 'the movement' and who ultimately gave his life in the quest for full equality.

Recent scholarship addressing the American Civil Rights Movement criticizes the dearth of information and understanding that capsule histories reveal.[1] Rather, this scholarship suggests that it is important to provide students a more sophisticated understanding than is available in most textbooks. Traditional treatments tend to place the Movement in what is generally termed the 'master narrative' of American history – that of ever-expanding freedoms. In this version, legal segregation and discrimination are presented as temporary hurdles, as impediments overcome through the valiant efforts of principled leaders and particularly through the valiant leadership of Dr. King, who in the period 1955 through his assassination in 1968 served to set the country on a course consonant with its founding and governing documents. This treatment, current scholars argue,

1

is simplistic; it ignores and underplays the deep-seated, intransigent nature of racism in American life in its failure to acknowledge the context for the Movement; it tends to emphasize the role of prominent males, largely neglecting the contributions of women, other than Rosa Parks; and it fails to leave students of the Movement and students in general with a comprehensive and coherent basis for understanding the significance of today's unresolved issues of racial and social justice, and equality.

In this work we endeavor to advance a brief documentary history that contributes to a more nuanced view of the Movement. This history is presented as an anthology composed of period documents including excerpts from letters; laws and other government documents; speeches; popular press articles; court decisions; and relevant published personal narratives. Framed by a unit that sets the context of life in the Jim Crow South and a unit that treats residual issues, the bulk of the documents reflect three areas of activity within the Movement (ca. 1954–68): social activism – addressing the protests, boycotts, and related civil actions from the viewpoint of the activists; the legal struggle in the courts; and civil rights legislation. This approach allows us to broaden the narrative and identify the multifaceted elements of the Movement: legal versus direct action, the bravery of the 'foot soldiers,' roles of women and youth, the contrasting and complementary views of leadership, the importance of community centers of resistance, the challenge to nonviolence.

Throughout this text the reader will note our inclusion of diverse Black voices, as well as the voices of White segregationists, moderates, and liberals. Prefaced by introductory essays and headnotes that provide a narrative and/or analytical framework, the documents tell the story. That story, we trust, provides a rich picture of the struggle – a picture that can be more evocative than the best secondary narratives.

Note

1 See, for example, J. B. Armstrong, S. H. Edwards, H. B. Roberson, and R. Y. Williams, eds., *Teaching the American Civil Rights Movement: Freedom's Bittersweet Song* (New York: Routledge, 2002).

1

'Nobody knows the trouble I've seen': dimensions of Jim Crow

Any treatment of the modern Civil Rights Movement in the United States should be grounded in an understanding of the nature of life for African Americans under Jim Crow. Although originally associated with a derogatory, stereotypical Black figure in White minstrel shows, 'Jim Crow' came to represent the complex system of laws and customs that buttressed White supremacy and segregated and oppressed African Americans in the American South. The roots of Jim Crow certainly antedate the Civil War and Reconstruction, although historians most typically use the term to refer to the period between the late nineteenth century, when Southern states began to codify segregation, and the beginning of the modern Civil Rights Movement in the 1950s. Historian Richard Bardolph, for example, located the first post-Reconstruction segregation laws in Tennessee in the early 1880s. By the end of the first decade of the twentieth century, segregation laws were firmly entrenched throughout the South.[1]

Jim Crow regulated the lives of Blacks politically, economically, and socially. In Southern politics, White reaction against Black political participation that began with the re-establishment of the White power structure during and after Reconstruction culminated in the nearly complete disfranchisement of Blacks by the early twentieth century. In the Southern economy, Whites typically expected African Americans to hold only the most menial jobs. Managerial and skilled positions were to be reserved for Whites. Blacks who aspired to economic advancement had little or no opportunity and, furthermore, faced sanctions for such aspirations. Social segregation – from requirements for separate accommodations in public facilities to ordinances maintaining separate Black and White neighborhoods – stamped Blacks with a badge of inferiority maintained through legal and extra-legal means.

Figure 1 Sandy Run Store. The ugliness of Jim Crow was not hidden.

Our exploration of the political, economic, and social dimensions of Jim Crow begins with a sampling of Jim Crow laws in various Southern states, the legal means by which White superiority was maintained. The sampling of state constitutional provisions and laws included in the first section of the chapter gives one a sense of the pervasiveness of segregation in the life of the South. While such legal codes imposed social separation in public transportation, schooling (even in the use of textbooks in some cases!), entertainments, neighborhoods, jails, and even cemeteries, constitutional provisions such as that of Mississippi (**1.1.A**) disfranchised African Americans, leaving them politically powerless.

The justification for legal segregation was the claim by Southern states that they were merely maintaining the health, safety, and welfare of the community (that is, applying what are known as the 'police powers' of the state). These laws did not violate the principle of equal protection of the law found in the Fourteenth Amendment to the Constitution, argued their defenders, because they called for '*equal* but separate' facilities. This logic was challenged by a group of African Americans based in New Orleans. Attorneys for Homer Plessy, arrested for violating the Louisiana railway coach law of

1890 (**1.1.B**), argued that the object of that law was merely 'to separate the Negroes from the Whites in public conveyances for the gratification and recognition of the sentiment of White superiority and White supremacy of right and power ...' Such laws fostered unreasonable distinctions and violated the equal protection clause. The United States Supreme Court, however, in *Plessy* v. *Ferguson* (1896), agreed with the state of Louisiana. Distinguishing between political rights and social customs, the Court found that the Louisiana legislature 'is at liberty to act with reference to the established usages, customs and traditions of the people, and with a view for the promotion of their comfort, and the preservation of the public peace and good order.' The Court concluded: 'We consider the underlying fallacy of the plaintiff's argument to consist in the assumption that the enforced separation of the two races stamps the colored race with a badge of inferiority. If this be so, it is not by reason of anything found in the act, but solely because the colored race chooses to put that construction upon it.'[2] Thus, the Court affirmed segregation as legal.

In *Plessy*, the Court focused narrowly on social customs; Blacks, however, clearly suffered loss of political rights under Jim Crow. Additional to the standard devices noted in Document **1.1.A** for limiting Black political participation, poll taxes and literacy requirements were used to avoid the Fifteenth Amendment's prohibition against denial of the franchise based on race. White Southerners were not bashful in admitting their motives. In 1895, for example, South Carolina adopted a similar constitutional provision to that of Mississippi. South Carolina Senator Benjamin Tillman argued, 'We did not disfranchise the negroes until 1895. Then we had a constitutional convention convened which took the matter up calmly, deliberately, and avowedly with the purpose of disfranchising as many of them as we could under the Fourteenth and Fifteenth Amendments. We adopted the educational qualification as the only means left to us ...'.[3] Historically, such devices were complemented by extra-legal measures used to deny Blacks' voting rights.

Document **1.2**, excerpts from a US Senate investigation into the 1946 primary campaign of Mississippi Senator Theodore Bilbo, provides a sense of the intimidating tactics used by Whites in the South to keep Blacks from the polls. Mississippi Blacks had complained to the Senate over the racist nature of Bilbo's campaign. The excerpts from exhibits and testimony during the Senate inves-

tigation demonstrate a number of aspects of political disfranchisement: attitudes of Southern White politicians, tactics of registrars,
and collusion of police in physical abuse of Blacks attempting to
register and vote. While the document provides a rich description
of the racist culture and terror tactics pursued during the era of Jim
Crow, it also reflects the resilience of African Americans in pursuit
of their constitutional rights.

Whites typically resented Blacks whom they perceived to be
'too prosperous for a nigger.' Document **1.3** provides a sense of the
prescribed roles of the vast majority of African Americans in the
economy of the South. 'Debt slavery' and sharecropping kept rural
Blacks at the bottom of the economic ladder. When Blacks moved
beyond 'their place,' retribution often followed.

Documents **1.4** and **1.5** provide a sense of the social conventions
under which African Americans lived during the era of Jim Crow.
Segregated facilities, injustices in the legal system, and hypocrisy
characterized a racist system. Perhaps the most hypocritical aspect
of Southern life was the exploitation of Black women by White men.
The source of mulatto children in the South was not the Black, male
beast of White mythology; rather, it was a system that condoned the
exploitation of Black women by White men in positions of domination.
As Ann Pointer (**1.5**) put it, 'the Klan [is] talking about they want a
pure race. Now who mixed up this race, you understand me?'

The ultimate tool of Black subjugation was the lynch mob. Statis-
tics compiled by Tuskegee Institute researchers suggest that between
1882 and 1968, over 3,200 African Americans were lynched in the
South and border states.[4] In Document **1.6**, Clark Foreman describes
a lynching.

It is important to note that while legal discrimination was confined
largely to Southern and border states, Blacks faced discrimination
in the North as well. James Baldwin wrote (**1.7**), 'I knew about the
south, of course, and about how southerners treated Negroes and
how they expected them to behave, but it had never entered my
mind that anyone would look at me and expect me to behave that
way. I learned in New Jersey that to be a Negro meant, precisely, that
one was never looked at but was simply at the mercy of the reflexes
the color of one's skin caused in other people.'

Taken together, the following documents provide insight to the
effective, total segregation of Blacks from Whites – in virtually every
aspect of life.

1.1 Jim Crow laws, 1890–1947

The following state constitutional provisions and laws give one a sense of the pervasiveness of segregation in the life of the South. The 1890 Mississippi Constitutional provision (**1.1.A**) was designed to disfranchise African Americans and served as a model for disfranchisement throughout the South. Of course, the tax, conviction, and educational provisions also disfranchised some Whites, so many states adopted 'grandfather clauses' that exempted Whites from the exclusionary provisions. The Louisiana law providing separate railroad coaches (**1.1.B**) is of particular interest as it was the law that was unsuccessfully challenged in *Plessy v. Ferguson* (1896). In that case, the US Supreme Court accepted Louisiana's argument that such legislation was a reasonable expression of the police power of the state and that 'separate but equal' provisions did not violate the equal protection clause of the Fourteenth Amendment to the Constitution. As the selections below reveal, Jim Crow laws regulated many aspects of life.

A Voting
Every male inhabitant of this state, except idiots, insane persons, and Indians not taxed, who is a citizen of the United States, twenty-one years old and upwards, who has resided in this state two years, and one year in the election district, or in the incorporated city or town in which he offers to vote, and who is duly registered, and who has never been convicted of bribery, burglary, theft arson, obtaining money or goods under false pretenses, perjury, forgery, embezzlement, or bigamy, and who has paid, on or before the first day of February on the year in which be shall offer to vote, all taxes which may have been legally required of him, and which he has had an opportunity of paying according to law, for the two preceding years, and who shall produce to the officers holding the election satisfactory evidence that he has paid said taxes, is declared to be a qualified elector …

A uniform poll-tax of two dollars, to be used in aid of the common schools … is hereby imposed on every male inhabitant of this state between the ages of twenty-one and sixty years, except certain physically handicapped persons … said tax to be a lien only upon taxable property …

On and after the first day of January, A.D. 1892, every elector shall, in addition to the foregoing qualifications, be able to read any section of the constitution of this state; or he shall be able to understand the same when read to him, or give a reasonable interpretation thereof …

Electors shall not be registered within four months next before any election at which they may offer to vote ...

Constitution of Mississippi, Art. 12, 1890, in *Annotated Code of Mississippi*, 1892, p. 80, reproduced in Bardolph, *The Civil Rights Record*, p. 138.

B Railway cars

Be it enacted by the General Assembly of the State of Louisiana, That all railway companies carrying passengers in their coaches in this State, shall provide equal but separate accommodations for the white, and colored races, by providing two or more passenger coaches for each passenger train, or by dividing the passenger coaches by a partition so as to secure separate accommodations; provided that this section shall not be construed to apply to street railroads. No person or persons, shall be permitted to occupy seats in coaches, other than the ones assigned to them on account of the race they belong to.

Acts of Louisiana, 1890, No. 111, pp. 152–154, reproduced in Bardolph, *The Civil Rights Record*, pp. 132–133.

C Interracial marriage

The legislature shall never pass any law to authorize or legalize any marriage between any white person and a negro, or descendant of a negro.

Constitution of Alabama (1901), Art. IV, sec. 102. See *Code of Alabama*, 1903, III, p. 82, reproduced in Bardolph, *The Civil Rights Record*, p. 131.

D Schools

The legislature shall establish, organize, and maintain a liberal system of public schools throughout the state for the benefit of children thereof between the ages of seven and twenty-one years. Separate schools shall be provided for white and colored children, and no child of either race shall be permitted to attend schools of the other race.

Constitution of Alabama (1901), Art. XIV, sec. 256. See *Code of Alabama*, 1903, III, p. 187, reproduced in Bardolph, *The Civil Rights Record*, pp. 135–136.

E Jails

That in the State penitentiary and in all county jails, stockades, convict camps, and all other places where State or county prisoners may at any time be kept confined, separate apartments shall be provided and maintained for white and negro prisoners.

That separate bunks, beds, bedding, separate dining tables and all other furnishings, shall be provided and kept by the State and counties, respectively, for the use of white and negro prisoners, [and such items] after having been assigned to the use of, or after having been used by white or negro prisoners [shall never] be changed the one for the use of the other.

That it shall be unlawful for any white prisoner to be handcuffed or otherwise chained or tied to a negro prisoner.

Acts of Arkansas, 1903, No. 95, p. 161, reproduced in Bardolph, *The Civil Rights Record*, p. 161.

F Streetcars

That all street, inter-urban railway companies, engaged as common carriers ... shall ... set apart so much of the front portion of each car operated by them as shall be necessary, for occupation by the white passengers therein, and shall likewise provide and set apart so much of the rear part of said car as shall be necessary, for occupation by the colored passengers therein, and shall require as far as practicable the white and colored passengers to each occupy the respective parts of such car so set apart for them ...

Public Laws and Resolutions of North Carolina, 1907, chap. 850, pp. 1238–1239, reproduced in Bardolph, *The Civil Rights Record*, p. 134.

G Neighborhoods

Be it enacted by the general assembly of Virginia, That in the cities and towns of this commonwealth where this act shall be adopted ... the entire area within the respective corporate limits thereof shall ... be divided into districts, the boundaries whereof shall be plainly designated in such ordinance and which shall be known as 'segregation districts.' ...

That after twelve months from the passage of the ordinances adopting the provisions of this act, it shall be unlawful for any colored person, not then residing in a district so defined and designated as a white district, or who is not a member of a family then therein residing to move into and occupy as a residence any building or portion thereof in such white district, and it shall be unlawful, after the expiration of said period of twelve months from the passage of the ordinance adopting the provisions of this act, for any white person not then residing in a district so defined and designated as a colored district, or who is not a member of a family then therein residing, to move into and occupy as a residence any building, or portion thereof, in such colored district ...

Acts of Virginia, 1912, chap. 157, pp. 330–332, reproduced in Bardolph, *The Civil Rights Record*, pp. 197–198.

H Public entertainment

All circuses, shows and tent exhibitions, to which the attendance of the public of more than one race is invited or expected to attend shall provide for the convenience of its patrons not less than two ticket offices with individual ticket sellers, and not less than two entrances to the said performance, with individual ticket takers and receivers, and in the case of outside or tent performances, the said ticket offices shall not be less than twenty-five feet apart; that one of the said entrances shall be exclusively for the white race, and another exclusively for persons of the colored race ...

Acts of Louisiana, 1914, No. 235, sec. 1, p. 465, reproduced in Bardolph, *The Civil Rights Record*, p. 197.

I Telephone booths

The Corporation Commission is hereby vested with power and authority to require telephone companies in the state of Oklahoma to maintain separate booths for white and colored patrons when there is a demand for such separate booths ...

Laws of Oklahoma, 1915, chap. 26, p. 513, reproduced in Bardolph, *The Civil Rights Record*, p. 197.

J Advocacy of racial equality

Races – social equality, marriages between – advocacy of punished. – Any person, firm or corporation who shall be guilty of printing, publishing or circulating printed, typewritten or written matter urging or presenting for public acceptance or general information, arguments or suggestions in favor of social equality or of intermarriage between whites and negroes, shall be guilty of a misdemeanor.

Laws of Mississippi, 1920, chap. 214, p. 307, reproduced in Bardolph, *The Civil Rights Record*, p. 197.

K Textbooks

No textbook issued or distributed under this act to a white school child shall ever be reissued or redistributed to a colored school child, and no textbook issued or distributed to a colored school child shall ever be reissued or redistributed to a white school child.

Acts of Kentucky, 1928, chap. 48, sec. 11, p. 188, reproduced in Bardolph, *The Civil Rights Record*, p. 195.

L Cemeteries

Racial restrictions as to use of cemeteries for burial of dead. In the event ... property has been heretofore used exclusively for the burial of members of the Negro race, then said cemetery or burial ground so established shall remain and be established as a burial ground for the Negro race. In the event said property has been heretofore used exclusively for the burial of members of the White race, then said cemetery ground so established shall remain and be established as a burial ground for the White race.

North Carolina Session Laws, 1947, chap. 821, sec. 2, p. 1115, reproduced in Bardolph, *The Civil Rights Record*, p. 263.

1.2 Maintaining disfranchisement

Disfranchisement of Black voters was foundational to White supremacy in the Jim Crow South. The legal means by which Black voting was limited have previously been noted (see **1.1.A**), but extra-legal means were also used. The following selection, excerpts from a Senate investigation into the 1946 primary campaign of Senator Theodore Bilbo of Mississippi, suggests that intimidation of Black voters was alive and well after World War II. The investigation resulted from Black Mississippians' complaints that Bilbo's campaign – despite the Supreme Court's decision in *Smith* v. *Allwright* (see **2.9**) – was characterized by appeals to race hatred and thinly veiled threats to Black citizens who might attempt to vote. The document contains excerpts from various newspaper and magazine articles exhibited as evidence in the investigation and excerpts from the testimony of one of the many Blacks who had attempted to vote. Testimony of a White registrar is also included.

EXHIBIT 1

[From Jackson (Miss.) Daily News, June 25, 1946]

Senator Bilbo said he defied 'Tom Clark, the Department of Justice, and the FBI to try and keep the white people of this State from running the white Democratic primaries as we think they should be run.

'In the first place they would have to get a grand jury of Mississippians to indict a man. And, second, they would have to get a jury of 12 good and true Mississippi white men to convict them.'

Senator Bilbo volunteered his 'legal services to anybody that gets in trouble,' and he said, 'I'm a damn good lawyer. I've defended people in 11 murder cases in my life and got them off free. How I did it is my business.'

[From Jackson (Miss.) Daily News, June 23, 1946]

LAUREL (Special) – Citizens of Mississippi were again called on here Saturday by Senator Theo. G. Bilbo 'to resort to any means' to keep Negroes from the polls in the July 2 Democratic Primary.

'And if you don't know what that means, you are just not up on persuasive measures,' said Senator Bilbo as he completed a week of stump speaking in South Mississippi.

'Spurred on by the CIO [Congress of Industrial Organisation] and the PAC [Political Action Committee],' the senior Senator said, 'Negroes are going to make an all-out effort to vote next Tuesday week, and if you don't know what that means, you are not awake to the crisis ahead,' he said …

'The white people of Mississippi are sleeping on a volcano,' he warned, 'and it is left up to you red-blooded men to do something about it. The white men of this State have a right to resort to any means at their command to stop it.' …

[Exhibit 1 quotes from a Bilbo campaign speech]

… 'I believe in white superiority, white domination and the integrity of my white blood. Why, we have behind us 4,000 years of culture, learning, education, and wisdom … And the nigger – I got nothing against the nigger. I'm his best friend – but the poor devil is only 150 years removed from the jungle and eating his own kind.' …

'Why, I read a book written by 14 nigger leaders and every one of them wanted the same thing: social equality, intermarriage and interbreeding.' …

'The poll tax won't keep 'em from voting. What keeps 'em from voting is section 244 of the Constitution of 1890 that Senator George wrote. It says that a man to register must be able to read and explain the Constitution or explain the Constitution when read to him … And then Senator George wrote a Constitution that damn few white men and no niggers at all can explain.' …

[Individual Testimony]

Testimony of Varnado R. Collier, Gulfport, Miss.

… Mr. Collier. Well, on July 2, between 12 and 1 o'clock, my wife and I approached the city hall in Gulfport, and as we started up the steps we met a police officer who was coming out of the city hall, and I asked him if this was the place where the North Gulfport voting precinct was, and he said it was, and he escorted us on into the main corridor of the building, and he said, 'Now pull off your hat.' And I did that. And he pointed down the east wing corridor of the building and said, 'Go right down this hall and go through the door that is open there, and that is where you vote.'

Just as I turned or we turned to go down the east wing corridor, one of a group of 10 or 15 white men put his arm up in front of me and said, 'You people don't vote here today; come back tomorrow.' And before I could make a reply, they all were all over me, beating me up and knocking me down, and drug me out and threw me out on the porch.

The Chairman. What became of your wife?

Mr. Collier. Well, the last I know, she was hollering, 'Officer, stop them, don't let them beat my husband up,' and one of them hit her, and as I hit the porch – I suppose at about that time I was unconscious, part of the time – and when I hit the porch evidently the jar brought me back to consciousness, and I got up and patted my pockets to see what I had lost, and so forth, and I missed my hat. And I attempted to go back into the building to get my hat, and one of the group pulled out a long knife and said, 'Don't come back in here; keep going, buddy. If you don't, you will never walk out alive.'...

Testimony of Clifford R. Field, Natchez, Miss. [White Registrar]

... The Chairman. Will you tell the committee of a few instances when a colored person did apply and you turned him down, and give the reasons why you turned him down, if you know?

Mr. Field. Yes, sir. When they first started coming in there they came in without having two poll-tax receipts. They would not have been qualified if I had registered them. So I told them, I said, 'What is the use of me cluttering up these books with you all registering here when you are not going to be able to vote if you do register?'

The Chairman. The law doesn't provide that in order to be registered the poll taxes should be paid, does it?

Mr. Field. No, sir. .

The Chairman. Why did you put that restriction on them?

Mr. Field. Because it is just a matter of cluttering up the books with a lot of people's names who could not vote; they would not be eligible to vote even if they did register.

The Chairman. Do you require that same thing as to white people?

Mr. Field. No, sir.

The Chairman. Why not?

Mr. Field. Well, because I knew that eventually the white people would become qualified, but I didn't think –

The Chairman. Why didn't the same thing apply to the colored?

Mr. Field. I didn't think they would be qualified; they never were before, and I didn't think they ever would be.

The Chairman. Well, it is strange that you should have had a different method with the colored than with the whites.

Mr. Field. Yes, I expect it is, but I did it ...

The Chairman. What other restrictions did you place on the colored applying to register, in contrast to the whites, other than the requirement as to the production of the poll-tax receipt?

Mr. Field. The only other thing I did was to ask them to read the section of the constitution of the State of Mississippi where it explains the election of the Governor of the State of Mississippi. I did not require that of the whites, but I did require it of the colored.

The Chairman. Why did you make the exception?

Mr. Field. I didn't require it, that is all. I have no other reason than that they were colored.

The Chairman. Well, to be truthful about it, you made it a little harder for the colored to register than the whites; isn't that true?

Mr. Field. That is right.

Hearings before the Special Committee to Investigate Senatorial Campaign Expenditures, 1946, U.S. Senate, Seventy-Ninth Congress (Washington, DC: United States Government Printing Office, 1947), pp. 7–9, 197–198, 204–205.

1.3 Labor for the White South

The following passage demonstrates some of the methods used to maintain economic power relations in the South. Richard Wright describes how landowners kept Black sharecroppers entangled 'in this hateful web of cotton culture.'

... Most of the flogging and lynchings occur at harvest time, when fruit hangs heavy and ripe, when the leaves are red and gold, when nuts fall from the trees, when the earth offers its best. The thought of harvest steals upon us with a sense of an inescapable judgment. It is time now to settle accounts with the Lords of the Land, to divide the crops and pay old debts, and we are afraid. We have never grown used to confronting the Lords of the Land when the last of the cotton is ginned and baled, for we know beforehand that we have lost yet another race with time, that we are deeper in debt. When word reaches us that the Lords of the Land are bent over the big books down at the plantation commissary, we lower our eyes, shake our heads, and mutter:

A naught's a naught,

Five's a figger;

All for the white man,
None for the nigger ...

And after we have divided the crops we are still entangled as deeply as ever in this hateful web of cotton culture. We are older; our bodies are weaker; our families are larger; our clothes are in rags; we are still in debt; and, worst of all, we face another year that holds even less hope than the one we have just endured. We know that this is not right, and dark thoughts take possession of our minds. We know that to tread this mill is to walk in days of slow death. When alone, we stand and look out over the green, rolling fields and wonder why it is that living here is so hard. Everything seems to whisper of the possibility of happiness, of satisfying experiences; but somehow happiness and satisfaction never come into our lives. The land upon which we live holds a promise, but the promise fades with the passing seasons.

And we know that if we protest we will be called 'bad niggers.' The Lords of the Land will preach the doctrine of 'white supremacy' to the poor whites who are eager to form mobs. In the midst of general hysteria they will seize one of us – it does not matter who, the innocent or guilty – and, as a token, a naked and bleeding body will be dragged through the dusty streets. The mobs will make certain that our token-death is known throughout the quarters where we black folk live. Our bodies will be swung by ropes from the limbs of trees, will be shot at and mutilated.

And we cannot fight back; we have no arms; we cannot vote; and the law is white. There are no black policemen, black justices of the peace, black judges, black juries, black jailers, black mayors, or black men anywhere in the government of the South. The Ku Klux Klan attacks us in a thousand ways, driving our boys and girls off the jobs in the cities and keeping us who live on the land from protesting or asking too many questions.

This is the way the Lords of the Land keep their power. For them life is a continuous victory; for us it is simply trouble in the land. Fear is with us always, and in those areas where we black men equal or outnumber the whites fear is at its highest. Two streams of life flow through the South, a black stream and a white stream, and from day to day we live in the atmosphere of a war that never ends. Even when the sprawling fields are drenched in peaceful sunshine, it is war. When we grub at the clay with our hoes, it is war. When we sleep, it is war. When we are awake, it is war. When one of us is born, he enters one of the warring regiments of the South. When there are days of peace, it is a peace born of a victory over us; and when there is open violence, it is when we are trying to push back the encroachments of the Lords of the Land ...

Richard Wright, 'Inheritors of Slavery', from *Twelve Million Black Voices: A Folk History of the Negro in the United States* (New York: Viking Press, 1941), pp. 41–42, 43–46.

15

1.4 Jim Crow social conventions

Jim Crow social conventions demeaned Blacks in the South. In an oral interview, Kenneth Young and Mai Young describe some of their experiences in the 1930s and 1940s. Note the resentment that shows clearly through their recollections. As Kenneth Young declared, 'They did everything they could to make you feel inferior.'

Kenneth Young: ... The black folks learned early their place in life and you got along fine as long as you didn't step over the line. You knew who was white, you knew who was black and you don't make a mistake. In other words, white men and women were addressed as 'Mr. and Mrs.' You didn't address blacks that way. And don't make a mistake talking to a white person about a black person and call him 'Mr.' I know when I first came back home to teach I'd been away four years to boarding school, and I had northern teachers while I was away. I picked up a little northern brogue. I was talking about some black woman who was supervisor of the schools for black folks and I kept saying 'Miss So-and-So.' Finally, the white woman stopped me and said 'Young, that woman you're talking about, is she black or white?' I said, 'She's black.' 'Well, don't Miss her to me then. Just call her by her first name. Don't ever Miss a black person to me.' I said, 'No ma'am.' So before we'd get very far I had an occasion to say 'Miss So-and-So' again. She stopped and looked at me: 'Told you about that!' 'I won't make that mistake anymore.' So you had to watch your tongue. White folks Mr. and Mrs., blacks by their first name.

Very seldom [did black folks break those rules]. Sometimes they'd do it without thinking but very few deliberate attempts to ignore the southern custom. We all lived here together, and I know when I went to be principal there in the southern part of the state [in 1930] the superintendent of the school system had come from my home county about 100 miles up north. I went to see him. They'd sent me to him when I got here. He said, 'Oh yeah boy.' Never called a Negro man a man, it was always boy. 'Yeah boy,' [he] says, 'I know you. Your daddy's name is Sam Young.' 'Yes sir, he is.' 'Well, I'll be damned. Ain't that something.' [Laughter.] He said, 'I told them you'd get along fine because you knew the white folks.' 'I sure do.' What he meant by that, you know the customs and you will not ignore the customs down here. 'You've been up north?' I said, 'Well I went to Tennessee, that's not up north but from Alabama that's a long ways.' He said, 'Well you know the customs and you aren't going to do anything that's against the customs.' 'No sir.' So I didn't. I stayed within, you know, the boundaries as long as I was there.

Mai Young: I never shall forget ... we went to Columbus to take the

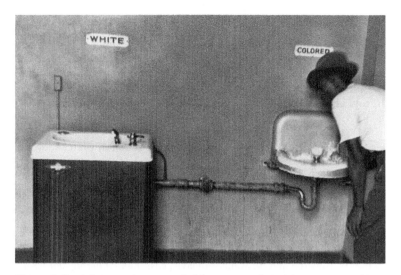

Figure 2 Racial separation extended from water fountains to cemeteries.

children for something, buy them some clothes I think. We adopted two children at the same time and we took them over there and Pat wanted some water. Pat said, 'Why can't I have it?' I think he [gestures to Mr. Young] gave her some.

KY: They had one cup up there and the white person drank. White person drank out of the fountain, had a cup hanging there and you had to drink out of that. So I had my youngest girl, and Pat, [who] was about two and a half, three years old, said, 'Daddy I want some water.' She was standing, and I put her up to the fountain and let her drink. This is a white fountain. This white guy ran over there and said: 'Can't you read!?!' The sign said white only. Said, 'Can't you read!' I said, 'The baby can't read.' I stood and looked at him. I didn't move. First thing crossed my mind [is] I'm going to die here today because if he'd snatched that child away from that fountain while she's trying to drink I'm going to hit him. He just turned and walked on off. I guess he looked in my eyes and saw death because I'm going to kill him today ...

MY: We had an experience like that down in Montgomery. We had gone to a game I believe, and I went in the restroom and the guy at the filling station came and knocked on the door. Kenneth said, 'Don't you go in there.'

KY: I was outside. He saw her go in but he ran to the door, bam, bam. I said, 'My wife's in there mister and don't you go in!'

MY: 'She's not supposed to go in there.'

17

KY: I said, 'I don't care if she's not, she's in there and don't you go in!' I said, 'If you want some trouble you go in now and I'll die here today.' Turned around and said to somebody: 'That's a fool.' Anytime a Negro outside and you didn't do anything about it they considered you a fool. So he told us, 'That's a fool.' But I said, 'My wife went in there and don't you go in.'...

MY: I'm telling you, those were the days.

KY: Eating together and using restrooms the southern white, he would die before he'd let you do it ...

They did everything they could to make you feel inferior. They didn't miss a trick. If they had two fountains they'd put another cup up there for the blacks. Everything they could do to make you feel inferior they did it ...

W. H. Chafe, R. Gavins, and R. Korstad with P. Ortiz, R. Parrish, J. Ritterhouse, K. Roberts, and N. Waligora-Davis, eds., *Remembering Jim Crow: African Americans Tell about Life in the Segregated South* (New York: The New Press, 2001), pp. 180–182.

1.5 White men and Black women

White domination often led to sexual abuse of African American women. The product was mixed-race children. In the following passage, Ann Pointer reveals dimensions of sexual exploitation in the Jim Crow South.

Everywhere the [white] man has got, maybe from eight to fifteen tenants, on his place, there is a woman there that he is messing with. Then you going to see the flowers start to blooming, the children start to popping. A white woman told me one time – we were talking about a situation – she say, 'What if your husband built a house right adjacent in the back of your house, and he slept with another woman and was having children by her right in your yard? What would you do?' I said, 'I wouldn't stay there. I would leave.' She said, 'Well, I didn't go anywhere because, when he asked for my hand in marriage, he asked my father could I be controlled. My father told him Yes because my father was guilty of the same thing.' She said, 'I stayed there and while this woman worked in the field, I had to tend to the children.' Now that happened right here in Macon County, and his wife had to take that.

I told her, 'I wouldn't have taken that because I would've been gone, and I wouldn't [have] went back to my father, neither. He wouldn't know where I went. My husband get brazen enough to bring a woman in my house and he going to stay there and have children by her – uh-uh it ain't going to happen with me. I wouldn't put up with it.' But a lot of these white women have had to put up with it and helped raise the children. Now, I know what I'm talking about. They all have been pushed about like that because this man is going to do what he want to. You don't know what he's doing until the flowers start to blooming, that's what they say. When you see these mixed-up children come out [snap] from there, you know that he's stirr ng about. This woman that's got these children, she's going to dress better than anybody in the community, and she got money all the time, and her children [are] well taken care of. He does it undercover, but everybody know what's going on. But they ain't going to say nothing. They talk about it, but they can't do nothing about it because the man own them. It's like I say, what is slavery? Yes, they abolished the chains, they abolished this here, abolished that, but you still a slave – you understand me? – in so many words because that greenback dollar can make you a slave. When you don't have anything and you trying to make it, you're still a slave. Most people look down on that word, but they'll find out that they are.

You don't have to wonder about these flowers blooming. You can just look at the population and tell. Haven't you paid attention to that? Different people mixed up. You don't know what they are. They got some everything in them, and you can see that there's been visitation by someone just [by] looking at the group, this bouquet. That's what I'm saying. And the Klan [is] talking about they want a pure race. Now who mixed up this race, you understand me? The bouquets have been made now. In the classroom, if you look at a class of 32 children, you see some of everything. You know what I'm saying. It's been like that all of the time, and it brought about a lot of dissension among the blacks as well as whites. If a black man's got a wife, and she have a white baby, he on the man's place [and] he can't say nothing. You see what I'm talking about. Do you see the injustice in that? Even though he doesn't like it. Now you know what he's going to do? He's going to mistreat his wife under the cover and give her a very, very bad time, and this child will be knocked about, which is wrong. Going back to the [wh te] man, he done stood it all up and he gone on about his business, left it like that ...

Chafe *et al.*, eds., *Remembering Jim Crow*, pp. 52–53.

1.6 Lynching

The ultimate instrument of terror and intimidation in the Jim Crow South was, of course, the lynching. In the following passage, Clark Foreman, a young White college student, describes the lynching of a Black man in Athens, Georgia, in February, 1921. With deputies at the location evidently preoccupied, a mob broke into the courthouse in Athens where John Lee Eberhardt was being confined, dragged him to an automobile, and drove him outside the city.

The negro was carried to the place of the murder. He was shown the lady he was supposed to have murdered in the hopes that he would confess. The lady was about 23, fair and beautiful. She had a baby eighteen months old and was expecting another in June. The negro would not confess. He was brought out in the yard and tied to a pine tree, about a hundred yards from the house. The crowd of about three thousand people gathered around the tree in a large circle. A leader made a speech forbidding any shooting on

Figure 3 Lynching: The ultimate terrorist tactic.

account of the danger of onlookers. Strict order was preserved. Everyone was made to sit down, so that the ones behind them might see with ease the ghastly spectacle that was about to take place. A fire was built about the negro's feet and lit. Neither gasoline nor kerosene was used, in order that the job might not be done too fast. The family was brought to the center of the ring so that the negro might have one more chance to confess. He pleaded to God to testify his innocence. More wood was thrown on the fire. The negro yelled for mercy.

The fire leaps up and seems to burn him too fast. Some hardened onlooker smolders it so that the negro might suffer longer. He tries to choke himself, his hands tied behind him. Finally with a monster effort he bends over far enough to swallow some flame. He dies amid the jeers of the crowd.

The people ... grab souvenirs from the branches of the guilty tree. Even the dead negro is not spared. Fingers and toes are pulled from the scorched corpse to remind the participants of the deed. At this juncture a woman comes forth with a pistol and asks to be allowed to shoot the negro. The request is granted. More wood is piled on, and the funeral pyre flares up and lights the faces of the watchers. The mob disperses each to his home, with an air of conquest and satisfaction rather than horror and condemnation.

Clark Foreman Papers, Cambridge, Mass.

1.7 James Baldwin and Northern discrimination

While Jim Crow – at least in its *de jure* sense – was primarily a Southern phenomenon, racial discrimination was not limited to that section. Here James Baldwin describes experiences while he worked in the defense industry in New Jersey in the early 1940s.

... I had been living in New Jersey, working in defense plants, working and living among southerners, white and black. I knew about the south, of course, and about how southerners treated Negroes and how they expected them to behave, but it had never entered my mind that anyone would look at me and expect me to behave that way. I learned in New Jersey that to be a Negro meant, precisely, that one was never looked at but was simply at the mercy of the reflexes the color of one's skin caused in other people. I acted in New Jersey as I had always acted, that is as though I thought a great deal of myself – I had to *act* that way – with results that were, simply, unbelievable. I had scarcely arrived before I had earned the enmity, which was extraordinarily ingenious, of all my superiors and nearly all my co-workers.

In the beginning, to make matters worse, I simply did not know what was happening. I did not know what I had done, and I shortly began to wonder what *anyone* could possibly do, to bring about such unanimous, active, and unbearably vocal hostility. I knew about jim-crow but I had never experienced it. I went to the same self-service restaurant three times and stood with all the Princeton boys before the counter, waiting for a hamburger and coffee; it was always an extraordinarily long time before anything was set before me; but it was not until the fourth visit that I learned that, in fact, nothing had ever been set before me: I had simply picked something up. Negroes were not served there, I was told, and they had been waiting for me to realize that I was always the only Negro present. Once I was told this, I determined to go there all the time. But now they were ready for me and, though some dreadful scenes were subsequently enacted in that restaurant, I never ate there again.

It was the same story all over New Jersey, in bars, bowling alleys, diners, places to live. I was always being forced to leave, silently, or with mutual imprecations. I very shortly became notorious and children giggled behind me when I passed and their elders whispered or shouted – they really believed that I was mad. And it did begin to work on my mind, of course; I began to be afraid to go anywhere and to compensate for this I went places to which I really should not have gone and where, God knows, I had no desire to be. My reputation in town naturally enhanced my reputation at work and my working day became one long series of acrobatics designed to keep me out of trouble. I cannot say that these acrobatics succeeded. It began to seem that the machinery of the organization I worked for was turning over, day and night, with but one aim: to eject me. I was fired once, and contrived, with the aid of a friend from New York, to get back on the payroll; was fired again, and bounced back again. It took a while to fire me for the third time, but the third time took. There were no loopholes anywhere. There was not even any way of getting back inside the gates.

That year in New Jersey lives in my mind as though it were the year during which, having an unsuspected predilection for it, I first contracted some dread, chronic disease, the unfailing symptom of which is a kind of blind fever, a pounding in the skull and fire in the bowels. Once this disease is contracted, one can never be really carefree again, for the fever, without an instant's warning, can recur at any moment. It can wreck more important things than race relations. There is not a Negro alive who does not have this rage in his blood – one has the choice, merely, of living with it consciously or surrendering to it. As for me, this fever has recurred in me, and does, and will until the day I die …

J. Baldwin, *Notes of a Native Son* (Boston: Beacon Press, 1955), pp. 92–94.

Notes

1 R. Bardolph, *The Civil Rights Record: Black Americans and the Law, 1849–1970* (New York: Thomas Y. Crowell, 1970), p. 45.
2 *Plessy* v. *Ferguson*, 163 U.S. 537 (1896).
3 *Congressional Record* (56th Congress, 1st Session), March, 1900, pp. 3223–3224.
4 Lynchings by State and Race, 1882–1968 (Tuskegee Institute, 1979); see www.law.umkc.edu/faculty/projects/ftrials/shipp/lynchingsstate. html (accessed December, 2008).

2

'Walk together children': elements of resistance

The Civil Rights Movement did not dramatically materialize with Rosa Parks's refusal to relinquish her seat on a bus in Montgomery, Alabama, one December evening in 1955. Rather, a number of developments, domestic and international, converged to create a climate suitable for the Movement. By the early 1950s, a long tradition of resistance to injustice had become a part of the African American experience in the United States. Whether one is speaking of 'communities of resistance,'[1] challenges to the power structure through 'daily conversations, folklore, jokes, songs, and other cultural practices,'[2] or the work of formal organizations such as the National Association for the Advancement of Colored People (NAACP), African Americans had developed practices and associations that either confronted or were poised to confront discrimination. Concurrently, at least in the North, African Americans had begun to exert political influence. Black voters became an important part of Franklin Delano Roosevelt's New Deal coalition, and Presidents Roosevelt and Truman demonstrated a willingness to respond at least selectively to Blacks' concerns. On the world stage, the United States had just emerged from a global conflict cast as a struggle against totalitarian government and fascist racism. The 1950s found the country deeply engaged in a Cold War against Communist totalitarianism. Principles of democracy, liberty, and justice were touted in defense of the American way in both struggles. Furthermore, as former European colonies struggled toward independence and the Cold War developed into a competition between the United States and the Soviet Union for influence with Third World nations, American commitment to those ideals was seen by many as central to its efforts. The United States' embrace of those principles in foreign relations sensitized some Americans to the abridgement and denial of the same principles at home. This chapter presents documents and oral histories that reflect a range of expressions of resistance to discrimination as well as early successes that were foundational to the Civil Rights Movement.

Despite, or in some cases in response to, segregation and discrimination, Black communities developed and strengthened life-affirming institutions that provided and sustained a base for challenges to segregation. Black churches, fraternal and similar community organizations, and unions were among institutions poised for action. Historically, the Black Church was central among such institutions. 'Any serious attempt to catalogue the growth and development of the Black community in America centers in the Black Church enterprise,'[3] wrote Wyatt T. Walker. In the antebellum South, '[e]ven before the erection of physical places of worship, the 'invisible churches' of the Southern plantations gave cohesion and commonality to an oppressed people ...'[4] After the Civil War, the significance of the church continued.

> Following the Emancipation Proclamation, armed with their simple but profound faith that God had delivered them from 'Egypt land,' the ex-slaves set about the task of building their own centers of social intercourse and the citadel of hope against the unfulfilled promises of Emancipation. [The Black Church] provided the cocoon of insulation that softened the impact of disorientation produced by America's hypocrisy regarding freedom.[5]

The newly freed slaves turned inward, building their church as refuge from the failures of the Freedmen's Bureau; from widespread social, economic, and political disfranchisement; and from despair wrought of their prolonged deprivation and 'trained incapacity' for the rigors either of rural or urban living. Furthermore, wrote Walker, 'Personal and social development took refuge under the umbrella of the Black Church. Burial societies, insurance companies, and business enterprises of every stripe frequently began in the church.'[6] By the 1950s, wrote sociologist Aldon D. Morris, 'The Black church supplied the civil rights movement with a collective enthusiasm generated through a rich culture ... that spoke directly to the needs of an oppressed group.'[7] Walker noted that 'at center of this struggle were the forces of the Black Church, not only as the authors of confrontation but also as the sustaining force that provided the dynamics and vitality of the movement.'[8]

A key component of the rich culture of the church was the music. Negro spirituals, a folk music arising from the slave experience and continuing through segregation, expressed both spiritual themes of hope and redemption as well as earthly aspirations for freedom and justice. The themes were intertwined as the spirituals often emphasized means by which 'God delivered the faithful from impossible circumstances.'[9] The words of these gospel songs would readily be redacted to meet contemporary challenges during the Civil Rights Movement as singers substituted or added terms, events, names, and places for traditional lyrics. 'Up above my head, I hear music in the air' became 'Up above my head, I hear freedom in the air' or 'I will overcome' became 'We shall overcome,' an old gospel tune that, through the Highlander Folk School, became the anthem for the Movement. In this volume, we have used the titles of traditional Negro spirituals as metaphorical titles for our chapters.

The Black Church also provided much of the leadership of the Movement. Many Black pastors 'preached that oppression is sinful and that God sanctions protest aimed at eradicating social evils.'[10] Rev. Joseph Lowery provides insights into the role of the African American pastor and church (**2.1**).

The church was at the core, but Black communities formed other centers of resistance. Jo Ann Robinson describes a number of the local organizations and leading individuals in Montgomery, Alabama, prior to the 1955 boycott (**2.2**). One such individual, E. D. Nixon, was a leader in the Brotherhood of Sleeping Car Porters (BSCP), a union of Black workers. On the national level, the BSCP was a vocal advocate for African American concerns. The union's president, A. Philip Randolph, planned a March on Washington in 1941 (**2.3**) to protest discrimination against Blacks in the work force. The plan provided a model for the later mass action characteristic of the Civil Rights Movement. Although the march was canceled, its possibility prompted President Franklin Roosevelt to create a federal Fair Employment Practices Committee (FEPC) to 'reaffirm' the federal policy of nondiscrimination in hiring. Thus the potential of direct action, combined with the growing political power of Blacks in the North, influenced both the Roosevelt and Truman administrations, which were more willing than previous administrations to acknowledge Blacks' concerns and conditions and to take executive action in support of those concerns. Truman's executive order creating a Civil Rights Committee to study issues of race and that Committee's subsequent publication, *To Secure these Rights* (**2.4**), served to bring national attention to civil rights issues.

In the South, the creation and actions of the FEPC were condemned and on occasion were met with violent reactions among Whites. Bayard Rustin's description of these reactions provided a platform from which he advocated nonviolence, a concept that would become a defining element of the Civil Rights Movement (**2.5**). Rustin also revealed a number of other issues, including the clear frustration shared by many Blacks at the beginning of World War II.

Aldon Morris notes the importance of 'movement halfway houses' as elements critical to the success of the Civil Rights Movement. 'A movement halfway house,' writes Morris, 'is an established group or organization ... [whose] participants are actively involved in efforts to bring about a desired change in society.'[11] The Fellowship of Reconciliation (FOR), a national, pacifist organization, and the Highlander Folk School, in Monteagle, Tennessee, engaged in adult education for social change, are specific examples. James Farmer (**2.6**) recounts the formation from FOR and the first activity of the Congress of Racial Equality (CORE) in the early 1940s. Septima Clark (**2.7**) describes Rosa Parks's experience at the Highlander Folk School. Highlander, the Fellowship of Reconciliation (FOR), and CORE would all play significant roles in the Civil Rights Movement as training grounds for leadership, nonviolent action, and citizen education.

The principal national organization struggling for equal rights was the NAACP. Formed in 1909, the NAACP advocated an activist approach (as opposed to Booker T. Washington's accommodationist approach) to issues facing African Americans. The organization called for enforcement of civil and political rights guaranteed under the Fourteenth and Fifteenth Amendments as well as equal educational opportunities. Among various strategies, legal action was that most successfully pursued by the NAACP. Committed to the belief that the U.S. Supreme Court had erred in its decision in *Plessy* v. *Ferguson* (1896), the NAACP systematically supported and pursued a series of lawsuits that sought to highlight the actual inequities manifested in the application of 'separate but equal' as well as other inconsistencies between state law and the U.S. Constitution. Victories that the NAACP experienced in its legal challenges to contrivances such as arbitrary court decisions (**2.8**), the all-White primary election (**2.9**), interstate travel (**2.10**), and segregated education (**2.11**) began to chip away at the legal foundations of Jim Crow and set the stage for a direct challenge to the reasoning in *Plessy*.

Finally, as these various groups mounted challenges to White supremacy, it should be noted that very different strategies were adopted. CORE, for example, based its activism on nonviolent, direct action. The NAACP, on the other hand, was often perceived as committed to a slower, legalistic approach to change. Bayard Rustin's response to criticism of direct action from NAACP attorney Thurgood Marshall (**2.12**) reflects some of these differences.

2.1 The central role of Black ministers

In the following passage, the Rev. Joseph Lowery talks about both the role of the minister and a theology of liberation in the Black Church. Central to the Black experience, both were foundational to the Civil Rights Movement.

… I think there are two or three things in the black community that are not fully understood in the white community as it relates to the preacher … In the black community, historically, it's been the preacher who has been the principal community leader. Now there are several reasons for this. One was, of course, educational. He usually could read and write – and had exposure to educational experiences that gave him some advantage. But beneath that was the fact that he was the freest leader in the community. The black congregation supported him, so even though he did solicit a lotta support from the white community for various church causes, actually he was more independent than any other black person in the community …

Aside from that … the black preacher in slavery and the spirituals which grew up out of slavery after blacks were introduced to the Christian faith, their exegesis, their interpretation of the Christian faith always saw Jesus as a liberator. And when the Christian faith talked about the brotherhood of man, they believed that and they expressed it in songs like 'All God's Children Got Shoes.' Now, what they were talkin' about was that even though they were barefooted and the white folks, the slave owners, had shoes, they said, 'Well, all God's children got shoes and when we get to Heaven, we'll put on our shoes.'

Now, he wasn't always talkin' about a place after death. Heaven had a dichotomy in its meaning. To some extent, they meant afterlife, but to an equal extent, if not greater, they were talkin' about somewhere outside slavery. When they sang 'Steal Away to Jesus,' they were singing at night that the Underground Railroad was at work, and Jesus was the symbol of their

28

freedom – try to get up North where there wasn't no slavery. And when they talked about the other song I mentioned, 'All God's Children Got Shoes,' they'd say, 'Heav'n, Heav'n, everybody talkin' 'bout Heav'n, ain't goin' there.' They were talking about the white folks were up there singing about the Lord, God, Love, and Peace and then holding them in slavery, see.

So they saw an hypocrisy in the faith, but they saw the fault not with the religion, but with those who were practicing it. And they adopted the religion, and Jesus became a symbol of freedom and liberty. And the gospel to them was a liberating gospel, because when they read about God delivering Moses and the Children of Israel [thumping his desk for emphasis], they saw the parallel between the experience of the Israelites and the black experience. And they figured that God was gonna deliver them. And so, without always articulating it in theological terms, the black church has always seen God as being identified with the downcast and the suffering. Jesus' first text he used when he preached his first sermon was taken from Isaiah, which is, 'The Lord has anointed me to preach the gospel to the poor, to deliver the oppressed, to free the captive ...'

Howell Raines, *My Soul Is Rested: The Story of the Civil Rights Movement in the Deep South* (New York: Penguin Books, 1983), pp. 68–69.

2.2 African American civic organizations and leaders

Jo Ann Robinson, an English professor at Alabama State College in Montgomery, was a key figure in the Montgomery bus boycott of 1955–56. Here she discusses some of the civic organizations that characterized Black Montgomery during the 1940s and 1950s. These organizations, typical of those in Black communities in cities throughout the South, provided a network of Black self-help and resistance to White supremacy.

This organization [the Women's Political Council] of black women had been founded in 1946, nine years before the [Montgomery bus] boycott began, by Dr. Mary Fair (Mrs. N. W. or 'Frankye') Burks, chairman of the English department at Alabama State College. She became the WPC's first president, and it was she who organized the women who would work together as leader and followers, giving and taking suggestions, and who would never reveal the secrets of the WPC ...

The WPC was formed for the purpose of inspiring Negroes to live above mediocrity, to elevate their thinking, to fight juvenile and adult delinquency, to register and vote, and in general to improve their status as a group. We were 'woman power,' organized to cope with any injustice, no matter what, against the darker sect ...

The early WPC members all lived in the general neighborhood of the college. Most were professional women. There were competent educators, supervisors, principals, teachers, social workers, other community workers, nurses – women employees from every walk of life. Many of the women from Alabama State College were members; so were many public school teachers ...

The Progressive Democratic Association, of which Mr. E. D. Nixon was president, was an old, well-established organization of black leaders, men and women. Some of the best political minds in Montgomery were in this group.

Mr. Nixon was well known throughout the city, county, and much of the state of Alabama and was highly respected by white and black citizens alike ...

In Montgomery, Mr. Nixon was a vital force to be reckoned with. In addition to being president of the Progressive Democratic Association, a leader of the Brotherhood of Sleeping Car Porters and a former president of the local and state branches of the National Association for the Advancement of Colored People, he had been a leader in the 'human rights' movement for many years prior to the boycott. Although he lacked formal training, Nixon was acquainted with most of the members of the police and sheriffs departments, with the judges and jailers, and with people at city hall. Also he knew most of the lawyers in the city, white and black ...

If a black person had been arrested on what amounted to a misdemeanor, Mr. Nixon could often get him freed or exonerated just by going to the place of incarceration. If the trouble was more serious, he knew what to do and whom to call to bring about a solution to the problem. If he had to, he would take a lawyer with him to get arrested persons out of jail. He posted bond for many and accepted responsibility for those who were released in his care ... He was a friend to all ... especially those who could not help themselves.

Mr. Rufus Lewis, president of the Citizens' Steering Committee, fought in an entirely different way. His organization saw to it that people registered to vote as soon as their age level permitted ...

For years he had worked faithfully with his race, encouraging every person twenty-one years old and older to become registered voters. His philosophy on voting was often expressed as: 'A voteless people is a hopeless people.' He often said that if enough black voters had been registered, the present city administrators, who were strong segregationists, would never have been elected. Any man who did not have a voter registration card Mr. Lewis considered not worthy of his time. For a man was not a man, he felt, until he became a registered voter ...

Jo Ann Robinson, *The Montgomery Bus Boycott and the Women Who Started It* (Knoxville: University of Tennessee Press, 1987), pp. 22–29.

2.3 March on Washington

In May, 1941, A. Philip Randolph, President of the BSCP, summoned African Americans to mass, non-violent direct action to address discrimination in employment. A 'March on Washington,' he contended, would pressure President Roosevelt to issue an executive order abolishing discrimination in government agencies and national defense jobs. Roosevelt did, in fact, issue such an order, and Randolph agreed to call off the march. Randolph's arguments portended strategies of two decades later.

We call upon you to fight for jobs in National Defense.

We call upon you to struggle for the integration of Negroes in the armed forces, such as the Air Corps, Navy, Army and Marine Corps of the Nation.

We call upon you to demonstrate for the abolition of Jim-Crowism in all Government departments and defense employment.

An Hour of Crisis

This is an hour of crisis. It is a crisis of democracy. It is a crisis of minority groups. It is a crisis of Negro Americans.

What is this crisis?

To American Negroes, it is the denial of jobs in Government defense projects. It is racial discrimination in Government departments. It is widespread Jim-Crowism in the armed forces of the Nation ...

Self-Liberation

With faith and confidence of the Negro people in their own power for self-liberation, Negroes can break down the barriers of discrimination against employment in National Defense. Negroes can kill the deadly serpent of race hatred in the Army, Navy Air and Marine Corps, and smash through and blast the Government, business and labor-union red tape to win the right to equal opportunity in vocational training and re-training in defense employment.

Most important and vital to all, Negroes, by the mobilization and coordination of their mass power, can cause PRESIDENT ROOSEVELT TO ISSUE AN EXECUTIVE ORDER ABOLISHING DISCRIMINATIONS

IN ALL GOVERNMENT DEPARTMENTS, ARMY, NAVY, AIR CORPS
AND NATIONAL DEFENSE JOBS ...

Negroes can build a mammoth machine of mass action with a terrific
and tremendous driving and striking power that can shatter and crush the
evil fortress of race prejudice and hate, if they will only resolve to do so and
never stop, until victory comes.

Dear fellow Negro Americans, be not dismayed in these terrible times.
You possess power, great power. Our problem is to harness and hitch it up
for action on the broadest, daring and most gigantic scale.

Aggressive Mass Action

In this period of power politics, nothing counts but pressure, more pressure, and still more pressure, through the tactic and strategy of broad,
organized, aggressive mass action behind the vital and important issues of
the Negro. To this end, we propose that ten thousand Negroes MARCH
ON WASHINGTON FOR JOBS IN NATIONAL DEFENSE AND EQUAL
INTEGRATION IN THE FIGHTING FORCES OF THE UNITED
STATES ...

But what of national unity?

We believe in national unity which recognizes equal opportunity of black
and white citizens to jobs in national defense and the armed forces, and in
all other institutions and endeavors in America. We condemn all dictator-
ships, Fascist, Nazi and Communist. We are loyal, patriotic Americans, all.

But, if American democracy will not defend its defenders; if American
democracy will not protect its protectors; if American democracy will not
give jobs to its toilers because of race or color; if American democracy will
not insure equality of opportunity, freedom and justice to its citizens, black
and white, it is a hollow mockery and belies the principles for which it is
supposed to stand ...

However, we sternly counsel against violence and ill-considered and
intemperate action and the abuse of power. Mass power, like physical
power, when misdirected is more harmful than helpful ...

Freedom from Stigma

Today, we call upon President Roosevelt, a great humanitarian and idealist,
to follow in the footsteps of his noble and illustrious predecessor and take
the second decisive step in this world and national emergency and free American Negro citizens of the stigma, humiliation and insult of discrimination
and Jim-Crowism in Government departments and national defense.

The Federal Government cannot with clear conscience call upon private
industry and labor unions to abolish discrimination based upon race and
color as long as it practices discrimination itself against Negro Americans.

The Black Worker, 14 (May, 1941).

2.4 'To Secure These Rights'

The Roosevelt and Truman administrations were more responsive to civil rights activists than were their predecessors. Both issued Executive Orders that promoted the rights of African Americans. For example, in June, 1941, President Roosevelt issued Executive Order 8802, asserting 'that there shall be no discrimination in the employment of workers in defense industries or government because of race, creed, color, or national origin.' With Executive Order 9809 in 1946, President Truman established a Committee on Civil Rights. Excerpts from the summary of that committee's 1947 report, *To Secure These Rights*, are found below. That report formed the basis for comprehensive civil rights legislation that Truman requested from Congress. Although segregationist Senators derailed such legislation, civil rights issues had been brought to the attention of the nation. In July, 1948, Truman issued Executive Order 9981, calling for 'equality of treatment and opportunity for all persons in the armed forces without regard to race, color, religion, or national origin.' While it took some time, by the end of the 1950s, the military had been desegregated.

I. TO STRENGTHEN THE MACHINERY FOR THE PROTECTION OF CIVIL RIGHTS, THE PRESIDENT'S COMMITTEE RECOMMENDS:

1. The reorganization of the Civil Rights Section of the Department of Justice to provide for ... a substantial increase in its appropriation and staff to enable it to engage in more extensive research and to act more effectively to prevent civil rights violations ...
2. The establishment within the FBI of a special unit of investigators trained in civil rights work.
3. The establishment by the state governments of law enforcement agencies comparable to the federal Civil Rights Section.
4. The establishment of a permanent Commission on Civil Rights in the Executive Office of the President, preferably by Act of Congress; And the simultaneous creation of a joint Standing Committee on Civil Rights in Congress.
5. The establishment by the states of permanent commissions on civil rights to parallel the work of the Federal Commission at the state level.
6. The increased professionalization of state and local police forces.

II. TO STRENGTHEN THE RIGHT TO SAFETY AND SECURITY OF THE PERSON, THE PRESIDENT'S COMMITTEE RECOMMENDS:

1. The enactment by Congress of new legislation ... which would impose the same liability on one person as is now imposed on two or more [anti-civil rights] conspirators ...
4. The enactment by Congress of a new statute, specifically directed against police brutality and related crimes.
5. The enactment by Congress of an antilynching act.
6. The enactment by Congress of a new criminal statute on involuntary servitude ...

III. TO STRENGTHEN THE RIGHT TO CITIZENSHIP AND ITS PRIVILEGES, THE PRESIDENT'S COMMITTEE RECOMMENDS:

1. Action by the states or Congress to end poll taxes as a voting prerequisite.
2. The enactment by Congress of a statute protecting the right of qualified persons to participate in federal primaries and elections against interference by public officers and private persons.
3. The enactment by Congress of a statute protecting the right to qualify for, or participate in, federal or state primaries or elections against discriminatory action by state officers based on race or color, or depending on any other unreasonable classification of persons for voting purposes ...

V. TO STRENGTHEN THE RIGHT TO EQUALITY OF OPPORTUNITY, THE PRESIDENT'S COMMITTEE RECOMMENDS:

1. In general:
   The elimination of segregation, based on race, color, creed, or national origin, from American life. The conditioning by Congress of all federal grants-in-aid and other forms of federal assistance to public or private agencies for any purpose on the absence of discrimination and segregation based on race, color, creed, or national origin.
2. For employment:
   The enactment of a federal Fair Employment Practice Act prohibiting all forms of discrimination in private employment ... The enactment by the states of similar laws; The issuance by the President of a mandate against discrimination in government employment and the creation of adequate machinery to enforce this mandate.

3. For education:
   Enactment by the state legislatures of fair educational practice laws for public and private educational institutions, prohibiting discrimination in the admission and treatment of students ...
4. For housing:
   The enactment by the states of laws outlawing restrictive covenants; Renewed court attack, with intervention by the Department of Justice, upon restrictive covenants.
5. For health services:
   The enactment by the states of fair health practice statutes forbidding discrimination and segregation ... in the operation of public or private health facilities.
6. For public services:
   The enactment by Congress of a law stating that discrimination and segregation ... is contrary to public policy; The enactment by the states of similar laws ... The enactment by Congress of a law prohibiting discrimination or segregation ... in interstate transportation and all the facilities thereof, to apply against both public officers and the employees of private transportation companies; The enactment by the states of laws guaranteeing equal access to places of public accommodation, broadly defined ...

VI. TO RALLY THE AMERICAN PEOPLE TO THE SUPPORT OF A CONTINUING PROGRAM TO STRENGTHEN CIVIL RIGHTS, THE PRESIDENT'S COMMITTEE RECOMMENDS:

A long-term campaign of public education to inform the people of the civil rights to which they are entitled and which they owe to one another ...

To Secure These Rights: The Report of the President's Committee on Civil Rights (Washington, DC: U.S. Government Printing Office, 1947), pp. 151–173.

2.5 Bayard Rustin on nonviolence

Rustin, later to become an influential, behind-the-scenes advisor to Martin Luther King, Jr., was a pacifist and advocate of Gandhian nonviolence. He served as youth organizer for Randolph's March on Washington, then became a staff member of FOR and helped form the Congress (originally Committee) of Racial Equality (CORE) from that body (see **2.6**). He participated in CORE's 'Journey of Reconciliation,' an inter-racial bus ride in 1947 through the upper South testing the Supreme Court's decision in *Morgan* v. *Virginia* (see **2.10**). The 'Journey' served as the model for the 1961 'Freedom Rides.' The following piece provides a sense of the frustration felt by African Americans as the US entered World War II: violence against Blacks, continued discrimination, practices inconsistent with the liberty for which the US supposedly was fighting. Despite this frustration, and a growing desire among Blacks to meet violence with violence, Rustin calls for nonviolent, direct action.

Since the United States has entered the war, white-Negro tension has increased steadily. Even in normal times, changes in social and economic patterns cause fear and frustration, which in turn lead to aggression. In time of war, the general social condition is fertile soil for the development of hate and fear, and transference of these to minority groups is quite simple ...

Negro soldiers often are forced to wait at Jim Crow ticket windows while whites are being served, frequently missing their buses and trains. Often bus drivers refuse to pick up any Negroes until all whites are seated, sometimes causing them hours' delay. Scores of Negroes have been beaten and arrested in Memphis, Tennessee; Beaumont, Texas; Columbus, Georgia; and Jackson, Mississippi [sites of major military installations], for insisting on transportation on buses overcrowded because of war conditions. Beaumont has threatened severe punishment for violation of Jim Crow bus laws.

There have been numerous wildcat strikes, in both North and South, where white employees refuse to work with Negroes. Several white and Negro CIO [Congress of Industrial Organizations] officials have been attacked. One was twice assaulted by white workers for trying to get jobs for Negroes.

Negro soldiers and civilians have been killed by whites....

A soldier was shot in the streets of Little Rock, Arkansas, because he refused to tip his hat to a local policeman and address him as 'sir.' The world-famous singer Roland Hayes was beaten and jailed because his wife, who had taken a seat a 'few yards forward' in a Georgia shoe store, insisted upon being served 'where she was' or trading elsewhere. On July 28, two Texas policemen, Clyde and Billy Brown, forced Charles Reco, a Negro soldier, into the back seat of a police car and drove him to the police station because in a Beaumont bus he took a vacant seat reserved for a white. During the ride they shot him once in the shoulder and once in the arm.

Racial feeling has increased since June 1942, when the Fair Employment Practices Committee began hearings on anti-Negro discrimination in Birmingham, Alabama. It has been fed by the anti-Negro propaganda stirred up by Governor Dixon of Alabama, Governor Talmadge of Georgia, and

Representative John Rankin of Mississippi. This propaganda has encouraged such minor politicians as Horace C. Wilkinson, who has suggested developing a 'League of White Supremacy,' to make sure 'that this menace to our national security and our local way of life will disappear rapidly.' Governor Dixon, in refusing to sign a government war contract because it contained a nondiscrimination clause, said, 'I will not permit the citizens of Alabama to be subject to the whims of any federal committee, and I will not permit the employees of the state to be placed in the position where they must abandon the principles of segregation or lose their jobs.' Following this statement, Alabama's Senator John Bankhead wrote General Marshall, army chief of staff, demanding that no Negro soldiers be brought South for military training ...

An increasingly militant group has it in mind to demand *now*, with violence if necessary, the rights it has long been denied. 'If we must die abroad for democracy we can't have,' I heard a friend of mine say, 'then we might as well die right here, fighting for our rights.'

This is a tragic statement. It is tragic also how isolated the average Negro feels in his struggle. The average Negro has largely lost faith in middle-class whites. In his hour of need he seeks not 'talk' but dynamic action ... He describes with disgust the efforts in his behalf by most middle-class Negro and white intellectuals as 'pink tea methods – sometimes well-meanin' but gettin' us nowhere.' ...

Many Negroes see mass violence coming. Having lived in a society in which church, school, and home problems have been handled in a violent way, the majority at this point are unable to conceive of a solution by reconciliation and nonviolence ... I have heard hundreds of Negroes hope for a Japanese military victory, since 'it don't matter who you're a slave for.'

These statements come not only from bitterness but from frustration and fear as well. In many parts of America the Negro, in his despair, is willing to follow any leadership seemingly sincerely identified with his struggle if he is convinced that such leadership offers a workable method. In this crisis those of us who believe in the nonviolent solution of conflict have a duty and an opportunity ...

Certainly the Negro possesses qualities essential for nonviolent direct action. He has long since learned to endure suffering. He can admit his own share of guilt and has to be pushed hard to become bitter ... He is creative and has learned to adjust himself to conditions easily. But above all he possesses a rich religious heritage and today finds the church the center of his life ...

Those who argue for an extended educational plan are not wrong, but there must also be a plan for facing *immediate* conflicts. Those of us who believe in nonviolent resistance can do the greatest possible good for the Negro, for those who exploit him, for America, and for the world by becoming a real part of the Negro community, thus being in a position to suggest methods and to offer leadership when troubles come ...

Bayard Rustin, 'The Negro and Nonviolence,' in *Time on Two Crosses: The Collected Writings of Bayard Rustin*, ed. Devon W. Carbado and Donald Weise (San Francisco: Cleis Press, Inc., 2003), pp. 6–10.

2.6. The origin of the Congress of Racial Equality

CORE was one of the organizations that would play a significant role in the Civil Rights Movement. CORE was an offspring of the Fellowship of Reconciliation (FOR), described by Aldon Morris as one of the 'half-way houses' of the movement, an important part of the network of activism for civil rights. FOR, established in England in 1914, was a Christian-based organization advocating nonviolent solutions to social conflict. As such, it was the source of much of the training that civil rights activists received in Gandhian principles. CORE was the creation in 1942 of a group of FOR activists, including James Farmer, Bayard Rustin, and James Peck. Farmer would serve as CORE's national director from 1961 to 1966. In the following excerpt, Farmer describes the origin of CORE and its first direct-action effort in Chicago.

In the course of my work there, I began studying Gandhi, Gandhi's program, his work in India in nonviolence ... I sent a memorandum to A. J. Muste, who was executive director of the Fellowship of Reconciliation, proposing that the FOR take the lead in starting an organization which would seek to use Gandhi-like techniques of nonviolent resistance – including civil disobedience, noncooperation, and the whole bit – in the battle against segregation ...

The decision was that the FOR would not sponsor it and assume that measure of responsibility for its outcome, its success or failure, but ... I was authorized on their payroll to try to set up a local group of the sort I had suggested – in one city – and the FOR would not sponsor it. They would just pay my salary, fifteen dollars a week, while I was doing that ...

That was an all-night session by the way, deciding what the name was going to be. And one fellow – I have no idea where he is now – name of Bob Chino, who was half Chinese and half Caucasian, came up with a name during this all-night meeting. He said, 'Why don't we call it CORE because it's the core of things. It's the center around which all else is built.' Then the problem was, what does C-O-R-E stand for? [Laughs] We then decided that it should be Committee of or on Racial Equality. A lengthy debate transpired on whether it was to be on or of Racial Equality. And my side won ... it became *of.*

Our first project then was a sit-in, or stand-in, I guess you'd call it, at a roller skating rink that was appropriately named White City Roller Skating Rink [laughs], which was at the corner of Sixty-third Street and South Park Avenue in southside Chicago ... This was in the ghetto, really, several blocks within the ghetto, but all white. Blacks were not admitted.

I should say that at this same time we met and consulted with an Indian, a Hindu, a Brahmin named Krishnalal Shridharani, who had been a disciple of Gandhi's in India, was with Gandhi on the famous march to the sea, the Salt March. He at this time was working on his Ph.D. at Columbia in sociology and his dissertation was a book analyzing Gandhi's technique, Gandhi's method. It was entitled *War Without Violence*, and this caught our imagination because that was precisely what we were aimed at. It was not acquiescence, as most people at that time, when they heard of nonviolence, assumed that it was ... In this book Shridharani had outlined Gandhi's steps of investigation, negotiation, publicity, and then demonstration. And we adopted those steps as our method of action.

At White City we first investigated in order to confirm what we already knew existed by having blacks go in and try to skate and they were stopped, of course, and told, 'I'm sorry, we can't sell you tickets. You can't come in.' This was done several times to be sure that there was no mistake about the policy ... Then we had whites, several whites, try to go in, with no apparent connection with the black group, and they were promptly admitted and skated around. Then we had an interracial group go in and seek admission, and this threw White City persons into confusion. Obviously they were part of one group, so what were they going to say?

So finally they had to use the club-night line and they said, 'I'm sorry, it's club night, and you can't come in unless you have a club card.' And our group said, 'Are there no exceptions?' 'Absolutely no exceptions, nobody gets in without a club card.' 'You know, that's strange. Some of our friends are already skating in there, and we know that they have no club card. They are not members of a club.' 'Well, are sure of that?' 'Yes, we are sure of that. We see them skating right through the door there, and one of them waved at us.' So they then consulted with the manager and everything else and said, 'I'm just sorry, you can't come in. '

We stood in line for a while, ... then went back every night to do the same thing, and finally tied up the line so that nobody else could get to the gate, and it became pretty rough. A little violence when some of the young tough whites wanted to skate badly... . This campaign against White City went on for several months before there was a conclusion, and finally we were victorious. White City admitted everybody after [our] picket lines and standing in line and cutting down on their profit, virtually bringing things to a halt. They began admitting blacks.

... during White City – the thing was dragging on for several months
– somebody suggested, 'Well, why don't we sue? Let's go to court and sue
on the basis of century-old civil rights laws.' We rejected this because that
would be reverting to the old techniques which we knew could work under
certain circumstances, but it would not tell us whether nonviolence would
work here, direct-action techniques ...

Raines, *My Soul Is Rested*, pp. 27–29.

2.7 Septima Clark on Rosa Parks at Highlander Folk School

The Highlander Folk School, in Monteagle, Tennessee, was established by Myles Horton, who believed that social change could be
fostered through adult education. Horton believed that oppressed
people themselves knew best how to address their problems, once
they engaged in group analysis of those problems. The school would
recruit leaders from among the people and provide workshops in
which the teacher's job was to engage students actively in identifying problems, raising questions, and developing their own solutions. Horton's philosophy drew from Christian social gospel and
Marxism, and originally the Highlander Folk School focused on
labor issues in support of unionization. In the 1940s, the school,
which had always been integrated, began to focus on racial issues,
fostering leadership in opposition to White supremacy. One such
leader was Septima Clark, from Charleston, South Carolina. Originally recruited as a community leader, she joined the Highlander
staff after being fired from her teaching job in Charleston as a result
of her membership in the NAACP. In the following passage Septima
Clark talks about Rosa Parks. She also mentions Virginia Durr, one
of the very few White liberals in the South who openly supported
Black efforts at desegregation.

I went to Highlander twice the first summer in '54, and the following summer
I used my car to transport three groups of six persons each to Highlander
workshops. At the end of that summer, we held a workshop to develop
leadership, which I was directing. That was when I met Rosa Parks.
    At that time Mrs. Parks lived in Montgomery, Alabama. Her husband
was a barber, and he used to shave and cut hair for all of the high-class

whites. Rosa was working with the youth group of the National Association for the Advancement of Colored People, or the N, double A, C, P, for short.

Rosa got to Highlander because she knew Virginia Durr, a great friend of Myles Horton, the director of the Highlander. Rosa and Virginia got to know each other by Rosa being a seamstress and Virginia's husband being the only lawyer in Montgomery who would take the legal cases brought by the NAACP. Working with the NAACP, Rosa was under fire. Virginia stayed under fire because she was a white woman who dared to take sides with blacks.

First Virginia Durr wrote a letter and asked that we send money for Rosa to come up to Highlander, which we did. Then Virginia took Rosa to Atlanta and saw her on a bus to Highlander.

We had a large group of people at that workshop. It was a two-week workshop on the United Nations. We knew that Rosa had been working with the youth group in Montgomery, so at the meeting I asked Rosa to tell how she was able to get the Freedom Train to come to Montgomery and get this youth group to go through the Freedom Train. She wouldn't talk at all at first.

Figure 4 Septima Clark and Rosa Parks at the Highlander Folk Center.

41

People at the workshop knew only a little bit about the Freedom Train. It was being sent by the government around the country from Washington, D.C. as a lesson in democracy. It carried an exhibit of the original U.S. Constitution and the Declaration of Independence. Anyone could go inside for free, but segregation was not permitted.

One night up there in the bedroom (there were about six beds in one dormitory) everyone started singing and dancing, white kids and all, and they said, 'Rosa, how in the world did you deal with that Freedom Train?'

Then she said, 'It wasn't an easy task. We took our children down when the Freedom Train came, and the white and black children had to go in together. They wouldn't let them go in otherwise, and that was a real victory for us:' But she said, 'After that, I began getting obscene phone calls from people because I was president of the youth group. That's why Mrs. Durr wanted me to come up here and see what I could do with this same youth group when I went back home.'

The next day in the workshop I say, 'Rosa, tell these people how you got that Freedom Train to come to Montgomery.' She hated to tell it. She thought that certainly somebody would go back and tell the white people. A teacher from Montgomery came at the same time, and she say she couldn't let them know she was coming to Highlander, because if these white people knew then she would have lost her job, too.

Anyway, Rosa got up and told that group about it. We had somebody there from the United Nations, and they said to her, 'If anything happens, you get in touch with me, and I'll be sure to see that you have your rights.'

After the workshop, Rosa was afraid to go from Highlander to Atlanta. Myles sent me with her. She was afraid that somebody had already spoken, and she didn't know what was going to happen. I went with her to Atlanta and saw her in a bus going down to Montgomery. She felt much better then.

I guess she kept thinking about the things at the workshop. At the end of the workshops we always say, 'What do you plan to do back home?' Rosa answered that question by saying that Montgomery was the cradle of the Confederacy, that nothing would happen there because blacks wouldn't stick together. But she promised to work with those kids, and to tell them that they had the right to belong to the NAACP, that they had the right to do things like going through the Freedom Train. She decided that she was going to keep right on working with them.

Three months after Rosa got back to Montgomery, on December 1, 1955, she refused to get up from her seat on the bus. When I heard the news, I said, 'Rosa? Rosa?' She was so shy when she came to Highlander, but she got enough courage to do that …

Cynthia Stokes, ed., *Septima Clark and the Civil Rights Movement: Ready from Within* (Trenton, NJ: Africa World Press, Inc., 1990), pp. 31–34.

2.8 *Brown* v. *Mississippi* (1936)

Often, 'justice' for Blacks accused of crimes in the South devolved to lynch law. Even when defendants did receive trials, they were typically arbitrary and characterized by the absence of basic due process protections. In this case, in order to get confessions, Brown and two others accused of murder were beaten, whipped, and twice hanged and cut down. Although the only evidence against them was the coerced confessions, the trial court found them guilty and the Mississippi State Supreme Court upheld the convictions. NAACP attorneys argued that these defendants' due process rights were violated, and the US Supreme Court agreed, overturning the convictions.

... Because a State may dispense with a jury trial, it does not follow that it may substitute trial by ordeal. The rack and torture chamber may not be substituted for the witness stand. The State may not permit an accused to be hurried to conviction under mob domination – where the whole proceeding is but a mask – without supplying corrective process ... It would be difficult to conceive of methods more revolting to the sense of justice than those taken to procure the confessions of these petitioners, and the use of the confessions thus obtained as the basis for conviction and sentence was a clear denial of due process.

In the instant case, the trial court was fully advised ... of the way in which the confessions had been procured. The trial court knew that there was no other evidence upon which conviction and sentence could be based.

Yet it proceeded to permit conviction and to pronounce sentence ... It was challenged before the Supreme Court of the State by the express invocation of the Fourteenth Amendment ... but that court declined to enforce petitioners' constitutional right. The court thus denied a federal right fully established and specially set up and claimed and the judgment must be reversed.

297 U.S. 278 (1936).

2.9 *Smith* v. *Allwright* (1944)

Throughout the 'solid South,' Democratic primaries were the only significant elections, with victory at that level tantamount to election to office. The primaries, however, had excluded Black voters (see **1.2**). In *Grovey* v. *Townshend* (1935), the US Supreme Court had recognized political parties as private entities, free to determine their own participation rules. By the time the NAACP challenged the constitutionality of the Texas all-White primary in *Smith* v. *Allwright*, the Court had reconsidered its position, and the NAACP persuaded the Court to find the all-White primary unconstitutional.

It may now be taken as a postulate that the right to vote in ... a primary for the nomination of candidates without discrimination by the State, like the right to vote in a general election, is a right secured by the Constitution ... By the terms of the Fifteenth Amendment that right may not be abridged by any state on account of race ...

The party takes its character as a state agency from the duties imposed upon it by state statutes ... When primaries become a part of the machinery for choosing officials ... the same texts to determine the character of discrimination or abridgement should be applied to the primary as are applied to the general election. If the state requires a certain electoral procedure, prescribes a general election ballot made up of party nominees so chosen and limits the choice of the electorate in general elections for state offices, practically speaking to those whose names appear on such a ballot, it endorses, adopts or enforces the discrimination against Negroes, practiced by a party entrusted by Texas law with the determination of the qualifications of participants in the primary. This is state action within the meaning of the Fifteenth Amendment ...

[T]he opportunity for choice is not to be nullified by a state through casting its electoral process in a form which permits a private organization to practice racial discrimination in the election. Constitutional rights would be of little value if they could be thus indirectly denied ... *Grovey v. Townsend is* overruled.

321 U.S. 649 (1944).

2.10 *Morgan* v. *Virginia* (1945)

In *Morgan* v. *Virginia*, the NAACP argued that state-imposed segregation in interstate travel impeded interstate commerce and was thus unconstitutional. The Supreme Court agreed. Later, in *Henderson* v. *U.S. Interstate Commerce Commission and Southern Railway* (1950), the Court extended its decision to also invalidate carrier-imposed segregation in interstate travel as well.

In weighing the factors that entered into our conclusion as to whether this statute so burdens interstate commerce or so infringes the requirements of national uniformity as to be invalid, we are mindful of the fact that conditions vary between northern or western states such as Maine or Montana, with practically no colored population; industrial states such as Illinois, Ohio, New Jersey and Pennsylvania with a small, although appreciable, percentage of colored citizens; and the states of the deep South ... Local efforts to promote amicable relations in difficult areas by legislative segregation in interstate transportation emerge from the latter racial distribution. As no state law can reach beyond its own border nor bar transportation of passengers across its boundaries, diverse seating requirements for the races in interstate journeys result. As there is no federal act dealing with the separation of races in interstate transportation, we must decide the validity of the Virginia statute on the challenge that it interferes with commerce, as a matter of balance between the exercise of the local police power and the need for national uniformity in the regulation of interstate travel. It seems clear to us that seating arrangements for the different races in interstate motor travel require a single, uniform rule to promote and protect national travel. Consequently, we hold the Virginia statute in controversy invalid ...

328 U.S. 373 (1945).

2.11 *McLaurin* v. *Oklahoma State Regents* (1950)

In *McLaurin* and its companion case, *Sweatt* v. *Painter*, the Supreme Court considered issues where states went through the motions of admitting African American students or creating an 'equivalent' school. McLaurin was admitted to the all-White University of Oklahoma's Graduate School in education. However, he was segregated in separate desks in the classroom , library, and cafeteria. Sweatt was admitted to a jury-rigged 'law school' for Blacks rather than the law school of the University of Texas. Both states argued that these provisions secured substantially equal treatment. The Court disagreed. With the decisions in *McLaurin* and *Sweatt*, the Court was indicating that it would accept nothing less than truly equal facilities under the doctrine of 'separate but equal.' An excerpt from the *McLaurin* decision follows.

Following the *Sipuel* decision, the Oklahoma legislature amended these statutes to permit the admission of Negroes to [white] institutions of higher learning ... in cases where [they] offered courses not available in the Negro schools. The amendment provided, however, that in such cases the program of instruction 'shall be given at such colleges or institutions of higher education upon a segregated basis.' Appellant was thereupon admitted to the University of Oklahoma Graduate School [and] ... his admission was made subject to 'such rules and regulations as to segregation as the President of the University shall consider to afford to Mr. G. W. McLaurin substantially equal educational opportunities as are afforded to other persons seeking the same education in the Graduate College,' a condition which does not appear to have been withdrawn. Thus he was required to sit apart at a designated desk in an anteroom adjoining the classroom; to sit at a designated desk on the mezzanine floor of the library, but not to use the desks in the regular reading room; and to sit at a designated table and to eat at a different time from the other students in the school cafeteria.

In the interval between the decision of the court below and the hearing in this Court, the treatment afforded appellant was altered. For some time, the section of the classroom in which appellant sat was surrounded by a rail on which there was a sign stating, 'Reserved for Colored,' but these have been removed. He is now assigned to a seat in the classroom in a row specified for colored students; he is assigned to a table in the library on the main floor; and he is permitted to eat at the same time in the cafeteria as other students, although here again he is assigned to a special table.

It is said that the separations imposed by the State in this case are in form merely nominal. McLaurin uses the same classroom, library and cafeteria as students of other races; there is no indication that the seats to which he is assigned in these rooms have any disadvantage of location. He may wait in line in the cafeteria and there stand and talk with his fellow students, but while be eats he must remain apart.

These restrictions signify that the State, in administering the facilities it affords for professional and graduate study, sets McLaurin apart from the other students ... Such restrictions impair his ability to study, to engage in discussions and exchange views with other students, and ... to learn his profession.

Our society grows increasingly complex, and our need for trained leaders increases correspondingly. Appellant's case represents, perhaps, the epitome of that need, for he is attempting ... to become ... a leader and trainer of others. Those who will come under his guidance ... must be directly affected by the education he receives. Their own education and development will necessarily suffer to the extent that his training is unequal to that of his classmates. State-imposed restrictions which produce such inequalities cannot be sustained ...

We conclude that the conditions under which this appellant is required to receive his education deprive him of his personal and present right to the equal protection of the laws. We hold that under these circumstances the Fourteenth-Amendment precludes differences in treatment by the state based upon race. Appellant ... must receive the same treatment at the hands of the state as students of other races ...

339 U.S. 737 (1950).

2.12 Rustin on Marshall's opposition to the Journey of Reconciliation

One of the characteristics of the Civil Rights Movement would be a variety of approaches to desegregation and the struggle against White supremacy. Activists such as Bayard Rustin believed in nonviolent, direct action. Thurgood Marshall, of the NAACP, often opposed direct action as counterproductive. In 1947, for example, Marshall was critical of CORE's Journey of Reconciliation. Here, Rustin responds to that criticism.

I am sure that Marshall is either ill-informed on the principles and techniques of non-violence or ignorant of the processes of social change. Unjust social laws and patterns do not change because supreme courts deliver just opinions. One need merely observe the continued practices of jim crow in interstate travel six months after the Supreme Court's decision to see the necessity of resistance. Social progress comes from struggle; all freedom demands a price.

At times freedom will demand that its followers go into situations where even death is to be faced ... Direct action means picketing, striking and boycotting as well as disobedience against unjust conditions, and all of these methods have already been used with some success by Negroes and sympathetic whites ...

I cannot believe that Thurgood Marshall thinks that such a program would lead to wholesale slaughter.... But if anyone at this date in history believes that the 'white problem,' which is one of privilege, can be settled without some violence, he is mistaken and fails to realize the ends to which man can be driven to hold on to what they consider privileges.

This is why Negroes and whites who participate in direct action must pledge themselves to non-violence in word and deed. For in this way alone can the inevitable violence be reduced to a minimum. The simple truth is this: unless we find non-violent methods which can be used by the rank-and-file who more and more tend to resist, they will more and more resort to violence. And court-room argumentation will not suffice for the activization which the Negro masses are today demanding.

'Our Guest Column: Beyond the Courts,' *Louisiana Weekly* (January 4, 1947).

Notes

1 See, for example, P. Sullivan, *Days of Hope: Race and Democracy in the New Deal Era* (Chapel Hill, NC: University of North Carolina Press, 1996).
2 See, for example, R. D. G. Kelley, ' 'We Are Not What We Seem': Rethinking Black Working-Class Opposition in the Jim Crow South,' *Journal of American History*, 80/1 (June, 1993), pp. 75–115.
3 W. T. Walker, *'Somebody's Calling My Name': Black Sacred Music and Social Change* (Valley Forge, Pa.: Judson Press, 1979), p. 19.
4 *Ibid.*, p. 19.
5 *Ibid.*, p. 20.
6 *Ibid.*, p. 20.
7 A. D. Morris, *The Origins of the Civil Rights Movement* (New York: The Free Press, 1984), p. 4.
8 Walker, *'Somebody's Calling My Name'*, p. 21.
9 *Ibid.*, p. 34.
10 Morris, *The Origins*, p. 4
11 *Ibid.*, p. 139.

3

'We are soldiers in the army': emergence of the Movement

African American resistance to Jim Crow preceding the modern Civil Rights Movement manifested itself in a number of ways and through a number of organizations. Just as these organizations had different approaches to issues of civil rights and social justice, the Movement emerged with varying configurations. Some students and scholars identify the beginning of the Movement with the success of Thurgood Marshall and the NAACP in persuading the US Supreme Court to overturn the 'separate but equal' doctrine as it applied to education (*Brown* v. *Board*). Others focus on the Montgomery Bus Boycott as the seminal event. Both events had antecedents. Nonetheless, the period 1954–55 is generally accepted as the 'beginning' of the modern Civil Rights Movement. These two manifestations of resistance also reflect differing approaches within the Movement. In this chapter we explore the various expressions of the Movement from *Brown* through the Civil Rights Act of 1957.

The NAACP's legal successes challenging educational inequality, culminating in the *Sweatt* and *McLaurin* cases (see **2.11**), provided Thurgood Marshall and his associates with a basis from which to launch a bolder assault, specifically on segregation in education, but thereby an assault on segregation writ large. Marshall first focused on inequalities in elementary and secondary public education, and then challenged the very notion that separate education and educational facilities could ever be equal. In a series of cases combined by the Supreme Court under *Brown* v. *Board of Education of Topeka* (**3.1**), Marshall sought to show that segregated education had never been equal and that race was not a reasonable basis for the classification of students. Furthermore, Marshall introduced evidence from social scientists to show the harmful psychological effects of segregation on Black students (**3.2**). Ultimately, Marshall's approach persuaded the Court to overturn longstanding precedent.

49

Throughout their deliberations, the Justices were aware of the stiff resistance to desegregation among the vast majority of Whites in the South and were concerned over the potential for violent, White reaction. The Court, therefore, postponed its relief decree for one year. In that decree, *Brown II*, although the Court required the school systems to 'make a prompt and reasonable start toward full compliance' with the decision, it recognized that time might be required for full implementation and charged the lower courts to make sure that the implementation effort was pursued with 'all deliberate speed.'[1]

The Justices were prescient in foreseeing the negative reaction among Southern Whites as, subsequent to the Court's decree, Southern states pursued policies and enacted legislation intended to undermine *Brown*. 'The Southern Manifesto' (3.3), signed by White US Congressmen and Senators from the South, laid out their basic argument and applauded 'the motives of those States which have declared the intention to resist forced integration by any lawful means.' Those 'lawful means' comprised a range of state legislative measures designed to impede desegregation, including 'nullification' and 'interposition' (3.4), the re-establishment of segregation laws (3.5), and school closing laws (3.6). A number of states passed anti-NAACP laws (3.7).

The crisis surrounding school desegregation in Little Rock, Arkansas, in the fall of 1957 illustrated a number of the issues related to the implementation of *Brown*. In an effort to meet the demands of *Brown*, the Little Rock school board had developed a plan for gradual desegregation of its schools. The plan was to begin with the desegregation of Central High School, where nine Black students were to be enrolled in the fall of 1957. The evening before school was to open, however, Governor Orval Faubus, ostensibly to maintain order, but evidently attempting to gain political capital with segregationists, ordered the Arkansas National Guard to prevent the students from entering the school. Faubus's actions incited segregationists, and White mobs also formed to greet the Black students. The ensuing series of events demonstrated the bravery of the Black students (3.8); the tactics segregationists used to intimidate; and, despite President Eisenhower's use of federal troops to enforce the rights of the students (3.9), the unwillingness of the federal government to interfere with local 'law and order' (3.10). The crisis also provided an opportunity for the Supreme Court to assert federal supremacy (**3.11**) over state 'interposition.'

The experiences of the Little Rock Nine and their supporters confirmed Rustin's argument (see **2.12**) that Supreme Court decisions alone would not bring social change. Rather, change required action by the people – boycotts, demonstrations, sacrifice. The efficacy of such tactics, ultimately central to the Civil Rights Movement, was demonstrated during the Montgomery Bus Boycott. Although the Montgomery story of 1955–56 included legal challenges to unjust laws, its special significance lay in its expression of a number of the Movement's key characteristics: an organized, mass movement centered in the churches and complemented by local Black organizations; nonviolent, direct action; charismatic leadership; and regional networking for change.

When Rosa Parks was arrested on December 1, 1955, for refusing to relinquish her seat to a White man upon the command of the bus driver, that event did not spontaneously generate the protest movement. Rather, Parks had been an active member of the NAACP and had attended training sessions at the Highlander Folk School (see **2.7**). As Jo Ann Robinson pointed out (**3.12**), members of the Black community in Montgomery had complained about abuses in the bus system for years, had attempted to negotiate change with the city, and had been contemplating a boycott. A number of Black leaders were aware of a brief and successful 1953 bus boycott in Baton Rouge, Louisiana, that might serve as a model. When Rosa Parks was arrested, Robinson's Women's Political Council distributed fliers calling for a one-day boycott, E. D. Nixon recruited support from clergy in Montgomery – including the new minister at the Dexter Avenue Baptist Church, Martin Luther King, Jr. – and, most important, the Montgomery Improvement Association (MIA), an 'organization of organizations,' was created. The MIA served as the nerve-center of the interconnected network of Black political, fraternal, and church groups that were the lifeline of the mass movement. The MIA quickly decided to organize the Black community for a boycott that would last until demands were met. Later, when the White leadership proved to be wholly intransigent, the MIA filed a federal lawsuit challenging local and state segregation laws.

Aldon D. Morris argues that mass movements 'are the products of organizing efforts and preexisting institutions.'[2] He concludes that the 'local movement center' was key to the organizing effort:

A local movement center is a social organization within the community of a subordinate group, which mobilizes, organizes, and coordinates collective action aimed at attaining the common ends of that subordinate group. A movement center exists in a subordinate community when that community has developed an interrelated set of protest leaders, organizations, and followers who collectively define the common ends of the group, devise necessary tactics and strategies along with training for their implementation, and engage in actions designed to attain the goals of the group.[3]

The MIA provided the local movement center in Montgomery and a blueprint for organizing mass movements in Black communities throughout the South. The MIA's executive committee organized weekly mass meetings, raised money, and organized a transportation system for Blacks who had relied on the buses to get to and from work. Central to the movement was the mass meeting, held in local churches and reflecting the structure and spirit, including the music and preaching, of a Black church service (3.13). The central figure was the charismatic preacher, and the MIA's selection of Martin Luther King, Jr. as its principal spokesperson was serendipitous. King was a highly educated product of the Black Church, able to appeal to a broad spectrum of the Black community. Morris

Figure 5 Congregants sing 'We shall overcome' at a mass meeting.

notes that 'King could attract large segments of oppressed blacks from the poolrooms, city streets, and backwoods long enough for trained organizers to acquaint them with the workshops, demands, and strategies of the movement.'[4] The defining philosophy of those workshops was nonviolent, direct action, and figures such as Bayard Rustin and Glenn Smiley, national field secretary of FOR, traveled to Montgomery to tutor King and provide training workshops.

During the course of the boycott, King became a nationally known figure. '[King's] signal contribution to nonviolent protest was to incorporate Gandhian principles and techniques into the black church culture that had nourished him,' wrote historian Stuart Burns.'King brought together [A. Philip] Randolph's Gandhian mass action with black social gospel to create a synthesis of visionary but pragmatic non-violent politics.'[5] Black social gospel posited the redemptive power of Christian love, and King was unmatched in articulating this vision.

> Love must be at the forefront of our movement if it is to be a successful movement ... When we speak of love, we speak of understanding goodwill toward all men. We speak of a redemptive, a creative sort of love ... So that as we look at the problem, we see that the real tension is not between the Negro citizens of Montgomery and the white citizens, but it is a conflict between justice and injustice, between the forces of light and the forces of darkness, and if there is a victory – and there will be a victory – the victory will not be merely for he Negro citizens and a defeat for the white citizens, but it will be a victory for justice and a defeat of injustice. It will be a victory for goodness in its long struggle with the forces of evil. This is a spiritual movement.[6]

Despite various efforts by the White leaders in Montgomery to stifle the boycott, including mass arrests and intimidation, the boycott was maintained until the Supreme Court endorsed an earlier federal court decision finding the Montgomery segregation laws unconstitutional (**3.14**). King, however, with the prompting of Bayard Rustin (**3.15**), understood that a broader coordinating structure was needed to maintain the momentum that the Montgomery boycott had brought to the Movement. A series of meetings that he organized along with colleagues Fred Shuttlesworth from Birmingham and C. K. Steel from Tallahassee, Florida, led to the formation of the Southern Christian Leadership Conference (SCLC). This organization, with King at its head, would link and coordinate church-based desegregation efforts throughout the South.

Developments in Montgomery and other Southern cities gained the attention of the US Congress, which, in September 1957, passed the first civil rights bill since Reconstruction (**3.16**). The bill was very much a compromise between liberal, labor, and religious groups on the one hand and Southern segregationists on the other, and it had only lukewarm support from the Eisenhower Administration. Blacks' general reaction to the bill as being inadequate to address historic inequities is reflected in Charles H. Thompson's analysis of the law (**3.17**). Nonetheless, change was in the air, and it appeared that the Movement had gained critical momentum.

3.1 *Brown* v. *Board of Education of Topeka* (1954)

The decisions of the Supreme Court in cases such as *McLaurin* v. *Oklahoma* (**2.11**) requiring truly equal opportunities under the concept of 'separate but equal' did not go unnoticed in the South. Southern states began to improve public school facilities for Blacks, trusting that the nearly half-century-old precedent would not be overturned. In the cases decided under *Brown* (from the states of Kansas, South Carolina, Virginia, and Delaware and the District of Columbia), however, the NAACP argued that segregation was inherently unequal and provided sociological evidence in support of that contention. The Court agreed. *Plessy* was overturned.

In the first cases in this Court construing the Fourteenth Amendment, decided shortly after its adoption, the Court interpreted it as proscribing all state-imposed discriminations against the Negro race. The doctrine of 'separate but equal' did not make its appearance in this Court until 1896 in the case of *Plessy v. Ferguson* ... involving not education but transportation. American courts have since labored with the doctrine for over half a century. In this Court, there have been six cases involving the 'separate but equal' doctrine in the field of public education ... In more recent cases, all on the graduate school level, inequality was found in that specific benefits enjoyed by white students were denied to Negro students of the same educational qualifications ... In none of these cases was it necessary to re-examine the doctrine to grant relief to the Negro plaintiff ...

In the instant cases, the question is directly presented. Here ... there are findings below that the Negro and white schools involved have been equalized, or are being equalized, with respect to buildings, curricula, qualifications and salaries of teachers ... Our decision, therefore, cannot turn on merely the comparison of these tangible factors in the Negro and white schools involved in each of the cases. We must look instead to the effect of segregation itself on public education. In approaching this problem, we cannot turn the clock back to 1868 when the Amendment was adopted, or even to 1896 when *Plessy v. Ferguson* was written. We must consider public education in the light of its full development and its present place in American life throughout the Nation. Only in this way can it be determined if segregation in public schools deprives these plaintiffs of the equal protection of the laws.

Today, education is perhaps the most important function of state and local governments ... It is required in the performance of our most basic public responsibilities, even service in the armed forces. It is the very foundation of good citizenship. Today it is a principal instrument in awakening the child to cultural values, in preparing him for later professional training, and in helping him to adjust normally to his environment ...

We come then to the question presented: Does segregation of children in public schools solely on the basis of race, even though the physical facilities and other 'tangible' factors may be equal, deprive the children of the minority group of equal educational opportunities? We believe that it does ...

To separate them from others of similar age and qualifications solely because of their race generates a feeling of inferiority as to their status in the community that may affect their hearts and minds in a way unlikely ever to be undone. The effect of this separation on their educational opportunities was well stated by a finding in the Kansas case by a court which nevertheless felt compelled to rule against the Negro plaintiffs:

'Segregation of white and colored children in public schools has a detrimental effect upon the colored children. The impact is greater when it has the sanction of the law; for the policy of separating the races is usually interpreted as denoting the inferiority of the Negro group. A sense of inferiority affects the motivation of a child to learn. Segregation with the sanction of law, therefore, has a tendency to retard the education and mental development of Negro children and to deprive them of some of the benefits they would receive in a racially integrated school system.' Whatever may have been the extent of psychological knowledge at the time of *Plessy v. Ferguson*, this finding is amply supported by modern authority. Any language in *Plessy v. Ferguson* contrary to this finding is rejected.

We conclude that in the field of public education the doctrine of 'separate but equal' has no place. Separate educational facilities are inherently unequal. Therefore, we hold that the plaintiffs and others similarly situated for whom the actions have been brought are, by reason of the segregation complained of, deprived of the equal protection of the laws guaranteed by the Fourteenth Amendment ...

347 U.S. 483 (1954).

3.2 How children learn about race

An unprecedented aspect of the NAACP's argument in *Brown* was the submission of sociological evidence indicating the harmful effects of segregation on Black children. That research was conducted by Kenneth B. Clark. The excerpt below summarizes his findings.

Racial attitudes appear early in the life of children and affect the ideas and behavior of children in the first grades of school. Such attitudes – which appear to be almost inevitable in children in our society – develop gradually.

According to one recent study, white kindergarten children in New York City show a clear preference for whites and a clear rejection of Negroes. Other studies show that Negro children in the kindergarten and early elementary grades of a New England town, in New York City, in Philadelphia, and in two urban communities in Arkansas know the difference between Negroes and whites; realize they are Negro or white; and are aware of the social meaning and evaluation of racial differences.

The development of racial awareness and racial preferences in Negro children has been studied by the author and his wife. To determine the extent of consciousness of skin of color in these children between three and seven years old, we showed the children four dolls all from the same mold and dressed alike; the only difference in the dolls was that two were brown and two were white ... These children reacted with strong awareness of skin color. Among three-year-old Negro children in both northern and southern communities, more that 75 percent showed that they were conscious of the difference between 'white' and 'colored.' Among older children, an increasingly greater number made the correct choices.

These findings clearly support the conclusion that racial awareness is present in Negro children as young as three years old. Furthermore, this knowledge develops in stability and clarity from year to year, and by the age of seven, it is a part of the knowledge of all Negro children. Other investigators have shown that the same is true of white children ...

There is now no doubt that children learn the prevailing social ideas about racial differences early in their lives. Not only are they aware of race in terms of physical characteristics such as skin color, but also they are generally able to identify themselves in terms of race ...

In addition to Negro children's awareness of differences in skin color, the author and his wife studied the ability of these children to identify themselves in racial terms ... We asked the children to point out the doll 'which is most like you.' Approximately two-thirds of all the children answered correctly. Correct answers were more frequent among the older ones....

Many personal and emotional factors probably affected the ability of these Negro children to select the brown doll ... The majority of these Negro children at each age indicated an unmistakable preference for the white doll and a rejection of the brown doll.

... Learning about races and racial differences, learning one's own racial identity, learning which race is to be preferred and which rejected – all these are assimilated by the child as part of the total pattern of ideas he acquires about himself and the society in which he lives ... Furthermore, as the average child learns to evaluate these differences according to the standards of the society, he is at the same time required to identify himself with one or another group ... The child therefore cannot learn what racial group he belongs to without being involved in a larger pattern of emotions, conflict, and desires which are part of his growing knowledge of what society thinks about his race ...

The fact that young Negro children would prefer to be white reflects their knowledge that society prefers white people. White children are generally found to prefer their white skin – an indication that they, too, know that society like whites better. It is clear, therefore, that the self-acceptance or self-rejection found so early in a child's developing complex of racial ideas reflects the awareness and acceptance of the prevailing racial attitudes in his community ...

Kenneth B. Clark, *Prejudice and Your Child* (Boston: Beacon Press, 1963), pp. 18–19, 22–24.

3.3 Southern Manifesto

The 'Declaration of Constitutional Principles,' signed in 1956 by nineteen US Senators and seventy-nine members of the House of Representatives – all from the South – represented the fundamental constitutional position from which the White power structure in the South criticized the Brown decision for over a decade. (See the statement of Alabama Governor George Wallace, **5.8.**)

... We regard the decision of the Supreme Court in the school cases as a clear abuse of judicial power. It climaxes a trend in the Federal judiciary undertaking to legislate, in derogation of the authority of Congress, and to encroach upon the reserved rights of the States and the people.

The original Constitution does not mention education. Neither does the 14th amendment nor any other amendment. The debates preceding the submission of the 14th amendment clearly show that there was no intent that it should affect the system of education maintained by the States.

The very Congress which proposed the amendment subsequently provided for segregated schools in the District of Columbia.

In the case of *Plessy* v. *Ferguson* in 1896 the Supreme Court expressly declared that under the 14th amendment no person was denied any of his rights if the States provided separate but equal public facilities. This decision has been followed in many other cases. It is notable that the Supreme Court, speaking through Chief Justice Taft, a former President of the United States, unanimously declared in 1927 in *Lum* v. *Rice* that the 'separate but equal' principle is 'within the discretion of the State in regulating its public schools and does not conflict with the 14th amendment.'

This interpretation, restated time and again, became a part of the life of the people of many of the States and confirmed their habits, customs, traditions, and way of life. It is founded on elemental humanity and common sense, for parents should not be deprived by Government of the right to direct the lives and education of their own children.

This unwarranted exercise of power by the Court, contrary to the Constitution, is creating chaos and confusion in the States principally affected. It is destroying the amicable relations between the white and Negro races that have been created through 90 years of patient effort by the good people of both races. It has planted hatred and suspicion where there has been heretofore friendship and understanding.

We reaffirm our reliance on the Constitution as the fundamental law of the land.

We decry the Supreme Court's encroachments on rights reserved to the States and to the people, contrary to established law, and to the Constitution.

We commend the motives of those States which have declared the intention to resist forced integration by any lawful means.

We appeal to the States and people who are not directly affected by these decisions to consider the constitutional principles involved against the time when they too, on issues vital to them, may be the victims of judicial encroachment.

We pledge ourselves to use all lawful means to bring about a reversal of this decision which is contrary to the Constitution and to prevent the use of force in its implementation.

In this trying period, as we all seek to right this wrong, we appeal to our people not to be provoked by the agitators and troublemakers invading our States and to scrupulously refrain from disorder and lawless acts.

Congressional Record, 84th Congress Second Session, 102/4 (Washington, DC: Governmental Printing Office, March 12, 1956), 4459–4460.

3.4 Interposition and nullification

Although presumably discredited as a result of the American Civil War, the concept of state interposition between the action of the federal government and the 'rights' of their citizens, 'nullifying' federal action was reinstated by some Southern states in response to the federal court's ruling in *Brown*. The resolution passed by the state of Alabama is an exemplar. See 3.11 for the Supreme Court's response to such state actions.

WHEREAS the Constitution of the United States was formed by the sanction of the several states, given by each in its sovereign capacity; and

WHEREAS the states, being the parties of the constitutional compact, it follows of necessity that...they must decide themselves, in the last resort, such questions as may be of sufficient magnitude to require their interposition and

WHEREAS ... The Supreme Court of the United States asserts, for its part, that the states did ... upon the adoption of the Fourteenth Amendment, prohibit unto themselves the power to maintain racially separate public institutions; the State of Alabama ... asserts that it and its sister states have never surrendered such rights; and

WHEREAS this assertion ... constitutes a deliberate, palpable, and dangerous attempt by the court to prohibit to the states certain rights and powers never surrendered by them; and

WHEREAS the question of contested power asserted in this resolution is not within the province of the court to determine ... be it

RESOLVED By The Legislature of Alabama, Both Houses Thereto Concurring:

That until the issue between the State of Alabama and the General Government is decided by the submission to the States ... of a suitable constitutional amendment that would declare, in plain and unequivocal language, that the states do surrender their power to maintain public school and other public facilities on a basis of separation as to race, the Legislature of Alabama declares the decisions and orders of the Supreme Court of the United States relating to separation of races in the public schools are, as a matter of right, null, void, and of no effect ...

Laws of Alabama, Special Session, 1956, No. 42, I, 70, reproduced in R. Bardolph, *The Civil Rights Record: Black Americans and the Law, 1849–1970* (New York: Thomas Y. Crowell, 1970), pp. 379–380.

3.5 Louisiana segregation amendment

In response to *Brown*, Louisiana reasserted its segregation policies, repeating the traditional argument that separation was an expression of the police power of the state, that is, the state's inherent right to protect the health, safety, and welfare of its citizenry.

All public elementary and secondary schools in the State of Louisiana shall be operated separately for white and colored children. This provision is made in the exercise of the state police power to promote and protect public health, morals, better education and the peace and good order in the State, and not because of race. The Legislature shall enact laws to enforce the state police power.

Acts of Louisiana, 1954, No. 752, p. 1338.

3.6 Anti-desegregation statutes

Southern states pursued multiple measures to combat desegregation. As a corollary to its enactment of segregation provisions (3.5) the Louisiana legislature empowered the governor to close racially mixed schools.

The governor, in order to secure justice to all, preserve the peace, and promote the interest, safety, and happiness of all the people, is authorized and empowered to close any racially mixed public school or any public school which is subject to a court order requiring it to admit students of both the negro and white races ...

Acts of Louisiana, Regular Session, 1958, No. 256.

3.7 The NAACP and oppositional legislation

By the late 1950s, Southern states were targeting the NAACP. A number of states passed legislation comparable to the following Arkansas law. In 1956, Alabama effectively banned the NAACP through a state court order.

WHEREAS the National Association for the Advancement of Colored People has, through its program and leaders in the state of Arkansas, disturbed the peace and tranquility which has long existed between the White and Negro races, and has threatened the progress and increased understanding between Negroes and Whites; and

WHEREAS, the National Association for the Advancement of Colored People has encouraged and agitated the members of the Negro race in the belief that their children were not receiving educational opportunities equal to those accorded white children, and has urged ... every effort to break down all racial barriers existing between the two races in schools, public transportation facilities and society in general ...

Now therefore, be it enacted by the General Assembly of the State of Arkansas:

Section 1

It shall be unlawful for any member of the [NAACP] to be employed by the State, school district, county or any municipality thereof, so long as membership ... is maintained ...

Acts of Arkansas, 1959, No. 115.

3.8 Elizabeth Eckford at Central High School

When Arkansas Governor Orval Faubus called out the Arkansas National Guard to surround Little Rock's Central High School, supporters of the desegregating students, led by Daisy Bates, President of the Arkansas NAACP, decided that the students should appear at the school in a group. Unfortunately, Ms. Bates failed to get the message to Elizabeth Eckford. The following passage

61

from Bates's memoir recounts Elizabeth's harrowing experience in September 1957 as she faced both the White mob and the Arkansas Guardsmen.

That night I was so excited I couldn't sleep. The next morning I was about the first one up. While I was pressing my black-and-white dress – I had made it to wear on the first day of school – my little brother turned on the TV set. They started telling about a large crowd gathered at the school. The man on TV said he wondered if we were going to show up that morning ...

Before I left home, Mother called us into the living room. She said we should have a word of prayer. Then I caught the bus and got off a block from the school. I saw a large crowd of people standing across the street from the soldiers guarding Central.

As I walked on, the crowd suddenly got very quiet. Superintendent Blossom had told us to enter by the front door. I looked at all the people and thought, 'Maybe I will be safer if I walk down the block to the front entrance behind the guards.'

At the corner I tried to pass through the long line of guards around the school so as to enter the grounds behind them. One of the guards pointed across the street. So I pointed in the same direction and asked whether he meant for me to cross the street and walk down. He nodded 'yes.' So, I walked across the street conscious of the crowd that stood there, but they moved away from me.

Figure 6 Elizabeth Eckford braves hateful Whites outside Central High.

For a moment all I could hear was the shuffling of their feet. Then someone shouted, 'Here she comes, get ready!' I moved away from the crowd on the sidewalk and into the street. If the mob came at me I could then cross back over so the guards could protect me.

The crowd moved in closer and then began to follow me, calling me names. I still wasn't afraid. Just a little bit nervous. Then my knees started to shake all of a sudden and I wondered whether I could make it to the center entrance a block away. It was the longest block I ever walked in my whole life.

Even so, I still wasn't too scared, because all the time I kept thinking that the guards would protect me.

When I got in front of the school, I went up to a guard again. But this time he just looked straight ahead and didn't move to let me pass him. I didn't know what to do. Then I looked and saw the path leading to the front entrance was a little further ahead. So I walked until I was right in front of the path to the front door.

I stood looking at the school – it looked so big! Just then the guards let some white students go through.

The crowd was quiet. I guess they were waiting to see what was going to happen. When I was able to steady my knees, I walked up to the guard who had let the white students in. He too didn't move. When I tried to squeeze past him, he raised his bayonet and then the other guards moved in and they raised their bayonets.

They glared at me with a mean look and I was very frightened and didn't know what to do. I turned around and the crowd came toward me.

They moved closer and closer. Somebody started yelling, 'Lynch her! Lynch her!'

I tried to see a friendly face somewhere in the mob – someone who maybe would help. I looked into the face of an old woman and it seemed a kind face, but when I looked at her again, she spat on me.

They came closer, shouting, 'No nigger bitch is going to get in our school. Get out of here!'

I turned back to the guards but their faces told me I wouldn't get any help from them. Then I looked down the block and saw a bench at the bus stop. I thought, 'If I can only get there I will be safe.' I don't know why the bench seemed a safe place to me, but I started walking toward it. I tried to close my mind to what they were shouting, and kept saying to myself, 'If I can only make it to the bench I will be safe.'

When I finally got there, I don't think I could have gone another step. I sat down and the mob crowded up and began shouting all over again. Someone hollered, 'Drag her over to this tree! Let's take care of that nigger.' Just then a white man sat down beside me, put his arm around me and patted my shoulder. He raised my chin and said, 'Don't let them see you cry.'

Then, a white lady – she was very nice – she came over to me on the bench. She spoke to me but I don't remember what she said. She put me on the bus and sat next to me. She asked my name and tried to talk to me but I don't think I answered. I can't remember much about the bus ride, but the next thing I remember I was standing in front of the School for the Blind, where Mother works.

Daisy Bates, *The Long Shadow of Little Rock: A Memoir* (Fayetteville: University of Arkansas Press, 1962), pp. 72–75.

3.9 Eisenhower addresses nation

On September 20, 1957 a federal court issued an injunction prohibiting Governor Faubus's use of guards to prevent Black students from entering Central High School; the guard was withdrawn. The mob remained, however, and, when the Black students were admitted on September 23, rushed the police officers who were protecting the school. The Mayor of Little Rock requested that President Eisenhower send federal troops to enforce the law, and on September 24, Eisenhower sent elements of the 101st Airborne Division to the city and federalized the National Guard, taking control away from Governor Faubus. That evening Eisenhower addressed the nation. The next day, the Black students re-entered the school under the protection of some 1,000 soldiers of the 101st.

Good Evening, My Fellow Citizens. For a few minutes this evening I want to speak to you about the serious situation that has arisen in Little Rock ...

In that city, under the leadership of demagogic extremists, disorderly mobs have deliberately prevented the carrying out of proper orders from a Federal Court. Local authorities have not eliminated that violent opposition and, under the law, I yesterday issued a Proclamation calling upon the mob to disperse.

This morning the mob again gathered in front of the Central High School of Little Rock, obviously for the purpose of again preventing the carrying out of the Court's order relating to the admission of Negro children to that school.

Whenever normal agencies prove inadequate to the task and it becomes necessary for the Executive Branch of the Federal Government to use its powers ... the President's responsibility is inescapable ... I have today issued an Executive Order directing the use of troops under Federal authority to aid in the execution of Federal law at Little Rock, Arkansas ...

... As you know, the Supreme Court of the United States has decided that separate public educational facilities for the races are inherently unequal and therefore compulsory school segregation laws are unconstitutional.

Our personal opinions about the decision have no bearing on the matter of enforcement ... Local Federal Courts were instructed by the Supreme Court to issue such orders and decrees as might be necessary to achieve admission to public schools without regard to race – and with all deliberate speed.

During the past several years, many communities in our Southern States have instituted public school plans for gradual progress in the enrollment and attendance of school children of all races in order to bring themselves into compliance with the law of the land.

They thus demonstrated to the world that we are a nation in which laws, not men, are supreme.

I regret to say that this truth – the cornerstone of our liberties – was not observed in this instance ...

The proper use of the powers of the Executive Branch to enforce the orders of a Federal Court is limited to extraordinary and compelling circumstances. Manifestly, such an extreme situation has been created in Little Rock. This challenge must be met and with such measures as will preserve to the people as a whole their lawfully-protected rights in a climate permitting their free and fair exercise. The overwhelming majority of our people in every section of the country are united in their respect for observance of the Law – even in those cases where they may disagree with that law ...

Our enemies are gloating over this incident ... We are portrayed as a violator of those standards of conduct which the peoples of the world united to proclaim in the Charter of the United Nations. There they affirmed 'faith in fundamental human rights' and 'in dignity and worth of the human person' ...

And so, with deep confidence, I call upon the citizens of the State of Arkansas to assist in bringing to an immediate end all interference with the law and its processes ...

Thus will be restored the image of America and of all its parts as one nation, indivisible, with liberty and justice for all.

Public Papers of the Presidents of the United States: Dwight D. Eisenhower, 1957 (Washington, DC: Government Printing Office, 1958), entry 198, pp. 689–694.

3.10 Bates–White correspondence

A disappointing aspect of the period was the failure of the federal government to protect Black Americans who were trying simply to secure their rights as American citizens. Under the federal system, the protection of the safety and health of citizens is principally the responsibility of state and local governments. State and local governments in the South were bastions of White supremacy. Whites who harassed or even assaulted civil rights activists were not prosecuted, or, when prosecuted, not convicted. For example, the murderers of Emmitt Till, a Black teenager who allegedly flirted with a White woman in Money, Mississippi, in 1955, were charged with murder but quickly acquitted by an all-White jury. Shortly thereafter, they smugly admitted to the crime in a paid interview with *Look* magazine. Not infrequently, local officials even conspired with terrorist groups such as the Ku Klux Klan (KKK) (see **4.7**). In Little Rock, as Daisy Bates and other NAACP activists continued to push for their rights, violence against them was not countered by local authorities. The correspondence below reflects Mrs. Bates's frustration and the timidity of the Eisenhower administration.

[To the Attorney General of the United States]
Last night, July 7, 1959, at 10:08, a bomb hurled from an automobile exploded in our front yard. The bomb fell short of its target and only the lawn was damaged from the explosion which rocked dwellings for several blocks. As adviser to the litigants in the Little Rock school case, my home has been under constant attack since August 1957 by lawless elements of this state, and many threats have been made upon my life and the lives of my immediate family. Incendiary bombs have been thrown at our home from automobiles. Three KKK crosses have been burned on our lawn. Fire has been set to the house on two occasions. All the glass in the front of the house has been broken out and steel screens had to be made to cover the front windows to protect our home. To this date, no one has been apprehended by the law enforcement officers of this city or state. We have appealed to the city and county for protection, yet these attacks on us and our home continue. We have been compelled to employ private guards. Now as a last resort, we are appealing to you to give us protection in Little Rock, United States of America.

– Daisy Bates

The Attorney General and I have read the distressing account in your telegram of July 8, 1959, of the harassment which you have suffered since the institution of the Little Rock school desegregation case, culminating in the explosion of a bomb on July 7. After careful consideration, however, we are forced to conclude that there is no basis for federal jurisdiction. Any investigation and prosecution of persons responsible for the incidents which you described in your telegram would be within the exclusive jurisdiction of state and local authorities. Inability or failure on the part of such authorities to take effective action does not authorize the federal government to intervene. This department can take action only when there has been a violation of federal law. The information which you furnish in your telegram fails to disclose any such violation.

– Asst. Attorney General W. Wilson White

Bates, *The Long Shadow of Little Rock*, pp. 162–163.

3.11 *Cooper* v. *Aaron* (1958)

White segregationists were not the sole challengers of the Little Rock school board's plan for gradual desegregation. The local NAACP went to court arguing that the plan was too incremental, thus denying rights to Black students. The US district and circuit courts, however, approved the school board's plan. The NAACP appealed to the Supreme Court. In the meanwhile, the state legislature passed, and Faubus signed, a statute authorizing the Governor to close schools that had come under federal court desegregation orders – thereby challenging federal court orders and directly opposing a ruling of the Supreme Court. The Supreme Court asserted its supremacy.

As this case reaches us it raises questions of the highest importance to the maintenance of our federal system of government. It necessarily involves a claim by the Governor and Legislature of a State that there is no duty on state officials to obey federal court orders ... Specifically it involves actions by the Governor and Legislature of Arkansas upon the premise that they are not bound by our holding in *Brown* v. *Board of Education* ... We are urged to uphold a suspension of the Little Rock School Board's plan to do away with segregated public schools in Little Rock until state laws and efforts to upset and nullify our holding in *Brown* v. *Board of Education* have been further challenged and tested in the courts. We reject these contentions ...

The constitutional rights of respondents are not to be sacrificed or yielded to the violence and disorder which have followed upon the actions of the Governor and Legislature....

The controlling legal principles are plain. The command of the Fourteenth Amendment is that no 'State' shall deny to any person within its jurisdiction the equal protection of the laws ...

What has been said, in the light of the facts developed, is enough to dispose of the case. However, we should answer the premise of the actions of the Governor and Legislature that they are not bound by our holding in the *Brown* case. It is necessary only to recall some basic constitutional propositions which are settled doctrine.

Article VI of the Constitution makes the Constitution the 'supreme Law of the Land.' In 1803, Chief Justice Marshall [in *Marbury* v. *Madison*] ... declared the basic principle that the federal judiciary is supreme in the exposition of the law of the Constitution ...

Chief Justice Marshall spoke for a unanimous Court in saying that: 'If the legislatures of the several states may, at will, annul the judgments of the courts of the United States, and destroy the rights acquired under those judgments, the constitution itself becomes a solemn mockery ...'

... The Constitution created a government dedicated to equal justice under law. The Fourteenth Amendment embodied and emphasized that ideal. State support of segregated schools ... cannot be squared with the Amendment's command that no State shall deny to any person within its jurisdiction the equal protection of the laws ... The principles announced in [*Brown*] and the obedience of the States to them, according to the command of the Constitution, are indispensable for the protection of the freedoms guaranteed by our fundamental charter for all of us. Our constitutional ideal of equal justice under law is thus made a living truth.

358 U.S. 1 (1958).

3.12 A history of abuses

Alabama State College English Professor Jo Ann Robinson was President of the Women's Political Council (see 2.2) and principal organizer of the one-day boycott of the buses immediately after the arrest of Rosa Parks. In the excerpt below, Robinson recounts the legacy of indignities that Black citizens suffered from public transit operators in Montgomery.

The black Women's Political Council had been planning the boycott of Montgomery City Lines for months ... The idea itself had been entertained for years. Almost daily some black man, woman, or child had had an unpleasant experience on the bus and told other members of the family about it at the supper table or around the open fireplace or stove. These stories were repeated to neighbors, who re-told them in club meetings or to the ministers of large church congregations ...

Very little or nothing tangible had ever been done on the part of the darker race to prevent continuous abuse on city transit lines, except to petition the company and the City Commission for better conditions. Ten years before, when Mrs. Geneva Johnson, in the latest of a long string of similar incidents, was arrested for not having correct change and 'talking back' to the driver when he up-braided her, nothing was done. Charged with disorderly conduct, she paid her fine and kept on riding. A representation of Negro men complained to the bus company about the matter and about other mistreatments as well, but nothing came of it.

During the next few years, Mrs. Viola White and Miss Katie Wingfield were arrested, as well as two children visiting from New Jersey. All had committed the same offense – sitting in the front seats reserved for whites. The children were a sister and brother, ten and twelve years old, respectively, who had been accustomed to riding integrated transportation. They got on the bus and sat down by a white man and a boy. The white youngster told the older black youth to get up from beside him. The youngster refused. The driver commanded them to move, but the children refused. The driver again commanded them to move, but the children continued to sit where they were ... The police were called, and the two children were arrested. Relatives paid their fines, sent the children home, and the case became history ...

Three years later, in 1952, a white bus driver and a Negro man exchanged words over the dime the passenger put into the slot. The Negro man, Brooks, was not afraid ... He never quavered when the driver abused him with words and accused him of not putting the money into the meter box of the bus. Instead, he stood his ground and disputed the driver ...

What followed was never explained fully, but the driver called the police, and when the police came they shot and killed Brooks as he got off the bus. Newspaper reports stated that the coroner had ruled the case justifiable homicide because the man had resisted arrest. Many black Montgomerians felt that Brooks was intoxicated and had gotten 'out of his place' with the white bus driver. Others wondered if any man, drunk or sober, had to be killed because of one dime, one bus fare. Each had his own thoughts on the matter, but kept on riding the bus.

In 1953, Mrs. Epsie Worthy got on a bus at a transfer point from another bus, and the driver demanded an additional fare. He refused to take the transfer. Rather than pay again, the woman decided that she did not have far to go and would walk the rest of the way. The driver would not be daunted. He wanted another fare, whether she rode or got off, and insisted upon it. Words followed as the woman alighted from the vehicle. She was not quite quick enough, for by the time she was safe on mother earth, the driver was upon her, beating her with his hands. She defended herself, fighting back with all her might. For a few minutes there was a 'free-for-all,' and she gave as much as she took. But in the end she was the loser, for when the police were summoned, she was taken to jail and fined fifty-two dollars for disorderly conduct ...

Jo Ann Robinson, *The Montgomery Bus Boycott and the Women Who Started it* (Knoxville: University of Tennessee Press, 1987), pp. 20–22.

3.13 Mass meeting at Holt Street Baptist Church

Joe Azbell, a reporter for the *Montgomery Advertiser*, submitted the following article describing his experience at the first mass meeting of the MIA on December 5, 1955. Mass meetings replicated the form of Black church services and revivals, as spirituals were sung, prayers offered, and leaders such as King addressed the meeting in the fashion of traditional, interactive sermons. The mass meeting was key to fostering and maintaining mass participation.

... I went inside the church and stood at the front for a few minutes. The two rear doors were jammed with people and a long aisle was crammed with human forms like a frozen food package. I went to the rear of the church and it was the same. The Negro policemen pleaded with the Negroes to keep the aisles free so people could get out. In the end the policemen gave up in despair of correcting the safety hazard. Bodies at the front were packed one against the other. It required five minutes for a photographer to move eight feet among these people in trying to leave the building.

The purpose of this meeting was to give 'further instructions' on the boycott of city buses which had been started as a protest of the Negroes against the arrest, trial and conviction of Rosa Parks, 42–year-old seamstress, on a charge of violating segregation laws by refusing to give up her seat to a white person and move to the rear of a city bus ...

SPEAKERS UNIDENTIFIED

The meeting was started in a most unusual fashion. A Negro speaker – apparently a minister – came to the microphone. He did not introduce himself but apparently most of the Negroes knew him. He said there were microphones on the outside and in the basement, and there were three times as many people outside as on the inside. There was an anonymity throughout the meeting of the speakers. None of the white reporters could identify the speakers. Most of the Negroes did. The introduction[s] of Fred Daniels and Rosa Parks were clear and brief. Daniels was arrested in the boycott Monday.

WHITES LISTEN

The passion that fired the meeting was seen as the thousands of voices joined in singing *Onward Christian Soldiers*. Another hymn followed. The voices thundered through the church.

Then there followed a prayer by a minister. It was a prayer interrupted a hundred times by 'yeas' and 'uh-huhs' and 'that's right.' The minister spoke of God as the Master and the brotherhood of man. He repeated in a different way that God would protect the righteous.

As the other speakers came on the platform urging 'freedom and equality' for Negroes 'who are Americans and proud of this democracy,' the frenzy of the audience mounted. There was a volume of clapping that seemed to boom through the walls. Outside the loudspeakers were blaring the message for blocks. White people stopped blocks away and listened to the loud-speakers' messages.

THE HAT IS PASSED

The newspapers were criticized for quoting police authorities on reports of intimidation of Negroes who attempted to ride buses and for comparing the Negro boycott with the economic reprisals of White Citizens groups.

The remark which drew the most applause was: 'We will not retreat one inch in our fight to secure and hold our American citizenship.' Second was a statement: 'And the history book will write of us as a race of people who in Montgomery County, State of Alabama, Country of the United States, stood up for and fought for their rights as American citizens, as citizens of democracy.'

Outside the audience listened as more and more cars continued to arrive: Streets became Dexter traffic snarls. There was hymn singing between speeches. In the end there was the passing of the hats and Negroes dropped in dollar bills, $5 bills and $10 bills. It was not passive giving but active giving. Negroes called to the hat passers outside – 'Here, let me give.'

PEACEFUL MEANS

When the resolution on continuing the boycott of the bus was read, there came wild whoop of delight. Many said they would never ride the bus again. Negroes turned to each other and compared past incidents on the buses.

At several points there was an emotionalism that the ministers on the platform recognized could get out of control and at various intervals they repeated and again what 'we are seeking is by peaceful means.'

'There will be no violence or intimidation. We are seeking things in
a democratic way and we are using the weapon of protest,' the speakers
declared.
MORE HYMNS
I left as the meeting was breaking up ...
There was hymn singing as I drove away ...
The meeting was much like an old-fashioned revival with loud applause
added. It proved beyond any doubt there was a discipline among Negroes
that many whites had doubted. It was almost a military discipline combined
with emotion.

Montgomery Advertiser (December 7, 1955).

3.14 *Browder* v. *Gayle* (1956)

In January, 1956, with the support of the MIA and the NAACP, local
attorneys went to court and challenged the public transportation
segregation laws in Montgomery. In June, the majority of a three-
judge panel issued the following decision, finding the laws unconstitutional. This decision was unanimously upheld by the US Supreme
Court on November 13, 1956. The next day, the MIA voted to end
the boycott upon the implementation of the Supreme Court ruling.

... In the School Segregation Cases [decided under] *Brown* v. *Board of
Education* ... the separate but equal doctrine was repudiated in the area
where it first developed, i.e., in the field of public education. On the same
day the Supreme Court made clear that its ruling was not limited to that field
when it remanded 'for consideration in the light of the Segregation Cases
and conditions that now prevail' a case involving the rights of Negroes to
use the recreational facilities of city parks ...
Later the Fourth Circuit expressly repudiated the separate but equal
doctrine as applied to recreational centers ... Its judgment was affirmed by
the Supreme Court ... The doctrine has further been repudiated in holdings
that the cities of Atlanta and of Miami cannot meet the test by furnishing
the facilities of their municipal golf courses to Negroes on a segregated
basis ...
[A] judicial decision, which is simply evidence of the law and not the
law itself, may be so impaired by later decisions as no longer to furnish any
reliable evidence.

We cannot in good conscience perform our duty as judges by blindly following the precedent of *Plessy* v. *Ferguson* ... In fact, we think that *Plessy* v. *Ferguson* has been impliedly, though not explicitly, overruled, and that, under the later decisions, there is now no rational basis upon which the separate but equal doctrine can be validly applied to public carrier transportation within the City of Montgomery and its police jurisdiction. The application of that doctrine cannot be justified as a proper execution of the state police power.

We hold that the statutes and ordinances requiring segregation of the white and colored races on the motor buses of a common carrier of passengers in the City of Montgomery and its police jurisdiction violate the due process and equal protection of the law clauses of the Fourteenth Amendment to the Constitution of the United States ...

142 F. Supp. 707 (M.D. Ala. 1956).

3.15 Rustin describes the origin of the Southern Christian Leadership Conference

Bayard Rustin was influential in convincing King and other Black ministers that a regional organization was necessary to maintain the momentum of the Montgomery movement, to sustain and coordinate pressure to desegregate throughout the South. The resultant Southern Negro Leaders Conference on Nonviolent Integration, in January, 1957, soon evolved into the clergy-led Southern Christian Leadership Conference (SCLC), headed by Martin Luther King, Jr.

Within a few days [of the successful conclusion to the Montgomery boycott], protests similar to the one in Montgomery swept the South. In Atlanta, Birmingham, Baton Rouge, New Orleans, Norfolk, Tallahassee, and many other cities, Negroes 'moved up front.' Most Southern white persons accepted integration ... But by the beginning of January, the occasional beating or shooting had grown into organized terror. The terror was supported by legal subterfuge. It became clear that the opposition was planning to frustrate the court decision by organized violence and 'a century of hopeless litigation.'

At this point, Reverend Martin Luther King, Jr., of Montgomery, Reverend F. L. Shuttlesworth of Birmingham, and Reverend C. K Steele of Tallahassee ... came to several conclusions:

None of the other protests were apt to succeed if the one at Montgomery was defeated.

Integration might not win at Montgomery unless the protests continued to spread throughout other areas of the South.

The increasing violence was being carefully planned and organized on the theory that the Negroes would back down when faced with such incidents. *Therefore* Negroes had no alternative but to extend and intensify this struggle.

... Any hesitation or temporary retreat on the part of Negroes would confuse white persons and drive them back to the old pattern.

The time had come for Negro leaders to gather from all over the South to 'share thinking, discuss common problems, plan common strategy, and explore mutual economic assistance.'

King, Steele, and Shuttlesworth issued a call on January 5 for a two-day conference to be held in Atlanta, beginning five days later ...

Every major protest leader was present. Leaders struggling with economic boycotts and reprisals in South Carolina were standing in a corner exchanging views with the 'strong men' from the Mississippi Delta, who are forced to carry on their work at night, underground.

The first person to take the floor was a man who had been shot because he had dared to vote. Some had come for technical advice, others to find out more about the spirit and practice of nonviolence. But all of them were determined to respond to the call 'to delve deeper into the struggle.' ...

The final meeting of the conference may go down in history as one of the most important meetings that have taken place in the United States. Sixty beleaguered Negro leaders from across the South voted to establish a permanent Southern Negro Leaders Conference on Nonviolent Integration.

This was the beginning of a South-wide nonviolent resistance campaign against all segregation ...

[The] conference voted to accept as the slogan of the broader movement the motto:

Not one hair of one head of one white person shall be harmed ...

Bayard Rustin, 'Even in the Face of Death,' in *Time on Two Crosses: The Collected Writings of Bayard Rustin*, ed. Devon W. Carbado and Donald Weise (San Francisco: Cleis Press, Inc., 2003), pp. 102–106.

3.16 Civil Rights Act of 1957

In response to a growing awareness of Black action in the South, in 1957 Congress, for the first time since 1875, passed a Civil Rights Act. Among its provisions, key elements of which follow below, the law established a Commission on Civil Rights to investigate violations of voting rights and denials of equal protection, and it attempted to further guarantee voting rights.

PART I – ESTABLISHMENT OF THE COMMISSION ON CIVIL RIGHTS

Section 101. (a) There is created in the executive branch of the Government a Commission on Civil Rights (hereinafter called the 'Commission') ....

Duties of the Commission

Section 104. (a) The Commission shall –

(1) investigate allegations in writing under oath or affirmation that certain citizens of the United States are being deprived of their right to vote and have that vote counted ...

(2) study and collect information concerning legal developments constituting a denial of equal protection of the laws under the Constitution; and

(3) appraise the laws and policies of the Federal Government with respect to equal protection of the laws under the Constitution ...

Powers of the Commission

Section 105. ...

(f) The Commission, or ... any subcommittee of two or more members, ... may ... hold such hearings and act at such times and places as the Commission or such authorized subcommittee may deem advisable. Subpoenas ... may be issued in accordance with the rules of the Commission ...

PART IV – TO PROVIDE MEANS OF FURTHER SECURING AND PROTECTING THE RIGHT TO VOTE

Section 131. Section 2004 of the Revised Statutes (42 U.S.C. 1971), is amended as follows: ... (c) Add, immediately following the present text, four new subsections to read as follows:

'(b) No person, whether acting under color of law or otherwise, shall intimidate, threaten, coerce, or attempt to intimidate, threaten, or coerce any other person for the purpose of interfering with the right of such other person to vote for, or not to vote for, any candidate for the Office of President, Vice President, presidential elector, Member of the Senate, or Member of the House of Representatives, Delegates or Commissioners from the Territories or possessions, at any general, special, or primary election held solely or in part for the purpose of selecting or electing any such candidate.

'(c) Whenever any person has engaged or there are reasonable grounds to believe that any person is about to engage in any act or practice which would deprive any other person of any right or privilege secured by subsection (a) or (b), the Attorney General may institute for the United States, or in the name of the United States, a civil action or other proper proceeding for preventive relief, including an application for a permanent or temporary injunction, restraining order, or other order ...

'(d) The district courts of the United States shall have jurisdiction of proceedings instituted pursuant to this section and shall exercise the same without regard to whether the party aggrieved shall have exhausted any administrative or other remedies that may be provided by law ...'

71 U.S. *Statutes at Large*, p. 634.

3.17 Black reaction to the Civil Rights Act of 1957

Charles H. Thompson, editor of the *Journal of Negro Education*, amplified many African Americans' reservations regarding the Civil Rights Act of 1957. Central among these was a concern that the act failed to address discrimination in employment and other economic issues.

On September 9, 1957, it was announced that President Eisenhower had just signed the Civil Rights Bill which had been passed by the Congress some weeks previously. The announcement reiterated the conclusions voiced by a number of people immediately after the Congress had passed the Bill, that it was a 'historic' document – being the first Civil Rights Bill passed by the Congress since 1875. Time can only disclose how 'historic' this act was. Recent events, however, suggest that its significance was more psychological than practical in meeting the real problems of civil rights for Negroes ...

Whether this Act should be characterized as 'historic' or not, several observations should be noted. First, it would be very misleading to assume, as a number of the proponents of this Act have assumed, that if Negroes are assured the right to vote in all areas of this country, they can thereby secure for themselves all or even most of the civil rights to which they are entitled. While the untrammelled right of Negroes to vote would be very helpful in any effort to obtain and maintain their civil rights, events past and present indicate that it is not a decisive factor, and, in view of the Negro's minority status, could not be decisive.

What is even more important, however, is the fact that some of the most crucial civil rights of Negroes are outside of the area which possession of the ballot could be expected to protect; for example, the right to be free from discrimination in employment, or more recently, to be free from economic and other reprisals. The most serious and critical disadvantage which Negroes suffer at present is economic, and much, if not most, of it is due to race ... [A]ccording to a recent survey, for 1956 ... the median income of Negro families was only 59 percent of the median income of white families. The elimination of Title III from the current bill makes it practically impossible to do anything realistic about this situation ...

Journal of Negro Education, 26 (Fall, 1957), pp. 433–434.

Notes

1 349 U.S. 294 (1955).
2 A. D. Morris, *The Origins of the Civil Rights Movement* (New York: The Free Press, 1984), p. 19.
3 *Ibid.*, p. 40.
4 *Ibid.*, p. 61.
5 Stewart Burns, *Daybreak of Freedom: The Montgomery Bus Boycott* (Chapel Hill: University of North Carolina Press, 1997), p. 23.
6 *Ibid.*, pp. 24–25.

4
'I'm a rollin':
the Movement gains momentum

Momentum for civil rights activists was precisely what the White power structure feared most. A program of 'massive resistance' was pursued by Whites eager to defend separatism and White supremacy – 'the Southern way of life.' While increasingly identifying the federal courts as the enemy, Whites mounted pressures against challenges to the status quo. Extra-legal reaction ranged from economic pressure to harassment and physical intimidation of Blacks, including murder. The KKK, in its various manifestations, was joined by more 'reputable' White Citizens Councils to combat desegregation and preserve the coveted White supremacy. Bayard Rustin's discussion of the White Citizens Council (WCC) of Mississippi (4.1) provides a sense of those groups' activities.

Despite repression by Whites, African Americans in communities throughout the South continued to organize protests, including sit-ins. Assured that service would be denied, Blacks would stage a 'sit-in' at Whites-only lunch counters or other public accommodations, silently protesting such manifestations of White supremacy. Those demonstrations were sporadic, and with Dr. King and the SCLC leaders immersed in the details of organizing a nonviolent, direct-action, mass movement, little energy and attention remained for regionally organizing sit-ins.

The necessary energy materialized when a sit-in by Black college students in Greensboro, North Carolina, in February 1960 (4.2), captured national attention. Soon groups of Black youth were staging sit-ins throughout the South. Ella Baker, a long-time civil rights activist and, in 1960, the executive director of SCLC, saw the potential gain for the movement through student involvement and invited student representatives to a meeting at Shaw University in Raleigh, North Carolina. Over 300 students attended, the great majority from Black colleges throughout the South. Despite

SCLC's interest in placing the student activists under its umbrella, the students, following Baker's encouragement, created their own organization – the Student Nonviolent Coordinating Committee (SNCC).

A group composed of students from Black college campuses in Nashville was particularly influential in the Shaw meeting. Under the tutelage of Jim Lawson, that group had begun experimenting with nonviolent, direct-action practices in the late 1950s. John Lewis, a student at American Baptist Theological Seminary and later a major activist, described instruction under Lawson in a philosophy (**4.3**) that would animate many of the early student activists and inform the founding statement of SNCC (**4.4**).

Among Ella Baker's reasons for encouraging students to form their own organization was her growing disenchantment with the top-down, traditional, male-dominated, organizational structure of groups such as SCLC and NAACP. Rather, she advocated 'group-centered' organization (**4.5**). This emphasis on grass-roots organization, empowering the people themselves as leaders, would be a hallmark of the work of SNCC and, frequently, a source of friction between SNCC and King's SCLC.

Momentum for civil rights reform received a boost when John F. Kennedy was elected President of the United States in November, 1960. Kennedy ran on a platform that promised major civil rights legislation, and he appeared to have been instrumental in gaining the release of Martin Luther King, Jr. when, in October, King had been arrested in an Atlanta demonstration. Blacks' enthusiasm for Kennedy was significant in his razor-thin victory over Richard Nixon. Once he was in office, Kennedy's support for civil rights was manifested through a dramatic increase in the number of Blacks appointed to federal offices and a major overhaul of the Justice Department's Civil Rights Division, but deference to Southern Democrats and focus on foreign policy and Cold War tensions trumped civil rights. The administration failed to initiate major civil rights legislation, disappointing many Black supporters.

However, as the Kennedy administration organized, momentum within the movement generated by youth protests was enhanced by the Freedom Rides of 1961, another expression of nonviolent, direct action. As noted in Chapter 2, one of the first organizations to promote nonviolent, direct action was the Congress of Racial Equality (see **2.6**), the offspring of FOR. While CORE was a

Northern-based, secular organization, by the late 1950s its activists were operating in the South in support of desegregation. When the student movement erupted, CORE activists sought to provide disciplined training for the students in Gandhian, nonviolent protest. A close working relationship between CORE and SNCC resulted, as was demonstrated by the Freedom Rides.

In December, 1960, the US Supreme Court, in *Boynton* v. *Virginia* (**4.**6), ruled that state laws requiring segregated waiting rooms, lunch counters, restrooms, and other facilities in airports, bus stations and train stations violated interstate travelers' constitutional rights. The decision served as an extension of *Morgan*, in which the Court had found segregation on interstate buses unconstitutional; yet *Boynton*, as well as *Morgan*, for that matter, was being ignored throughout the Deep South. CORE decided to replicate its 1947 Journey of Reconciliation and employ direct action to attract national attention to the issue and force federal officials to uphold the rights of interstate travelers. Thirteen CORE activists, Blacks and Whites, would ride in two groups from Washington, DC, to New Orleans – one group on Greyhound, the other on Trailways – challenging segregated seating and terminal facilities throughout the South.

The story of the Freedom Rides demonstrated the heroism of the activists; the violent nature of the White opposition, including collusion between law enforcement officials and terrorist groups such as the KKK; and the federal government's continued hesitancy to interfere with local and state officials' failures to recognize the rights of Black citizens and control White violence. When the buses reached Alabama, one bus was bombed outside Anniston, and later, another was attacked by mobs in Birmingham (**4.**7), effectively ending the initial CORE effort. As the Kennedy administration tried to negotiate with the White supremacist governor of Alabama, John Patterson, to guarantee the safety of the Riders, student activists from Nashville decided to support CORE and continue the Rides. Despite assurances from Patterson that law and order would be maintained, this group also was attacked upon arrival in Montgomery (**4.**8). In both cases, Whites' violence was abetted by local White law-enforcement officials. Ultimately, it took federal marshals and the Alabama National Guard to subdue White mobs in Montgomery. The violence, however, served to foster broad support from civil rights groups, including King and the SCLC, for the Freedom Rides, and they continued into Mississippi and other parts of the South.

In Mississippi, state officials controlled overt violence, but Riders were arrested – typically on charges of disturbing the peace or trespassing rather than on violation of segregation ordinances – and imprisoned and, when local facilities became overcrowded, shipped to the infamous Parchman State Penitentiary. Ironically, covert, punitive measures experienced at Parchman generated a solidarity among the Riders that would buoy many key activists through later crises. In the absence of overt violence, however, federal authorities did not intervene, although the Kennedys successfully influenced the Interstate Commerce Commission to clarify its position on desegregation (**4.9**), giving federal authorities a tool to enforce desegregation in interstate travel. Nonetheless, resolution of the crisis of authority between the federal government and states' rights defenders of segregation awaited a later date. Ultimately, over 400 Riders participated in the Freedom Rides, establishing nonviolent, direct action as the central strategy of the Movement.

Despite the widespread adoption of nonviolent, direct action, a number of African Americans challenged the efficacy of the strategy. Robert F. Williams, the best-known critic during the early years of the Movement, argued that 'turning the other cheek' was an inadequate response to the violence of White supremacists (**4.10**).

4.1 Rustin on the White Citizens Council in the Mississippi Delta

Created to defend White supremacy and combat federal court decisions and legislation supporting African American rights, the WCC is described by Bayard Rustin, below, as 'the Ku Klux Klan in business suits.' The following excerpt explores White fears in Mississippi and the tactics used to fight desegregation.

THE 1950 UNITED STATES CENSUS records that there are about two million people in Mississippi. Almost half of these are Negroes, living predominantly in the northwestern corner of the state. This section, the cotton producing Delta, is the backbone of the state. There the real economic and political power is concentrated. Much of the remainder of Mississippi is poor and the people depressed.

It was with these facts in mind that Senator Eastland recently said at a meeting of the White Citizens Council: 'Whoever controls the Delta controls

Mississippi.' The Senator made this remark in discussing the potential registration and voting power of Negroes in the state. Before him stood a large map of the twenty counties in and around the Delta where the Negro population is two and three times larger than the white.

After carefully impressing these 'frightful figures' upon his audience he concluded, 'We must not be overrun; our way of life must not be taken away by usurping courts or by the subversive NAACP.' What he really meant was this: Under no circumstances must the Negro in the Delta vote ... If the Negro votes there, he will outvote the whites, integration will come, white economic privileges resting on segregation will be destroyed and ... the whites therefore enslaved ...

In a profound sense the Senator speaks for the Delta. It is the voice of fear: first, the white men's fear of losing their favored position; then, their fear that if ever the Negro wins equality, he will use his overwhelming political power to give the white man the same kind of treatment he has given the Negro – and which the white man feels he himself deserves ...

If one is fully to understand the forces at work in the Southern mind and heart today, one must know what fear has wrought upon the Delta:

– Emmett Till was kidnapped and brutalized there, and his confessed kidnapers and proved murderers released as 'innocent.'

– The NAACP is feared by many black men and hated by almost all white people.

– The legislature has provided for a private school system at state expense.

– Economic pressure is brought against the eight thousand Negroes who have dared to register and attempted to vote.

– Negro leaders are systematically driven from the state or murdered in cold blood.

– Negro farmers are driven from their land by intimidation and by economic double-dealing.

– Police brutality is widespread.

– The state has recently passed an amendment raising voter qualifications in an effort to disfranchise the Negro further.

– Federal agencies such as the Farm Home Administration are locally misused as a means of controlling and harassing Negro workers and farmers.

All this has begun in the Delta. It was, moreover, at Indianola, in the heart of the Delta, that the White Citizens Council was founded in 1954. Today this organization dedicated to white supremacy holds the state in its grip and dares pulpit, labor, press, or citizens openly to defy it. No one does. Fear has settled over the Delta.

Ku Klux Klan in Business Suits

On May 17, 1954, the United States Supreme Court outlawed segregation in public education. By October 12, 1954, the White Citizens Council of Indianola, Mississippi, had become a state-wide organization. Today its first major report of accomplishments boasts:

> In less than two years of activity, 65 of our 82 counties in Mississippi have been organized with a membership of 80,000 ... The state office has published over two million pieces of literature in the 48 states ... which give concrete, convincing reasons for the absolute necessity of maintaining segregation in the South. – REPORT TO EXECUTIVE COMMITTEE, AUGUST 1956 ...

Section two of the report deals with the NAACP:

> We have proven to our Negro citizens that the NAACP is a left-wing, power-mad organ of destruction that cares nothing about the Negro. We have the support of the thinking, conservative Negro people who believe in segregation. We want to help them develop social pride in a segregated society.

There is no shame expressed in the report as to how this 'support of the thinking, conservative Negro people' was in part obtained. It was done by the use of paid Negro agents who have carried tales, some true and many false, creating confusion and discord until no one knows whom he can trust. Many are thus afraid to act at all. The report puts it this way:

> Information is received by the Council concerning all activities of the NAACP. Sources of this information cannot be divulged. It is impor-tant that the NAACP leaders in all vicinities be known. A list of the NAACP membership is being compiled.

This compilation of the NAACP list has numerous ramifications. Profes-sional Negroes in the Delta are afraid of economic reprisals and do not now join the NAACP. Teachers, doctors, pharmacists, and businessmen are kept under terrific pressure.

A teacher in Cleveland, Mississippi, would receive me only after dark if I walked to her home. 'That NAACP man's car you ride in will cause a commotion. Anyhow, you're a stranger, and somebody may think you are from the NAACP. Come late and walk.' At the close of our conversation, she said: 'Well, I really don't know what to think, but I know Mr. Smith [a white businessman and member of the WCC] is correct. He said that integration can't happen in Mississippi and if I lose my job the NAACP can't give me one. You can't give me one either, so please don't come here any more and don't speak to me if you see me on the street.' ...

In the Delta the Negro church is bought and paid for by the Council, with very few exceptions. Many ministers are in debt to members of the

Citizens Council. These clergymen denounce the NAACP as radical and misguided. They call for 'a new Booker T. Washington – someone to lead who is not interested in racial equality.' ...

Where the bought clergy and frightened middle class don't pay off, stronger methods are used. A good example is the careful plan carried out by the WCC in Charleston, Mississippi ...

Mr. Patterson's Master Plan

Among the group of fourteen men who formed the first White Citizens Council in the living room of Dave Hawkins of Indianola, Mississippi, was one Robert Patterson. Patterson later became secretary of the Citizens Councils of Mississippi, and, in January 1956, he became executive secretary of the Citizens Councils of America upon its formation in New Orleans. The national headquarters is at Patterson's office in Greenwood, Mississippi.

According to its stated purpose, the national movement is 'dedicated to the maintenance of peace, good order and domestic tranquility in our communities and our state and to the preservation of states' rights.'

According to documents smuggled from Patterson's headquarters, read by this reporter, and hurriedly returned, it appears that his idea of the 'maintenance of peace, good order and domestic tranquility' begins with what he calls the master plan ...

His plan calls for at least 500,000 Negroes to leave Mississippi by 1966. About 200,000 will leave voluntarily, having been forced out by the tractor, the mechanical cotton picker, the desire of the younger generation to head for the cities, and the decline of the small independent farmer. Another 100,000 will leave 'if industries coming into the state are made to understand that Negroes are not to be hired.' The remaining 200,000 may need to be 'assisted to leave through economic pressure.' ...

The plan also calls for driving the radical NAACP element out of the state immediately. It is argued that the masses of Negroes 'will do what is for the common good' if only the dangerous leaders are curbed or driven out first. To understand how completely in earnest Mr. Patterson undoubtedly is requires only the most cursory recital of the fate of Negroes who have stood up for their rights in the Delta:

– On May 6, 1954, the Reverend George Lee of the Belzoni, Mississippi, NAACP was shot and killed on the street after refusing to stop distributing literature urging Negroes to vote.

– In November 1955, Gus Courts, chairman of the Belzoni NAACP, was shot for carrying on the fight in which Reverend Lee was killed. After a month in the hospital and a short stay in Jackson, Mississippi, he left the state for Texas.

– In Columbus, Mississippi, a cafe thought to belong to Dr. Emmett Stringer was forced to close. His wife was threatened night after night.

– Shots were fired into the home of Dr. McCoy, the president of the state NAACP conference, in Jackson.

– Professor Hennington, principal of the Negro school at Merigold, Mississippi, was found dead in Long Lake, near Whitney, Mississippi. Although spies accused him of NAACP membership, he did not actually belong to the organization.

In other words, to accept leadership in the NAACP means signing one's own death warrant ...

One point in Patterson's careful plan has already been achieved – the establishment of the Mississippi Sovereignty Committee. Set up by the legislature in the summer of 1956, it aims to sell segregation to the public. The committee has $250,000 appropriated for its use. Some small part of this has gone to pay Negroes and white people who spy on the NAACP. The committee, composed completely of WCC legislators, has power to seize records, sends speakers over the state and into the North, publishes anti-Negro literature, holds hearings, attacks the NAACP and the Urban League, and works with the press ...

Bayard Rustin, 'Fear in the Delta', in *Time on Two Crosses: The Collected Writings of Bayard Rustin*, ed. Devon W. Carbado and Weise (San Francisco: Cleis Press, Inc., 2003), pp. 66–76.

4.2 Joe McNeil discusses Greensboro

Frank McCain, Junior Blair, David Richmond, and Joe McNeil were freshmen at North Carolina Agricultural and Technical College who decided they should do something to demonstrate their support for the movement. In the excerpt below, McNeil describes his thinking and the beginning of the sit-ins in Greensboro, North Carolina, in February 1960.

I was particularly inspired by the people in Little Rock. I think if we had to have done that in the area where I was growing up at the time, I would have volunteered to participate. I was really impressed with the courage that those kids had and the leadership they displayed. I think children my age in general felt that way. We knew what they were going through was not easy, but somehow many of us wanted to make a contribution and be a part of something like that.

In 1959 I was fortunate enough to get an academic scholarship to A. and T. Junior Blair and I were roommates. Frank McCain lived down the

Figure 7 Student activists stage a sit-in at Woolworth's in Atlanta.

hall from us. David Richmond lived in the city. We were all in the same algebra class and we gravitated to each other and became friends. We would get together and discuss current events, political events, things that affected us pretty much as college kids do today. Bull sessions. The question became, What do we do and to whom do we do it against? There were many conspicuous forms that we could have chosen, but Woolworth seemed logical because it was national in scope and somehow we had hoped to get sympathies from without as well as from within.

I don't think there's any specific reason why that particular day was chosen. I had talked to a local merchant [Ralph Johns] who was extremely helpful to us in getting things rolling, in giving us some ideas. We had played over in our minds possible scenarios, and to the best of our abilities we had determined how we were gonna conduct ourselves given those scenarios. But we did walk in that day – I guess it was about four-thirty – and we sat at a lunch counter where blacks never sat before. And people started to look at us. The help, many of whom were black, looked at us in disbelief too. They were concerned about our safety. We asked for service, and we were denied, and we expected to be denied. We asked why couldn't we be served, and obviously we weren't given a reasonable answer and it was our intent to sit there until they decided to serve us. We had planned to come back the following day and to repeat that scenario. Others found out what we had done, because the press became aware of what was happening. So the next day when we decided to go down again, I think we went down with fifteen, and the third day it was probably a hundred and fifty, and then it probably mushroomed up to a thousand or so, and then it spread to another city. All rather spontaneously of course, and before long, I guess it was probably in fifteen or twenty cities, and that's when we had our thing going.

Henry Hampton and Steve Fayer, *Voices of Freedom: An Oral History of the Civil Rights Movement from the 1950s through the 1980s'* (New York: Bantam Books, 1991), pp. 56–57.

4.3 John Lewis on nonviolence

In the following passage, John Lewis describes his tutelage under Jim Lawson and his resultant philosophy of nonviolence. Lewis was one of several students from Black colleges in Nashville, including Diane Nash, James Bevel, Marion Barry, and Bernard LaFayette, who would become significant activists in the Movement.

[F]rom the autumn of 1958 into the following fall, [Clark Memorial United Methodist Church] played a major role in educating, preparing and shaping a group of young men and women who would lead the way for years to come in the nonviolent struggle for civil rights in America ...
    I was an eager student for this stuff, just voracious, and I couldn't have found a better teacher than Jim Lawson. I truly felt – and I still feel today – that he was God-sent. There was something of a mystic about him, something holy, so gathered, about his manner, the way he had of leaning back in his chair and listening – really *listening* – nodding his head, saying, 'Yes, go ahead,' taking everything in before he would respond. Very patient. Very attentive. Very calm. The man was a born teacher, in the truest sense of the word.
    And we learned. We learned about Reinhold Niebuhr and his philosophy of nonviolent revolution. We read Thoreau. We studied ancient Chinese thinkers like Mo Ti and Lao-tzu. We discussed and debated every aspect of Gandhi's principles, from his concept of ahimsa – the Hindu idea of nonviolent passive resistance – to satyagraha – literally, 'steadfastness in truth,' a grounding foundation of nonviolent civil disobedience, of active pacifism.
    We talked a lot about the idea of 'redemptive suffering,' ... I always

understood the idea of the ultimate redeemer, Christ on the cross. But now I was beginning to see that this is something that is carried out in every one of us, that the purity of unearned suffering is a holy and *affective* thing. It affects not only ourselves, but it touches and changes those around us as well ... Suffering puts us and those around us in touch with our consciences. It opens and touches our hearts. It makes us feel compassion where we need to and guilt if we must.

Suffering, though, can be nothing more than a sad and sorry thing without the presence on the part of the sufferer of a graceful heart, an accepting and open heart, a heart that holds no malice toward the inflictors of his or her suffering. This is a difficult concept to understand, and it is even more difficult to internalize, but it has everything to do with the way of nonviolence. We are talking about *love* here ... It is a love that recognizes the spark of the divine in each of us ... It is the ability to see through those layers of ugliness, to see further into a person than perhaps that person can see into himself that is essential to the practice of nonviolence.

... [I]t is not hard to find compassion in your heart. It is not hard to find forgiveness. And this, Jim Lawson taught us, is at the essence of the nonviolent way of life – the capacity to forgive ... [I]f you can understand and feel even in the midst of those critical and often physically painful moments that your attacker is as much a victim as you are, that he is a victim of the forces that have shaped and fed his anger and fury, then you are well on your way to the nonviolent life.

... If you want to create an open society, your means of doing so must be consistent with the society you want to create. Means and ends are absolutely inseparable. Violence begets violence. Hatred begets hatred. Anger begets anger, every minute of the day in the smallest of moments as well as the largest.

Dr. King would often say that we've got to love people no matter what. Most of all, he would say we must love the unlovable. Love the *hell* out of them, he would say. And he meant that literally. If there is hell in someone, if there is meanness and anger and hatred in him, we've got to *love* it out.

... Jim Lawson knew – though we had no idea when we began – that we were being trained for a war unlike any this nation had seen up to that time, a nonviolent struggle that would force this country to face its conscience. Lawson was arming us, preparing us, planting in us a sense of both rightness and righteousness – 'soul force' – that would see us through the ugliness and pain that lay ahead, all in pursuit of something both he and Dr. King called the Beloved Community ...

John Lewis with Michael D'Orso, *Walking with the Wind: A Memoir of the Movement* (Orlando: Harcourt Brace & Company, 1998), pp. 76–78.

4.4 Founding statement of the Student Nonviolent Coordinating Committee, May, 1960

The founding statement of SNCC reflected the influence of Lawson and the Nashville group of students.

We affirm the philosophical or religious ideal of nonviolence as the foundation of our purpose, the presupposition of our belief, and the manner of our action.

Nonviolence, as it grows from the Judeo-Christian tradition, seeks a social order of justice permeated by love. Integration of human endeavor represents the crucial first step towards such a society.

Through nonviolence, courage displaces fear. Love transcends hate. Acceptance dissipates prejudice; hope ends despair. Faith reconciles doubt. Peace dominates war. Mutual regards cancel enmity. Justice for all overthrows injustice. The redemptive community supersedes immoral social systems.

By appealing to conscience and standing on the moral nature of human existence, nonviolence nurtures the atmosphere in which reconciliation and justice become actual possibilities.

Although each local group in this movement must diligently work out the clear meaning of this statement of purpose, each act or phase of our corporate effort must reflect a genuine spirit of love and good-will.

James Lawson, Student Nonviolent Coordinating Committee Founding Statement, May, 1960, reproduced (incomplete) in Clayborne Carson, David J. Garrow, Gerald Gill, Vincent Harding, and Darlene Clark Hine, eds., *The Eyes on the Prize Civil Rights Reader* (New York: Penguin Books, 1991), pp. 119–120.

4.5 Ella Baker, 'Bigger than a hamburger'

Ella Baker often was at loggerheads with SCLC's leader-centered organization. Rather, she believed that leadership roles should be distributed throughout an organization, empowering many, thus organizing individuals for self-sufficiency rather than reliance on a charismatic leader. Her ideas were extremely influential in shaping the way SNCC worked with people. See, for example,

James Forman's concern about Martin Luther King, Jr.'s appearance in Albany (**5.1**).

RALEIGH, N.C. – The Student Leadership Conference made it crystal clear that current sit-ins and other demonstrations are concerned with something much bigger than a hamburger or even a giant-sized Coke.

Whatever may be the difference in approach to their goal, the Negro and white students, North and South, are seeking to rid America of the scourge of racial segregation and discrimination not only at lunch counters, but in every aspect of life.

In reports, casual conversations, discussion groups, and speeches, the sense and the spirit of the following statement that appeared in the initial newsletter of the students at Barber-Scotia College, Concord, N.C., were re-echoed time and again:

> We want the world to know that we no longer accept the inferior position of second-class citizenship. We are willing to go to jail, be ridiculed, spat upon and even suffer physical violence to obtain First Class Citizenship.

By and large, this feeling that they have a destined date with freedom, was not limited to a drive for personal freedom, or even freedom for the Negro in the South. Repeatedly it was emphasized that the movement was concerned with the moral implications of racial discrimination for the 'whole world' and the 'Human Race.'

This universality of approach was linked with a perceptive recognition that 'it is important to keep the movement democratic and to avoid struggles for personal leadership.'

It was further evident that desire for supportive cooperation from adult leaders and the adult community was also tempered by apprehension that adults might try to 'capture' the student movement. The students showed willingness to be met on the basis of equality, but were intolerant of anything that smacked of manipulation or domination.

This inclination toward *group-centered leadership*, rather than toward a *leader-centered group pattern of organization*, was refreshing indeed to those of the older group who bear the scars of the battle, the frustrations and the disillusionment that come when the prophetic leader turns out to have heavy feet of clay.

However hopeful might be the signs in the direction of group-centeredness, the fact that many schools and communities, especially in the South, have not provided adequate experience for young Negroes to assume initiative and think and act independently accentuated the need for guarding the student movement against well-meaning, but nevertheless unhealthy, over-protectiveness.

Here is an opportunity for adult and youth to work together and provide genuine leadership – the development of the individual to his highest potential for the benefit of the group.

Many adults and youth characterized the Raleigh meeting as the greatest or most significant conference of our period. Whether it lives up to this high evaluation or not will, in a large measure, be determined by the extent to which there is more effective training in and understanding of non-violent principles and practices, in group dynamics, and in the re-direction into creative channels of the normal frustrations and hostilities that result from second-class citizenship.

The Southern Patriot (June, 1960).

4.6 *Boynton* v. *Virginia* (1960)

Boynton was convicted for sitting in the White section of the Trailways terminal in Richmond, Virginia. He appealed his conviction to the Virginia Supreme Court, which upheld the lower court ruling. Boynton then appealed to the US Supreme Court, which found that the business collaboration of the bus company and the restaurant brought the restaurant within the scope of the ICC prohibition against discrimination.

The basic question presented in this case is whether an interstate bus passenger is denied a federal statutory or constitutional right when a restaurant in a bus terminal used by the carrier along its route discriminates in serving food to the passenger solely because of his color …

We think there are persuasive reasons … why this case should be decided … on the Interstate Commerce Act contention raised in the Virginia courts. Discrimination because of color is the core of the two broad constitutional questions presented to us by petitioner, just as it is the core of the Interstate Commerce Act question presented to the Virginia courts. Under these circumstances we think it appropriate not to reach the constitutional questions but to proceed at once to the statutory issue.

The Interstate Commerce Act, as we have said, uses language of the broadest type to bar discriminations of all kinds …

Section 216 (d) of Part II of the Interstate Commerce Act, 49 U.S.C. 316 (d), which applies to motor carriers, provides in part:

'It shall be unlawful for any common carrier by motor vehicle engaged in interstate or foreign commerce to make, give, or cause any undue or unreasonable preference or advantage to any particular person ... in any respect whatsoever; or to subject any particular person ... to any unjust discrimination or any unjust or unreasonable prejudice or disadvantage in any respect whatsoever ... '

... It follows ... as a matter of course that should buses in transit decide to supply dining service, discrimination of the kind shown here would violate 216 (d) ...

[I]f the bus carrier has volunteered to make terminal and restaurant facilities and services available to its interstate passengers as a regular part of their transportation, and the terminal and restaurant have acquiesced and cooperated in this undertaking, the terminal and restaurant must perform these services without discriminations prohibited by the Act. In the performance of these services ... under such conditions the terminal and restaurant stand in the place of the bus company in the performance of its transportation obligations ...

Interstate passengers have to eat, and the very terms of the lease of the built-in restaurant space in this terminal constitute a recognition of the essential need of interstate passengers to be able to get food conveniently on their journey and an undertaking by the restaurant to fulfill that need. Such passengers in transit on a paid interstate Trailways journey had a right to expect that this essential transportation food service voluntarily provided for them under such circumstances would be rendered without discrimination prohibited by the Interstate Commerce Act. Under the circumstances of this case, therefore, petitioner had a federal right to remain in the white portion of the restaurant. He was there under 'authority of law' - the Interstate Commerce Act - and it was error for the Supreme Court of Virginia to affirm his conviction ...

The judgment of the Supreme Court of Virginia is reversed and the cause is remanded to that Court for proceedings not inconsistent with this opinion ...

364 U.S. 454 (1960).

4.7 Law enforcement and Ku Klux Klan collusion

The federal government's insistence that it was up to local and state law enforcement to maintain order in the face of direct action often left Black activists at the mercy of the KKK. Rowe, an FBI informant during the early 1960s, later wrote the following account of the arrangement between the Birmingham police and the KKK in May, 1961.

The rioting that greeted [the Freedom Riders] in Birmingham was not the brainchild of the Klan ... it was instigated by members of the police department ...

When all the details were worked out, this was the final arrangement between the Klan and the police department:

Since the riders were arriving on Mother's Day – a holiday – only a skeleton force of men and dogs would be on duty and they would have orders to stay in headquarters in the parking area.

The Klan would be allowed 15 minutes from the time the buses entered the terminal to beat, stab, maim and terrorize the passengers.

Detectives Turner and Parker would warn us when the time was up; I was to look for Mike; when he waved his arm as a signal we were to get the hell out.

'If you don't get out you're going to be arrested,' [Officer] Collins told us, 'and we don't want anybody arrested! Can you do it in fifteen minutes?'

The Klan agreed 'it' could be done in 15 minutes, and this commitment

Figure 8 Freedom Riders' bus bombed outside Anniston, Alabama, May 14, 1961.

was considered so important that a fiery summons was sent out to muster the members. A fiery summons may not be ignored; it means an emergency, and all Klansmen must go even if they lose their jobs ...

We made an astounding sight, nearly 1,000 men running and walking down the streets of Birmingham on Sunday afternoon carrying chains, sticks and clubs. Everything was deserted; no police officers were to be seen except one on a street corner. He stepped off and let us go by, and we barged into the bus station and took it over like an army of occupation. There were Klansmen in the waiting rooms, in the rest rooms, in the parking area.

A bus official said, 'Get the shoeshine boy out; the Klan is here.'

A colored man started to run from the rest room to the front door, and at least 70 people hit or kicked him in that short distance. Then two Klansmen picked him up and threw him out in the middle of the street over the top of an automobile. Every part of his body was covered with blood.

'Here they are!' someone yelled.

Three buses were pulling in at about the same time and the door of one opened immediately to reveal a white man being led off by a big Negro. The first statement I remember hearing in all the confusion was 'Kill the black bastard; he's hurt the white man!'

When the Klansmen approached him to get the Negro, the white man held up his hand in the gesture of a traffic officer and said, 'Stop. We've had enough. You'll have to kill me before you hurt him.'

One of the Klansmen replied, 'That won't be any goddamn problem!'

Instantly there was a mass of human beings on the passengers; everybody who got off the bus was clubbed, kicked or beaten. There was fighting everywhere; blood splattered in the streets. When people looked up, I couldn't see their faces for blood. I could hear screaming, 'Don't kick me,' and 'Oh my God, I'm cut!'

The mob surrounded a photographer who came up to take a picture and beat him to his knees. As one Klansman lifted the man's camera over his head to smash it, an out-of-town member, thinking he was the photographer, hit him with a blackjack.

This scene had lasted perhaps 13 minutes when someone grabbed my right shoulder so hard he ripped the sleeve of my shirt. I turned around to find Detective Turner shouting instructions at me.

'Get the boys out of here,' he said. 'I'm ready to give the signal for the police to move in!'

Just at that moment a colored woman ran up and said, 'You're the police; I've seen you before. They cut my husband; he's dying! Help me!'

Turner said, 'Nigger, if you knew what I know, you'd get the hell away from here while you can!'

She started to say, 'What ...,' but before she could finish her question two other Klansmen came up. One slapped her and the other one pushed and kicked her. As she crumpled to the sidewalk, one of the Klansmen kicked her squarely between the eyes.

'Oh my God, I'm dying!' she cried, and another Klansman kicked her in the stomach.

Turner said, 'Goddamn it, Tom, I told you to get out of here! They're on the way!'

I shouted, 'Everybody run! Everybody run!' ...

Gary Thomas Rowe, Jr., *My Undercover Years with the Ku Klux Klan* (New York: Bantam Books, 1976), pp. 38–43.

4.8 John Lewis on the Freedom Ride to Montgomery, May, 1961

John Lewis was a member of the Nashville-coordinated Freedom Riders who continued the Ride from Birmingham after the original CORE Riders had been bombed and beaten. Here he describes events as the Riders departed from the bus in Montgomery. In the six days between the Birmingham riot and the Riders' departure for Montgomery, the federal government had tried to negotiate the Riders' safety in Alabama, but with a White supremacist governor and elected state officials determined to defend the 'Southern way of life,' such negotiations proved futile. Again, violent White mobs acted virtually at will. Ultimately, Attorney General Robert Kennedy ordered in federal marshals, and the Kennedy administration initiated plans to send in units of the US Army to protect the safety of Freedom Riders and Black parishioners attending a mass meeting at Montgomery's First Baptist Church. Order was restored when Alabama Governor John Patterson, to avoid the use of federal troops, called in the Alabama National Guard. Patterson, however, made it clear that he had no sympathy with Freedom Riders and that they, along with the federal government, were responsible for the outbreaks of violence. The federal government had no business interfering with state sovereignty in these circumstances, he argued.

It was 8:30 A.M., Saturday, May 20, six days since the bombing in Anniston and the beatings in Birmingham, eighteen hours since we had walked into this terminal to continue the ride. Now, finally, we were moving on, south to Montgomery ...

In less than two hours we reached the Montgomery city limits, and suddenly, as if on cue, the patrol cars turned away, the airplane banked off toward the horizon, and we were on the road alone. There were no Montgomery police cars to meet us. There was nothing on the road but our bus. As we slowed to the city speed limit and began turning toward the downtown station, it felt eerie, very strange.

The Montgomery Greyhound terminal looked almost deserted as we pulled up to the loading dock. The only people I could see were a couple of taxi drivers sitting in their cabs, a small group of reporters waiting on the platform and a dozen or so white men standing together over near the terminal door.

'This doesn't look right,' I said to William Harbour as we stepped off the bus. I didn't like the looks of those men by the door.

The journalists moved in. An NBC reporter and his cameraman stepped up to speak to me and Katherine Burke. Norm Ritter, a writer from *Life* magazine, started to ask me a question, but I didn't hear it. I was looking past Ritter, to those white men, who were suddenly coming toward us fast.

Ritter saw the look on my face, I guess, and turned around. I remember how he lifted his arms, holding them out wide, as if to protect us, as if he could hold these men back by himself.

There was a low wall behind us, with about an eight-foot drop to a concrete ramp below. I backed the others toward the wall. 'Do not run,' I told them. 'Let's stand here together.'

And then, out of nowhere, from every direction, came people. White people. Men, women and children. Dozens of them. Hundreds of them. Out of alleys, out of side streets, around the corners of office buildings, they emerged from everywhere, from all directions, all at once, as if they'd been let out of a gate. To this day I don't know where all those people came from. They carried every makeshift weapon imaginable. Baseball bats, wooden boards, bricks, chains, tire irons, pipes, even garden tools – hoes and rakes. One group had women in front, their faces twisted in anger, screaming, '*Git them niggers, GIT them niggers!*'

It was the press, though, who got it first. The NBC cameraman, a guy named Moe Levy, was kicked in the stomach by a fat man with a cigar in his teeth. Levy's camera – a big, heavy piece of equipment ... – fell to the ground and someone picked it up and began beating him with it. A *Life* photographer named Don Urbrock had his camera yanked from his neck and it, too, became a weapon, swung at his face. The scene quickly became a blur as the crowd moved in. One reporter – I don't know who he was – had blood just gushing from his head.

Now the mob was moving toward us, and Jim Zwerg became their target. They shouted '*Nigger lover!*' as several men clutching axe handles grabbed Jim and pulled him into the mob. All I could see were his legs as his body disappeared into this mass of people ...

It was madness. It was unbelievable. I could see some of our group trying to climb a nearby tree to get away. Others were scrambling to get up the wall of a building, which was impossible. Everywhere this crowd was screaming and reaching out and hitting and spitting. It was awful. They were like animals. I tried shouting directions about the way to get out of the lot and up the street. I knew Montgomery. I knew this terminal. But there was no way anyone could hear me. And there was no way to get through the crowd, which had now closed all around us.

There was still a way clear to the cabs, though, and we tried getting the women among us over there. They managed to reach one of the taxis, which had a black driver sitting at its wheel, but when the two white women among us began to climb in, the driver said no, he could not carry them. 'It's the law,' he said, referring to the city's segregation statutes. Katherine Burke yelled at him to move over then, that *she* would drive. But the man would not budge. So the two white women, Susan Wilbur and Sue Harmann, were left behind as the cab pulled away with our five black women inside.

This was all happening at once, all within seconds, really. I could see Jim Zwerg now, being horribly beaten. Someone picked up his suitcase, which he had dropped, and swung it full force against his head. Another man then lifted Jim's head and held it between his knees while others, including women and children, hit and scratched at Jim's face. His eyes were shut. He was unconscious.

So was William Barbee, a classmate of mine at American Baptist, who was now lying on the pavement, a crowd of men stomping on his head and shoulders.

And now they were all around me. Someone grabbed my briefcase, which I'd been holding in my right hand since stepping off the bus. I pulled back but it was ripped from my fingers. At that instant I felt a thud against my head. I could feel my knees collapse and then nothing. Everything turned white for an instant, then black.

I was unconscious on that asphalt. I learned later that someone had swung a wooden Coca-Cola crate against my skull. There was a lot I didn't learn about until later.

The two Susans – Wilbur and Harmann – were cornered by a group of men and women who began taunting and hitting them. A white man drove up on that scene and yelled at them to get in his car. It was [Attorney General Robert Kennedy's special assistant] John Seigenthaler ...

Seigenthaler was shocked by the scene he came upon. He could see our luggage being thrown in the air, the contents flying out. As he got out of his car to help Wilbur and Harmann, the mob moved in on him. He yelled at them to back away, that he was a federal agent. No sooner did he get those words out of his mouth than he was hit in the head with a pipe and knocked unconscious. For twenty minutes he lay there, a personal aide to the attorney general of the United States, clubbed to the parking lot pavement of an Alabama bus terminal.

By the time I regained consciousness, the scene was relatively under control. Floyd Mann, Alabama's state public safety director, had pushed his way into the mob, tried pulling some men off William Barbee's body, then raised a pistol and fired it in the air, warning the crowd away.

Montgomery police commissioner L. B. Sullivan and his men had finally arrived – Sullivan had reportedly sat in his car around the comer from the terminal during the worst of the attack, calmly waiting while the mob had its way ...

Lewis, *Walking with the Wind*, pp. 154–157.

4.9 Interstate Commerce Commission Order, 22 September 1961

The Kennedy administration moved cautiously on its civil rights agenda, fearing that activism might derail other reform efforts. The Kennedys preferred negotiation with segregationists and were hesitant to use federal power. This hesitancy was particularly evident in areas traditionally seen as within the domain of state and local officials: public order and safety. During the Freedom Rides, the federal government intervened only when public order was perceived to have broken down completely. However, Robert Kennedy did, in late May, 1961, petition the Interstate Commerce Commission (ICC) to adopt clear regulations prohibiting racial discrimination in interstate travel. In response, the ICC issued a series of regulations, including fines for violations, thereby providing a tool with which federal authorities could enforce desegregation.

§ 180a.1 Discrimination prohibited.

No motor common carrier of passengers subject to section 216 of the Interstate Commerce Act shall operate a motor vehicle in interstate or foreign commerce on which the seating of passengers is based upon race, color, creed, or national origin ...

§ 180a.4 Discrimination in terminal facilities.

No motor common carrier of passengers subject to section 216 of the Interstate Commerce Act shall in the operation of vehicles in interstate or foreign commerce provide, maintain arrangements for, utilize, make available, adhere to any understanding for the availability, or follow any practice which includes availability of, any terminal facilities which are so operated, arranged, or maintained as to involve any separation of any portion thereof, or in the use thereof on the basis of race, color, creed, or national origin ...

§ 180a.7 Reports of interference with regulations.

Every motor common carrier of passengers subject to section 216 of the Interstate Commerce Act operating vehicles in interstate or foreign commerce shall report to the Secretary of the Interstate Commerce Commission, within fifteen (15) days of its occurrence, any interference by any person, municipality, county, parish, state, or body politic with its observance of the requirements of the regulations in this part ...

Federal Register, 26/188 (September 29, 1961), pp. 9166–9167.

4.10 Robert F. Williams criticizes nonviolence

Robert F. Williams was a Korean War veteran and President of the Union County, North Carolina, chapter of the NAACP in the late 1950s. An advocate of the use of weapons for self-defense, he was sanctioned by the NAACP and suspended from his presidency when he became involved in a shootout with members of the KKK. Later, trumped-up charges of kidnapping forced him to flee the country. In the following piece, the prologue to his 1962 book, *Negroes with Guns*, he challenges the efficacy of nonviolence.

Why do I speak to you from exile?

Because a Negro community in the South took up guns in self-defense against racist violence – and used them. I am held responsible for this action, that for the first time in history American Negroes have armed themselves as a group to defend their homes, their wives, their children, in a situation where law and order had broken down, where the authorities could not, or rather would not, enforce their duty to protect Americans from a lawless mob. I accept this responsibility and am proud of it. I have asserted the right of Negroes to meet the violence of the Ku Klux Klan by armed self-defense – and have acted on it. It has always been an accepted right of Americans, as the history of our Western states proves, that where the law is unable, or unwilling, to enforce order, the citizens can, and must, act in self-defense against lawless violence. I believe this right holds for black Americans as well as whites.

Many people will remember that in the summer of 1957 the Ku Klux Klan made an armed raid on an Indian community in the South and were met with determined rifle fire from the Indians acting in self-defense. The nation approved of the action and there were widespread expressions of pleasure at the defeat of the Kluxers who showed their courage by running away despite their armed superiority. What the nation doesn't know, because it has never been told, is that the Negro community in Monroe, North Carolina, had set the example two weeks before when we shot up an armed motorcade of the Ku Klux Klan, including two police cars, which had come to attack the home of Dr. Albert E. Perry, vice-president of the Monroe chapter of the National Association for the Advancement of Colored People. The stand taken by our chapter resulted in the official re-affirmation by the NAACP of the right of self-defense. The Preamble to the resolution of the 50th Convention of the NAACP, New York City, July 1959, states: ' ... we do not deny, but reaffirm, the right of an individual and collective self-defense against unlawful assaults.'

Because there has been much distortion of my position, I wish to make it clear that I do not advocate violence for its own sake or for the sake of reprisals against whites. Nor am I against the passive resistance advocated by the Reverend Martin Luther King and others. My only difference with Dr. King is that I believe in flexibility in the freedom struggle. This means that I believe in non-violent tactics where feasible; the mere fact that I have a Sit-In case pending before the US Supreme Court bears this out. Massive civil disobedience is a powerful weapon under civilized conditions where the law safeguards the citizens' right of peaceful demonstrations. In civilized society the law serves as a deterrent against lawless forces that would destroy the democratic process. But where there is a breakdown of the law, the individual citizen has a right to protect his person, his family, his home and his property. To me this is so simple and proper that it is self-evident.

When an oppressed people show a willingness to defend themselves, the enemy, who is a moral weakling and coward, is more willing to grant concessions and work for a respectable compromise. Psychologically, moreover, racists consider themselves superior beings and are not willing to exchange their superior lives for our inferior ones. They are most vicious and violent when they can practice violence with impunity. This we have shown in Monroe. Moreover, when because of our self-defense there is a danger that the blood of whites may be spilled, the local authorities in the South suddenly enforce law and order when previously they had been complacent toward lawless, racist violence. This too we have proven in Monroe. It is remarkable how easily and quickly state and local police control and disperse lawless mobs when the Negro is ready to defend himself with arms.

Furthermore, because of the international situation, the Federal Government does not want racial incidents which draw the attention of the world to the situation in the South. Negro self-defense draws such attention, and the Federal Government will be more willing to enforce law and order if the local authorities don't. When our people become fighters, our leaders will be able to sit at the conference table as equals, not dependent on the whim and the generosity of the oppressors. It will be to the best interests of both sides to negotiate just, honorable and lasting settlements.

The majority of white people in the United States have literally no idea of the violence with which Negroes in the South are treated daily – nay, hourly. This violence is deliberate, conscious, condoned by the authorities. It has gone on for centuries and is going on today, every day, unceasing and unremitting. It is our way of life. Negro existence in the South has been one long travail, steeped in terror and blood – our blood. The incidents which took place in Monroe, which I witnessed and which I suffered, will give some idea of the conditions in the South, conditions that can no longer be borne. That is why, one hundred years after the Civil War began, we Negroes in Monroe armed ourselves in self-defense and used our weapons. We showed that our policy worked. The lawful authorities of Monroe and North Carolina acted to enforce order *only after, and as a direct result of, our being armed.* Previously they had connived with the Ku Klux Klan in the racist violence against our people. Self-defense prevented bloodshed and forced the law to establish order. This is the meaning of Monroe and I believe it marks a historic change in the life of my people ...

Robert F. Williams, *Negroes with Guns* (Detroit: Wayne State University Press, 1998), pp. 3–5.

5

'Up above my head':
Albany to the Civil Rights
Act of 1964

The September 1961 ICC ruling against discrimination in interstate travel was an important legal step, but it, as well as most of the positive legal developments in the struggle against Jim Crow, remained contested in the South. Southern communities and institutions were dominated by White supremacists determined to retain segregation. While SNCC and CORE activists spread throughout the South fostering grassroots protest movements, King and the SCLC sought to support such efforts but also to capture national attention and promote further federal action. Developments from the protests in Albany, Georgia, in late 1961 through the March on Washington in August 1963 reveal the ebb and flow of the Movement in the early 1960s. These developments bore fruit with the passage of the Civil Rights Act of 1964.

Albany

The African American community in Albany, Georgia, was one of many motivated by the Freedom Rides to challenge segregation. A budding movement accelerated when SNCC organizers Charles Sherrod and Cordell Reagon arrived in the fall of 1961, energizing youth in the community to push their elders. In November, various Black organizations founded the Albany Movement, an organization similar to Montgomery's MIA. When the city failed to address the Albany Movement's concerns and activists were arrested, mass protest ensued. James Forman, a SNCC activist and Freedom Rider who arrived in the city in early December, recounts some events of that fall (5.1). Forman's account addresses SNCC organizers' concerns about the presence of Martin Luther King, Jr. and particularly the difference between SNCC's emphasis on grass-roots, group-centered organizations and the SCLC's leader-centered organization. Indeed, there was considerable confusion when King and the SCLC arrived, fostering what many perceived as a setback to the Movement.

In mid-December, the President of the Albany Movement, Dr. William G. Anderson, had invited King to speak at a mass meeting and, consequently, participate in a march the following day. King's subsequent arrest, the attempt by SCLC staff to organize a broader effort in Albany without consulting local leaders or receiving their endorsement, and King's departure despite a pledge to stay in jail all served to tarnish King's reputation in some quarters. The mass movement continued, however, throughout the winter and into the summer, with local White officials remaining intransigent – in fact, repudiating earlier agreements. Arrests of protesters mounted, but to little effect as Police Chief Laurie Pritchett crafted a strategy that sapped the energy of the Albany Movement (**5.2**). Breach of peace and unlawful assembly arrests (rather than arrests for violating segregation ordinances) avoided direct conflict with federal policy (and successfully kept the Justice Department out of the picture); the transfer of detainees to nearby jurisdictions avoided overcrowding in Albany jails; and, most significantly, use of minimal force avoided the appearance of police violence. In the absence of large-scale violence, national attention to the situation in Albany waned. Despite King's return and re-arrest during the summer of 1962, little immediate progress was made in desegregating Albany, and by the end of the summer the mass demonstrations were suspended. Although this was perceived by many as the first major failure of King and the SCLC, nonetheless lessons were learned and attitudes of many local Blacks were changed. Dr. Anderson announced it a 'qualified success' (**5.3**).

In Albany, the SCLC learned the importance of coordinated planning with the local movement center. It was also clear that national attention and federal help were much more likely captured when nonviolent demonstrators met with violence. Those lessons were applied in Birmingham.

Birmingham

Many regarded Birmingham as the South's most segregated city. Local segregation ordinances were pervasive (**5.4**). Furthermore, the local Commissioner of Public Safety, Eugene 'Bull' Connor, was a fervid White supremacist with ties to the Ku Klux Klan. He had conspired to arrange the violent reception of the Freedom Riders in May 1961 (see **4.7**). Despite the city's history of violence to African Americans, a local movement center had developed under the leadership of Rev. Fred Shuttlesworth. When the state outlawed the NAACP in the mid-fifties, Shuttlesworth and other local, Black ministers and community leaders formed the Alabama Christian Movement for Human Rights (ACMHR). From its inception, under the guidance of the charismatic Shuttlesworth, the ACMHR had challenged the White power structure through both litigation and mass action, but to little avail (**5.5**). In the spring of 1963, Shuttlesworth invited Dr. King and the SCLC to Birmingham to coordinate collective action.

The plan for direct action in Birmingham called for a focus on downtown businesses, targeting segregation and employment discrimination in those businesses. The first two phases were composed of sit-ins and protest marches but, as in Albany, impact was slight. To motivate activists, King personally joined a protest march, violating a state court-ordered injunction. He was arrested and, during his incarceration, responded to a published letter from local White clergy criticizing his tactics and presence in Birmingham. His letter in response is widely considered one of the most eloquent expressions of the Civil Rights Movement's philosophy of non-violent, direct action. 'I submit,' wrote King, 'that an individual who breaks a law that conscience tells him is unjust and who willingly accepts the penalty of imprisonment in order to arouse the conscience of the community over its injustice, is in reality expressing the highest respect for law.'[1]

The confrontation with White authorities was running out of steam when SCLC staffer James Bevel advocated the recruitment of children as marchers (**5.6**). His plan was endorsed, children began to march on May 2, and by the second day of their involvement, Bull Connor began to employ dogs and high-pressure hoses against them. By May 6, some 2,000 children had been jailed and shocking television images, photographs, and stories of Connor's tactics had been broadcast around the world. Meanwhile, Justice Department representative Burke Marshall was dispatched to Birmingham, where he mediated negotiations between activists and the White business community. An agreement ending the demonstrations was endorsed on May 10 (**5.7**). White supremacists, however, responded with a series of bombings, leading President Kennedy to threaten the use of federal troops.

Direct action had advanced desegregation in Birmingham. Bull Connor's violence inspired disgust and indignation among many Americans and eroded sympathy for segregation.

University Desegregation

Events in Birmingham contributed to the timing of President Kennedy's decision to ask Congress for a comprehensive civil rights bill. Events surrounding the desegregation of the all-White state universities in Mississippi and Alabama also played a role.

In January, 1961, James Meredith, an African American, was denied admission to the University of Mississippi. Supported by the NAACP, Meredith's case ultimately was appealed to the Supreme Court, which in September, 1962 ordered his admission. Mississippi Governor Ross Barnett, however, defied the Court's order. The Attorney General and President Kennedy in turn attempted to negotiate with Barnett, arguing that federal court orders must be enforced, but to no avail. By the time federal marshals accompanied Meredith to campus on September 30, a mob – composed of some two thousand White supremacists whipped up by Barnett and others – had organized. The marshals were attacked by the mob, state law enforcement did not intervene, and President Kennedy was forced to send in federal troops to maintain order. Despite Barnett's efforts, the University of Mississippi was desegregated.

Shortly after the mass demonstrations in Birmingham, Alabama Governor George Wallace, who, in his inaugural address, had called for 'segregation today ... segregation tomorrow ... segregation forever,' also attempted to block the desegregation of that state's university (**5.8**). Casting himself as a defender of the US Constitution and states' rights, Wallace stood in the doorway of the University of Alabama admissions office until federal marshals backed by the Alabama National Guard ordered him aside. By this time, President Kennedy had decided that the issue of civil rights was a basic, moral question testing the nation's founding principles. He used the occasion of Wallace's action to address the nation and call for Congressional action on civil rights (**5.9**).

March on Washington

A. Philip Randolph (see **2.**3) felt that the time was ripe for a March on Washington. The venerable Randolph, again aided by Bayard Rustin, was this time able to recruit the broad spectrum of activist organizations in support of desegregation, nonviolence, and civil rights legislation. Aiding in the planning were Martin Luther King, Jr., of the SCLC, Whitney Young, Jr., of the National Urban League, Roy Wilkins of the NAACP, James Farmer of CORE, and John Lewis of SNCC. On August 28, 1963, some 250,000 demonstrators gathered before the Lincoln Memorial and pledged their support for the achievement of social peace through social justice. Although a wide range of speakers addressed the crowd, the most memorable moment came with King's closing address.

> And when we allow freedom to ring, when we let it ring from every village and hamlet, from every state and city, we will be able to speed up that day when all of God's children – black men and white men, Jews and Gentiles, Catholics and Protestants – will join hands and to sing in the words of the old Negro spiritual, 'Free at last, free at last; thank God Almighty, we are free at last.'[2]

The non-violent, even festive nature of the crowd and soaring rhetoric of Martin Luther King, Jr. envisioned a better day for African Americans. White supremacists, however, continued to resort to violence. Just one day after President Kennedy's televised address to the nation on June 11, 1963, civil rights worker Medgar Evers was murdered in Mississippi. Some two weeks after King's speech at the Lincoln Memorial, a Ku Klux Klan bomb killed four teenage girls at the Sixteenth Street Baptist Church in Birmingham.

The Civil Rights Act of 1964

Kennedy's assassination in November of 1963 stunned the world and, especially, the Civil Rights community. The developments of 1963, however, fueled support for the comprehensive civil rights legislation he had requested. Despite frustrations with his administration, most activists saw him as a friend of the Movement. His successor, Lyndon Johnson, a Texan and former defender of segregation, was regarded with anxiety. Johnson proved, despite his mixed history, to be a major advocate of civil rights reform, albeit frequently on his own terms. He adopted Kennedy's proposed civil rights bill as his own and, using his considerable political skills, pushed it through Congress. He signed the resultant Civil Rights Act of 1964 (5.10) on July 2.

5.1 James Forman on Albany

Forman's account gives his perception of the strategy used by police chief Laurie Pritchett, the hesitancy of federal officials to become involved, and the pride of SNCC organizers in fostering a grassroots movement. His reservations about asking King to join the Albany Movement reflect the differing leadership styles between SNCC and the SCLC. The city reneged on the settlement mentioned here.

In early October of [1961] field secretaries Sherrod and Reagon arrived and set up an office in a small, run-down building two blocks from the Shiloh Baptist Church. They began registering voters. Some people called them Freedom Riders, which gave the two SNCC workers a certain status with many blacks. But, in general, the black population of Albany was at first 'very apprehensive,' Sherrod relates.

> It was known that we had little money, and there were doubts as to who we really were ... But when people began to hear us ... they began to open up a bit. ... We mocked the system that teaches men to be good Negroes instead of good men. We gave an account of the many instances of injustice in the courts, in employment, registration, and voting. The people knew that such evils existed but when we pointed out time and time again and emphasized the need for concerted action against them, the people began to think ...

I came to Albany myself on December 10 – by way of a Freedom Ride. We had decided to test the allegedly segregated seating policy of the Georgia Central Railroad, four blacks and five whites. When the conductor told the blacks in our group to move to the next coach, we refused and there was no further incident. But arriving in Albany, where about three hundred blacks were at the station to meet us, we went into the white waiting room and the police closed the doors behind us. Chief Laurie Pritchett then moved in and arrested eight of our group, although by that time some of us were no longer in the waiting room but just standing outside the station.

Chief Pritchett told the press, 'We will not stand for these troublemakers coming into our city for the sole purpose of disturbing the peace and quiet

Figure 9 Charles Sherrod canvasses outside Albany, Georgia.

of the city of Albany.' Pritchett appeared to be following the same policy used by the Jackson, Mississippi, police toward the Freedom Riders of 1961: Arrest quickly, quietly, and imprison. Move before white mobs can form, avoid brutal actions which can mobilize national support. Play it cool. 'Peace and quiet,' of course, meant maintaining segregation and oppression ...

[T]he city dropped charges against me and seven others ... But we were rearrested in the courtroom on state charges of conspiring to breach the peace and unlawful assembly, and we went back to jail – this time for a week. By now some 560 people had been arrested and there were at least 300 still in jail. The jails of Albany and of several nearby counties were jammed. National Guardsmen had been called up by Georgia's governor and telegrams were flowing into Attorney General Kennedy's office. At this point, the mayor of Albany contacted the Albany Movement and requested 'a biracial meeting.'

By noon the next day, Friday, the city had agreed in principle to desegregate bus and train facilities and to release those jailed. We were on the verge of winning our immediate objectives. More importantly, we had helped to create a movement in which – for the first time since the sit-ins – not only students, but also adults were actively participating in large numbers ...

I was extremely proud of this achievement, for it had the potential of spreading to other areas of the Deep South ... We had helped to generate a people's movement without dominating it – our goal as a band of organizers ...

The potential effect of this people's movement on black people – in Albany, but even more so in the rest of the country – was the main reason why I had opposed Dr. Martin Luther King's being invited to Albany ...

I opposed the move, pointing out that it was most important to keep the Albany Movement a people's movement – to keep the focus on the ordinary people involved in it, especially the unusual number of adults – and that the presence of Dr. King would detract from, rather than intensify, this focus ... I knew how much harm could be done by interjecting the Messiah complex – people would feel that only a particular individual could save them and would not move on their own to fight racism and exploitation ...

I might have added ... a word about the striking inaction of the federal government throughout the events of December, 1961.

When Salyn McCollum notified us of the ejection of the nine young blacks from the Trailways terminal on November 1, this was reported to the FBI. There was no apparent result. On November 22, when five students were arrested for using terminal facilities, there was no federal action. When Chief Pritchett ordered the Freedom Riders outside the railroad waiting room on December 10, then arrested them in the street, there was no action. Every one of these actions by the police violated an express federal ruling. With the demonstrations and mass arrests that followed, the local police were violating not merely a single ruling, but broader American law – the Bill of Rights and its provisions for freedom of assembly, the right of petition.

Our telegrams to Attorney General Kennedy brought no response, although we were graciously informed through *The New York Times* on December 4 that, 'The Justice Department was watching developments closely.' ... The federal government could have stepped in at any time, with clear power to enforce its own orders. But it didn't; the black people of Albany had to see to it that a federal ruling was complied with. They did, with their suffering and sacrifice – not with federal authority ...

James Forman, *The Making of Black Revolutionaries* (New York: The Macmillan Company, 1972), pp. 249–260.

5.2 Sheriff Laurie Pritchett's strategy

In the following passage from a later interview with Howell Raines, Chief Pritchett revealed how he undermined the efforts of King and the Albany Movement through mass arrests and the avoidance of overt violence.

I researched Dr. King. I read about his early days in Montgomery, his methods there. I read that he was a great follower of Gandhi's ...
   We had planned for mass arrests. We had known that their plan was ... to overcrowd our jail conditions, thus makin' us have to give in. And this was based on Dr. King's philosophy of the Gandhi march to the sea, which I had read and was fully aware of – of how they had crowded the jails, overrode the British jails and finally had to be turned loose. I had studied this philosophy of his and methods and made preparations that at no time would any be housed in our facilities in Albany or Dougherty County. I had made arrangements, and we had it on a map – Lee County, which was ten miles, and then we'd go out twenty-five miles, go out fifty miles, a hundred miles – and all these places had agreed to take the prisoners. So we had buses. When we would book and fingerprint, photograph, they'd come right out and enter the buses and be taken to some other jail. We sent personnel along to see that they were not mistreated ... stayed with 'em in the jails to see that nobody in the other counties mistreated or mishandled 'em ... I think this is one thing that Dr. King was surprised at. This did away with his method of overextending the facilities.

Howell Raines, *My Soul Is Rested: The Story of the Civil Rights Movement in the Deep South* (New York: Penguin Books, 1983), pp. 361–362.

5.3 William G. Anderson on the Albany Movement

While Albany was perceived by many as a setback for King and the Movement, there were achievements and lessons learned. Note that Anderson, President of the Albany Movement, in the following oral history interview, sounded themes similar to those of James Forman (**5.1**) concerning grassroots involvement. Anderson disagreed with Forman on the role of King.

The Albany Movement was a qualified success ... The buses had become desegregated, the train station, the bus station. But these were being desegregated by federal edict. It was not a voluntary move on the part of the people of Albany. But the lunch counters, the parks, and other public accommodations were not desegregated and there were no blacks employed as clerks in the stores at the time the Albany Movement came to an end, that is, in the sense of no more mass demonstrations.

But the Albany Movement was an overwhelming success in that, first of all, there was a change in the attitude of the people: ... they would never accept that segregated society as it was, anymore. There was a change in attitude of the kids ... They were determined that they would never go through what their parents went through to get the recognition that they should have as citizens.

Secondly, the Albany Movement ... gave some direction. The mistakes that were made in Albany were not to be repeated. For example, that settlement on a handshake in December 1961. That would never be repeated anytime in the future.

Bringing in Dr. King was probably the smartest thing that we ever did. Not only did we get the benefit of having a well-established, well-experienced civil rights organization as a part of the Albany Movement, but it also brought in world attention. The eyes of the world were focused on Albany primarily because of Dr. King. There was not a major newspaper in the world that was not represented in Albany. Not a major television network in the United States that was not represented in Albany ...

Henry Hampton and Steve Fayer, *Voices of Freedom: An Oral History of the Civil Rights Movement from the 1950s through the 1980s* (New York: Bantam Books, 1991), pp. 113–114.

5.4 Birmingham's racial segregation ordinances

State constitutional and statutory Jim Crow provisions were often supplemented by those of localities. The following ordinances give one a sense of the forced separation in Birmingham.

SECTION 369 ...

It shall be unlawful to conduct a restaurant or other place for the serving of food in the city, at which white and colored people are served in the same room, unless such white and colored persons are effectually separated by a solid partition extending from the floor upward to a distance of seven feet or higher, and unless a separate entrance from the street is provided for each compartment.

SECTION 597 ...

It shall be unlawful for a Negro and a white person to play together or in company with each other in any game of cards, dice, dominoes, checkers, baseball, softball, football, basketball or similar games.

Any person, who being the owner, proprietor ... of any tavern, ... ballfield, stadium or other public house or public place, or the clerk, servant or employee of such owner, proprietor, keeper, or superintendent, knowingly permits a Negro and a white person to play together or in company with each other, at any game ... in his house or ... premises under his charge, supervision or control, shall, on conviction, be punished ...

SECTION 359 ...

(a) It shall be unlawful for any person in charge or control of any room, hall, theatre, ... or other indoor or outdoor place, to which both white persons and Negroes are admitted, to cause, permit or allow therein or thereon any theatrical performance, ... or educational or entertainment program of any kind whatsoever, unless such room, hall, theatre, ... or other place, has entrances, exists and seating or standing sections set aside for and assigned to the use of white persons, and other entrances, exits and seating or standing sections set aside for and assigned to the use of negroes ...

(b) It shall be unlawful for any member of one race to use or occupy any entrance, exit or seating or standing section set aside for and assigned to the use of members of the other race.

SECTION 1002 ...

Every common carrier engaged in operation [of] streetcars in the city for the carriage of passengers shall provide equal but separate accommodations ...

SECTION 1413 ...

Every owner or operator of any jitney, bus or taxicab in the city shall provide equal but separate accommodations ...

Birmingham's Racial Segregation Ordinances, Birmingham Civil Rights Institute, 520 Sixteenth Street North, Birmingham, Ala. 35203.

5.5 Alabama Christian Movement for Human Rights

The following two documents reflect the concerns of the Alabama Christian Movement for Human Rights in 1956 and at the outset of the 1963 campaign in Birmingham.

A Original Declaration of Principles, June 5, 1956

(A) As free and independent Citizens of the United States of America, and the State of Alabama, we express publicly our determination to press forward persistently for Freedom and Democracy, and the removal from our society any forms of Second Class Citizenship.

(B) We are not echoing the will or sentiments of Outsiders; but our own convictions and Will to be free, so help us God. We will not become Rabblerousers; but will be sober, firm, peaceful, and resolute, within the Framework of Goodwill.

(C) We believe in our Courts and in Justice administered by our Courts; but we now point out to the Nation's conscience a strange paradox: One State District Court Judge can rule and immediately it is obeyed over the entire State – even if questioned or disagreed with; But even a unanimous Decision by 9 Judges of the U. S. Supreme Court (set us by the constitution to be the Highest and Final Court), and Rulings by Federal District Judges, representing the whole United States of America, are not only questioned and disagreed with, but Openly Flaunted, Disregarded, and Totally Ignored.

(D) We believe in State's Rights; but we believe that any 'First RIGHTS' are HUMAN RIGHTS. And the first right of a State is to Protect Human Rights, and to guarantee to each of its Citizens the same Rights and Privileges.

(E) We heartily concur in and endorse the Rulings of the Federal Judiciary that All public Facilities belong to and should be open to All on the same and equal terms; and we Hope, Trust, and Pray that efforts to commence should be begun by Officials in the Spirit of Brotherhood and Goodwill; without the necessity of Lawsuits having to be filed.

(F) We most highly commend the activities of the Officials and Citizens everywhere for the efforts made for CIVIL RIGHTS, and we thank God for them. But especially do we applaud Negroes in Montgomery, Ala., and Tallahassee, Fla. conducting themselves in the struggle so valiantly, and without rancor, hate, and smear, and above all without violence.

(G) As to Gradualism, we hold that it means to move forward, slowly maybe, but surely; not vacillation, procrastination, or evasion. The hastily enacted laws and enflamed statements of Public Officials do not lead us to embrace Gradualism. We want a beginning NOW! WE HAVE ALREADY WAITED 100 YEARS!

(H)   We Negroes shall never become enemies of the White People: We are all Americans; But America was born in the struggle for Freedom from Tyranny and Oppression. We shall never bomb any homes or lynch any persons; but we must, because of History and the future, march to Complete Freedom – with unbowed heads, praying hearts, and an unyielding determination. And we seek Guidance from our Heavenly Father; and from all men, Goodwill and understanding.

Birmingham Historical Society Newsletter (June, 2006), p. 2.

B The Birmingham Manifesto, April 3, 1963

The patience of an oppressed people cannot endure forever. The Negro citizens of Birmingham for the last several years have hoped in vain for some evidence of good faith resolution of our just grievances.

Birmingham is part of the United States and we are *bona fide* citizens. Yet the history of Birmingham reveals that very little of the democratic process touches the life of the Negro in Birmingham. We have been segregated racially, exploited economically, and dominated politically. Under the leadership of the Alabama Christian Movement for Human Rights, we sought relief ... We were rebuffed. We then turned to the system of the courts ... finally winning the terminal, bus, parks and airport cases. The bus decision has been implemented begrudgingly and the parks decision prompted the closing of all municipally-owned recreational facilities with the exception of the zoo and Legion Field. The airport case has been a slightly better experience ...

We have always been a peaceful people, bearing our oppression with super-human effort. Yet we have been the victims of repeated violence, not only that inflicted by the hoodlum element but also that inflicted by the blatant misuse of police power. Our memories are seared with painful mob experience of Mother's Day 1961 during the Freedom Ride. For years, while our homes and churches were being bombed, we heard nothing but the rantings and ravings of racist city officials ...

We believe in the American Dream of democracy, in the Jeffersonian doctrine that 'all men are created equal and are endowed by their Creator with certain inalienable rights, among these being life, liberty and the pursuit of happiness.'

Twice since September we have deferred our direct action thrust in order that a change in city government would not be made in the hysteria of a community crisis. We act today in full concert with our Hebraic-Christian tradition, the law of morality and the Constitution of our nation. The absence of justice and progress in Birmingham demands that we make a moral witness to give our community a chance to survive. We demonstrate our faith that we believe that the beloved community can come to Birmingham.

We appeal to the citizenry of Birmingham, Negro and white, to join us in this witness for decency, morality, self-respect and human dignity. Your individual and corporate support can hasten the day of 'liberty and justice for all.' This is Birmingham's moment of truth in which every citizen can play his part in her larger destiny. The Alabama Christian Movement for Human Rights, in behalf of the Negro community of Birmingham.

Freedomways, 4 (Winter, 1964), pp. 20–21.

5.6 James Bevel discusses recruiting children

In the following interview, James Bevel discusses the decision to use children as demonstrators in Birmingham.

Up to this point, about five to ten, maybe twelve people would go and demonstrate each day. My position was you can't get the dialogues you need with a few. So the strategy was, okay, let's use *thousands* of people who won't create an economic crisis because they're off the job: *the high school students.* Besides, most adults have bills to pay, house notes, rents, car notes, utility bills, but the young people – wherein they can think at the same level – are not hooked with all those responsibilities ...

We started organizing the prom queens of the high schools, the basketball stars, the football stars, to get the influence and power leaders involved. They in turn got all the other students involved. The black community as a whole did not have that kind of cohesion or camaraderie. But the students, they had a community they'd been in since elementary school, so they had bonded quite well. So if one would go to jail, that had a direct effect upon another because they were classmates.

We held workshops to help them overcome the crippling fears of dogs, and jails, and to help them start thinking through problems on their feet. We also showed the 'NBC White Paper' [a network television documentary] about the Nashville sit-ins in all of the schools. Our approach to the students was that you are responsible for segregation, you and your parents, because you have not stood up. In other words, according to the Bible and the Constitution, no one has the power to oppress you if you don't cooperate. So if you say you are oppressed, then you are also acknowledging that you are in league with the oppressor; now, it's your responsibility to break the league with him.

The first response was among the young women, about thirteen to eighteen. They're probably more responsive in terms of courage, confidence, and the ability to follow reasoning and logic. Nonviolence to them is logical ... Then the elementary students, they can comprehend that too. The last to get involved were the high school guys, because the brunt of the violence in the South was directed toward the black male ...

Hampton and Fayer, *Voices of Freedom*, pp. 131–132

5.7 Birmingham truce agreement, May 10, 1963

The Birmingham protests resulted in the following agreement with the White leadership.

1. Within 3 days after close of demonstrations, fitting rooms will be desegregated.
2. Within 30 days after the city government is established by court order, signs on wash rooms, rest rooms and drinking fountains will be removed.

Figure 10 Police brutality in Birmingham contributed to national support for civil rights.

3. Within 60 days after the city government is established by court order, a program of lunchroom counter desegregation will be commenced.
4. When the city government is established by court order, a program of upgrading Negro employment will be continued and there will be meetings with responsible local leadership to consider further steps.

Within 60 days from the court order determining Birmingham's city government, the employment program will include at least one sales person or cashier.

Within 15 days from the cessation of demonstrations, a Committee on Racial Problems and Employment composed of members of the Senior Citizens' Committee will be established, with a membership made public and the publicly announced purpose of establishing liaison with members of the Negro community to carry out a program of up-grading and improving employment opportunities with the Negro citizens of the Birmingham community.

Burke Marshall Papers, John F. Kennedy Library, Boston, Mass.

5.8 Governor George Wallace's statement and proclamation, June 11, 1963

In rhetoric that King characterized as 'lips dripping with words of interposition and nullification,' Wallace asserted his executive responsibility to shield Alabamans from federal intrusion.

As Governor and Chief Magistrate of the State of Alabama I deem it to be my solemn obligation and duty to stand before you representing the rights and sovereignty of this State and its peoples.

The unwelcomed, unwanted, unwarranted and force-induced intrusion upon the campus of the University of Alabama today of the might of the Central Government offers frightful example of the oppression of the rights, privileges and sovereignty of this State by officers of the Federal Government. This intrusion results solely from force, or threat of force, undignified by any reasonable application of the principle of law, reason and justice. It is important that the people of this State and nation understand that this action is in violation of rights reserved to the State by the Constitution of the United States and the Constitution of the State of Alabama ...

I stand before you here today in place of thousands of other Alabamians whose presence would have confronted you had I been derelict and neglected to fulfill the responsibilities of my office. It is the right of every citizen, however humble he may be, through his chosen officials of representative government to stand courageously against whatever he believes to be the exercise of power beyond the Constitutional rights conferred upon our Federal Government. It is this right which I assert for the people of Alabama by my presence here today.

Again I state – this is the exercise of the heritage of the freedom and liberty under the law – coupled with responsible government.

Now, therefore, in consideration of the premises, and in my official capacity as Governor of the State of Alabama, I do hereby make the following solemn proclamation:

WHEREAS, the Constitution of Alabama vests the supreme executive powers of the State in the Governor as the Chief Magistrate, and said Constitution requires of the Governor that he take care that the laws be faithfully executed; and,

WHEREAS, the Constitution of the United States, Amendment 10, reserves to the States respectively or to the people, those powers not delegated to the United States; and,

WHEREAS, the operation of the public school system is a power reserved to the State of Alabama under the Constitution of the United States and Amendment 10 thereof; and,

WHEREAS, it is the duty of the Governor of the State of Alabama to preserve the peace under the circumstances now existing, which power is one reserved to the State of Alabama and the people thereof under the Constitution of the United States and Amendment 10 thereof.

NOW, THEREFORE, I, George C. Wallace, as Governor of the State of Alabama, have by my action raised issues between the Central Government and the Sovereign State of Alabama, which said issues should be adjudicated in the manner prescribed by the Constitution of the United States; and now being mindful of my duties and responsibilities under the Constitution of the United States, the Constitution of the State of Alabama, and seeking to preserve and maintain the peace and dignity of this State, and the individual freedoms of the citizens thereof, do hereby denounce and forbid this illegal and unwarranted action by the Central Government.

Alabama Department of Archives and History, Montgomery, Ala.

5.9 Kennedy's address on civil rights, June 11, 1963

In a national address, President Kennedy announced that he would ask Congress for a civil rights bill and called upon all Americans to work toward the ideals upon which the nation was based. Excerpts follow.

... This afternoon, following a series of threats and defiant statements, the presence of Alabama National Guardsmen was required on the campus of the University of Alabama to carry out the final and unequivocal order of the United States District Court of the Northern District of Alabama. That order called for the admission of two clearly qualified young Alabama residents who happened to have been born Negro.

That they were admitted peacefully on the campus is due in good measure to the conduct of the students of the University of Alabama, who met their responsibilities in a constructive way.

I hope that every American, regardless of where he lives, will stop and examine his conscience about this and other related incidents. This Nation was founded by men of many nations and backgrounds. It was founded on the principle that all men are created equal, and that the rights of every man are diminished when the rights of one man are threatened.

Today we are committed to a worldwide struggle to promote and protect the rights of all who wish to be free. And when Americans are sent to Viet-Nam or West Berlin, we do not ask for whites only. It ought to be possible, therefore, for American students of any color to attend any public institution they select without having to be backed up by troops.

It ought to be possible for American consumers of any color to receive equal service in places of public accommodation, such as hotels and restaurants and theaters and retail stores, without being forced to resort to demonstrations in the street, and it ought to be possible for American citizens of any color to register to vote in a free election without interference or fear of reprisal ...

But this is not the case ...

We are confronted primarily with a moral issue. It is as old as the scriptures and is as clear as the American Constitution ...

One hundred years of delay have passed since President Lincoln freed the slaves, yet their heirs, their grandsons, are not fully free. They are not yet freed from the bonds of injustice. They are not yet freed from social and economic oppression. And this Nation, for all its hopes and all its boasts, will not be fully free until all its citizens are free.

We preach freedom around the world, and we mean it, and we cherish our freedom here at home, but are we to say to the world, and much more importantly, to each other that this is the land of the free except for the Negroes ...

We face, therefore, a moral crisis as a country and as a people. It cannot be met by repressive police action. It cannot be left to increased demonstrations in the streets. It cannot be quieted by token moves or talk. It is time to act in the Congress, in your State and local legislative body and, above all, in all of our daily lives ...

Next week I shall ask the Congress of the United States to act, to make a commitment it has not fully made in this century to the proposition that race has no place in American life or law. The Federal judiciary has upheld that proposition in the conduct of its affairs, including the employment of Federal personnel, the use of Federal facilities, and the sale of federally financed housing.

But there are other necessary measures which only the Congress can provide, and they must be provided at this session. The old code of equity law under which we live commands for every wrong a remedy, but in too many communities, in too many parts of the country, wrongs are inflicted on Negro citizens and there are no remedies at law. Unless the Congress acts, their only remedy is in the street.

I am, therefore, asking the Congress to enact legislation giving all Americans the right to be served in facilities which are open to the public – hotels, restaurants, theaters, retail stores, and similar establishments ...

I am also asking the Congress to authorize the Federal Government to participate more fully in lawsuits designed to end segregation in public education. We have succeeded in persuading many districts to desegregate voluntarily. Dozens have admitted Negroes without violence. Today a Negro is attending a State-supported institution in every one of our 50 States, but the pace is very slow.

Too many Negro children entering segregated grade schools at the time of the Supreme Court's decision 9 years ago will enter segregated high schools this fall, having suffered a loss which can never be restored. The lack of an adequate education denies the Negro a chance to get a decent job.

The orderly implementation of the Supreme Court decision, therefore, cannot be left solely to those who may not have the economic resources to carry the legal action or who may be subject to harassment.

Other features will also be requested, including greater protection for the right to vote. But legislation, I repeat, cannot solve this problem alone. It must be solved in the homes of every American in every community across our country ...

My fellow Americans, this is a problem which faces us all – in every city of the North as well as the South ...

This is one country. It has become one country because all of us and all the people who came here had an equal chance to develop their talents ...

We cannot say to 10 percent of the population that you can't have that right; that your children cannot have the chance to develop whatever talents they have; that the only way that they are going to get their rights is to go into the streets and demonstrate. I think we owe them and we owe ourselves a better country than that.

Therefore, I am asking for your help in making it easier for us to move ahead and to provide the kind of equality of treatment which we would want ourselves; to give a chance for every child to be educated to the limit of his talents.

As I have said before, not every child has an equal talent or an equal ability or an equal motivation, but they should have an equal right to develop their talent and their ability and their motivation, to make something of themselves.

We have a right to expect that the Negro community will be responsible, will uphold the law, but they have a right to expect that the law will be fair, that the Constitution will be color blind, as Justice Harlan said at the turn of the century ...

Public Papers of the Presidents of the United States: John F. Kennedy, 1963, (Washington, DC: Government Printing Office, 1964), entry 237, pp. 468–471.

5.10 Civil Rights Act of 1964

The Civil Rights Act of 1964 was a major victory for both the Civil Rights Movement and the Johnson administration. Southern Congressmen and Senators had been able to weaken earlier civil rights legislation, but Johnson effectively marshaled lobbyists and applied his own influence to ensure the passage of a strong measure. Ironically, one attempt to weaken the bill, the radical idea of including women in the Title VII prohibition of discrimination in employment, was incorporated and would become an important tool in the women's rights movement. Other 'weakening' amendments, as well as a filibuster by Southern Senators, were defeated before the bill was signed into law on July 2, 1964. Excerpts from a Commission on Civil Rights publication amplify the provisions of the law.

Title I VOTING

The purpose of this section is to provide more effective enforcement of the right to vote in Federal elections (for President, Vice President, presidential electors or members of Congress) without regard to race or color. It also speeds up the procedure by which voting rights suits may be decided.

The Act:

a. requires that the same standards be applied to all individuals seeking to register and vote;

b. forbids denial of the right to vote because of some minor mistake or omission;

c. requires that only literacy tests that are written may be used as a qualification for voting; and that the tests and answers be available on request;

d. establishes that in voting rights law suits the court must presume that anyone who completed the sixth grade is literate, unless the State can prove otherwise ...

Title II PUBLIC ACCOMMODATIONS

Discrimination on the basis of race, color, religion or national origin is specifically forbidden in the following places of public accommodation:

a. hotels and motels, restaurants, lunch counters, movie houses, gasoline stations, theaters and stadiums;

b. any other establishment which offers its services to patrons of the covered establishment ... so long as the covered facilities either affect interstate commerce in their operations, or are supported in their discriminatory practices by State action.

In addition, discrimination is forbidden in any other place of public accommodation that is required to segregate by State or local laws ...

Places that are actually owned and operated as private clubs are exempted from coverage of this title except to the extent that they offer their facilities to patrons of a covered establishment, such as a country club that customarily allows guests of a hotel to use its golf course.

No person may intimidate, threaten or coerce anyone for the purpose of interfering with the rights created by this title ...

Title III PUBLIC FACILITIES

The Attorney General is authorized to bring a civil suit to compel desegregation of any publicly-owned or operated facility whenever he receives a written complaint of discrimination ... State or municipally owned or operated parks, libraries and hospitals are among the facilities covered.

Title IV PUBLIC EDUCATION

Under this title the U.S. Office of Education is authorized to:
    a. conduct a national survey to determine the availability of equal educational opportunity;
    b. provide technical assistance upon request, to help States, political subdivisions or school districts carry out school deseregation plans;
    c. arrange training institutes to prepare teachers and other school personnel to deal with desegregation problems;
    d. make grants enabling school boards to employ specialists for in-service training programs.
    In addition. the Attorney General is authorized to file civil suits seeking to compel desegregation of public schools, including public colleges ...

Title V COMMISSION ON CIVIL RIGHTS

... Title V gives the Commission added authority to:
    a. serve as a national clearinghouse for civil rights information;
    b. investigate allegations of vote fraud.
    Commission hearing procedures are amended to further protect the rights of individuals who may be affected by Commission proceedings.
    As a national clearinghouse, the Commission will provide civil rights information in such areas as voting, housing, education, employment and the use of public facilities to Federal, State and local government agencies and officials, organizations and businesses, and the general public.

Title VI FEDERALLY ASSISTED PROGRAMS

Under this title every Federal agency which provides financial assistance through grants, loans or contracts is required to eliminate discrimination on the grounds of race, color or national origin in these programs ...
    Action by a Federal agency to carry out the requirements of this title may include the terminating of programs where discrimination is taking place or refusal to grant assistance to such a program ...

Title VII EQUAL EMPLOYMENT OPPORTUNITY

This title establishes a Federal right to equal opportunity in employment. It creates an Equal Employment Opportunity Commission to assist in implementing this right.
    Employers, labor unions and employment agencies are required to treat all persons without regard to their race, color, religion, sex, or national origin. This treatment must be given in all phases of employment, including hiring, promotion, firing, apprenticeship and other training programs, and job assignments.

When this title goes into full effect [July 2, 1968] employers will be subject to its provisions if they have 25 or more regular employees in an industry that affects interstate commerce .... .

Not covered by this title are (1) public employers, (2) bona fide private clubs, (3) educational institutions with regard to employees working in educational activities and all employment in religious educational institutions, (4) employers on or near an Indian reservation with regard to preferential treatment of Indians; and (5) religious corporations, institutions, etc., with regard to employees working in connection with religious activities.

When someone believes he has been discriminated against because of race, color, religion, sex, or national origin in any phase of job placement or employment, he may bring his complaint within 90 days to the Equal Employment Opportunity Commission or to the Attorney General ...

Title VIII VOTING STATISTICS

The Secretary of Commerce is required to conduct a survey of persons of voting age by race, color, and national origin and to determine the extent to which such persons have registered and voted in such geographic areas as the Commission on Civil Rights recommends ...

Title IX INTERVENTION AND REMOVAL IN CIVIL RIGHTS CASES

The Attorney General is authorized to intervene in any Federal court action seeking relief from the denial of equal protection of the laws on account of race, color, religion or national origin. If a Federal court refuses to accept a civil rights case and sends it back to a State court, this action may be reviewed on appeal.

Title X COMMUNITY RELATIONS SERVICE

A Community Relations Service is established in the Department of Commerce to provide assistance to persons or communities requiring help with civil rights problems where discriminatory practices impair constitutional rights or affect interstate commerce ...

Civil Rights Digest, Special Bulletin, 'A Summary of the Civil Rights Act of 1964' (The U.S. Commission on Civil Rights, August, 1964).

Notes

1 Martin Luther King, Jr., 'Letter from Birmingham Jail', in A *Testament of Hope: The Essential Writings and Speeches of Martin Luther King, Jr.*, ed. James M. Washington, (New York: HarperCollins, 1986). The complete text is readily available online. See, for example, www.thekingcenter.org/prog/non/Letter.html (accessed December 2008).
2 Martin Luther King, Jr., 'I Have a Dream', in *ibid.*, p. 220. The complete text is readily available online. See, for example, www.americanrhetoric.com/speeches/mlkihaveadream.htm (accessed December 2008).

6

'I shall not be moved': Freedom Summer, Selma, and the Voting Rights Act of 1965

Events in the summer of 1964 and early 1965 revealed some of the divisions within the broad coalition supportive of the Movement. While Johnson shepherded the Civil Rights Act through Congress, he was not a supporter of the voting rights campaign being pursued in Mississippi in the summer of 1964, known in the Movement as 'Freedom Summer.' The SCLC also had reservations concerning the dangerous work in Mississippi. Nonetheless, youthful SNCC workers pushed on. Later, in early 1965, King and the SCLC joined forces with SNCC workers in Selma, Alabama, to march for voting rights. White violence in Mississippi and Alabama generated a backlash of support for civil rights legislation.

Freedom Summer

Mississippi was the violent stronghold of White supremacy in the South (see **4.1**). Nonetheless, beginning in late 1961 and early 1962, SNCC workers began to enter the state, and soon a coalition of SNCC, CORE, and the state NAACP was formed, the Council of Federated Organizations (COFO). By early 1962, the Kennedy administration had called for the Movement to focus on voter registration rather than direct action, and COFO, in order to access philanthropic funds that the administration helped secure, joined the effort. The Kennedy administration felt that voter registration as an issue was less confrontational than efforts to desegregate public facilities, but White Mississippi disagreed. Violence and economic sanctions kept all but the most independent and fearless Blacks from registering (**6.1**). COFO did, however, pursue a mock 'Freedom Party' election in 1963, successfully engaging some 60,000 Blacks in the process.

Violent White resistance led to a change in strategy for 1964, as leaders Bob Moses and Dave Dennis decided to recruit White students to help with COFO's project that summer. The nation still tended to ignore violence directed against Blacks, but Moses and Dennis felt that such would not be the case if White students were the victims (**6.2**). The national attention afforded to the murder of three civil rights workers in June, Michael Schwerner, James Chaney, and Andrew Goodman, tragically confirmed Moses's and Dennis's thinking. Violence in Mississippi continued, leading some individuals to question the nonviolent stance of the Movement (**6.3**).

Voter registration and citizenship education were two key components of COFO's efforts during Freedom Summer. With regard to voter registration, objectives were twofold: (1) to continue to register Blacks in the conventional, White-dominated system and (2) to build up the alternative political party, the Mississippi Freedom Democratic Party (**6.4**). With regard to education, COFO planned to offer 'Freedom Schools' for children and adults statewide (**6.5**). The most successful of these efforts was the development of the Mississippi Freedom Democratic Party (MFDP). Voters were registered, precincts were created, and a party convention was held to elect a delegation to the 1964 Democratic National Convention where the legitimacy of the White-dominated, Mississippi Democratic Party delegates would be challenged.

When the MFDP delegation arrived in Atlantic City for the Democratic National Convention and sought credentials for themselves as the legitimate delegation from Mississippi, however, they ran afoul of President Johnson's desire to maintain party unity going into the fall election. Despite widespread sympathy for the MFDP (except, of course, among Southern delegations), Johnson did everything in his power to avert a credentials battle. In effect, his wheeling, dealing, and resultant 'compromise' disfranchised the Mississippi Blacks, creating a great degree of resentment among them. Many civil rights workers felt abandoned by the White, liberal coalition that was presumed to have been their ally, contributing to the feeling that Blacks needed to depend on themselves alone if they were to effect real change. We can see that sentiment in the excerpt from Fannie Lou Hamer (**6.6**).

Selma and the Voting Rights Act of 1965

The attention afforded to events in Mississippi in 1964 revealed the degree to which the great majority of Blacks in the South remained disfranchised. After ten years of Civil Rights activities, fewer than half of voting-age Blacks in the region were registered to vote, and in Alabama and Mississippi the numbers were much lower (19.4% and 6.4%, respectively).[1] In many communities, one of which was Selma, county seat of Dallas County, Alabama, overt violence by White law enforcement officials (or failure to address the actions of White supremacist terrorists) maintained the status quo.

SNCC organizers were the first to target Selma. In early 1963, SNCC veteran Bernard Lafayette and others began to canvass the Black community, where only 355 of 15,000 eligible residents were registered to vote. Attempts to register Blacks met stiff resistance from election officials and, as Lafayette and others organized marches and meetings in support of registration, a state judge banned such activities. The ban was enforced by the County Sheriff, Jim Clark. Clark had a history of violence and had deputized White supporters into a paramilitary 'posse' that roamed the state, supporting 'law and order' to counter civil rights activities. Clark's methods successfully impeded progress in registering Black voters in Selma and, in order to move forward, local activists (despite reservations by SNCC youth) in late 1964 invited Martin Luther King, Jr. and the SCLC to Selma.

The situation in Selma was similar to that in Birmingham – a well-organized base in the Black community and a violence-prone law enforcement official. Basing himself in Selma in January, 1965, King recognized the opportunity to garner national attention and, he hoped, federal support for voting rights. In short order, SCLC attempts to register voters were met with bullying, beatings, and arrests (eventually some 3,000 people were arrested). Clark and his men were indiscriminate, beating clergy, women, and youths – sometimes in the presence of national media and federal officials. A supporting protest march in a nearby town led to the death of Jimmy Lee Jackson, shot as he tried to interfere with a state trooper assaulting his mother and grandfather. The ensuing national attention led President Johnson, by early March, to assure King that a voting rights bill would soon be introduced in Congress.

To foster public support for federal voting rights legislation, King planned an integrated march from Selma to Montgomery with the intention of submitting a petition to Governor George Wallace, a

MISSING CALL FBI

THE FBI IS SEEKING INFORMATION CONCERNING THE DISAPPEARANCE AT PHILADELPHIA, MISSISSIPPI, OF THESE THREE INDIVIDUALS ON JUNE 21, 1964. EXTENSIVE INVESTIGATION IS BEING CONDUCTED TO LOCATE GOODMAN, CHANEY, AND SCHWERNER, WHO ARE DESCRIBED AS FOLLOWS:

ANDREW GOODMAN   **JAMES EARL CHANEY**   **MICHAEL HENRY SCHWERNER**

RACE:	White	Negro	White
SEX:	Male	Male	Male
DOB:	November 23, 1943	May 30, 1943	November 6, 1939
POB:	New York City	Meridian, Mississippi	New York City
AGE:	20 years	21 years	24 years
HEIGHT:	5'10"	5'7"	5'9" to 5'10"
WEIGHT:	150 pounds	135 to 140 pounds	170 to 180 pounds
HAIR:	Dark brown; wavy	Black	Brown
EYES:	Brown	Brown	Light blue
TEETH:		Good: none missing	
SCARS AND MARKS:		1 inch cut scar 2 inches above left ear.	Pock mark center of forehead, slight scar on bridge of nose, appendectomy scar, broken leg scar.

Figure 11 FBI flyer: Goodman, Chaney, and Schwerner were murdered in Mis-i in June, 1964.

staunch defender of White supremacy, seeking protection for Blacks attempting to register. On 'Bloody Sunday,' March 7, 1965, the first of two abortive attempts to begin the march ended in unrestrained violence on the part of law enforcement agencies. Video clips of rampaging deputies, state troopers, and 'possemen' attacking, gassing, and beating peaceful demonstrators shocked the nation. In response to these outrages, President Lyndon Johnson, on March 15, addressed a joint session of congress and a national television audience, announcing the submission of the promised voting rights bill (**6.7**). Two days later, Judge Frank Johnson issued a restraining order against Alabama officials, allowing the march to take place (**6.8**). Governor Wallace, claiming that he could not guarantee the safety of the marchers, gave President Johnson an excuse to nationalize the Alabama National Guard to that end. From March 21 to 25, Black and White activists marched to Montgomery. Two more people would die as a result of events, though, as Unitarian minister Rev. James Reeb was beaten by White thugs in Selma between attempts to complete the march and, the evening after the marchers' triumphant rally in Montgomery, Viola Liuzzo, a human rights advocate from Detroit, was murdered by Klansmen as she shuttled Blacks back to Selma.

The rally in Montgomery on March 25 anticipated the high point of the Movement in the South. Representatives of all the major civil rights organizations were on hand: Roy Wilkins of the NAACP, Whitney Young of the Urban League, John Lewis of SNCC, Bayard Rustin, A. Philip Randolph, and, of course, Martin Luther King, Jr. King's speech again resonated with the crowd of onlookers, some 25,000 strong. The Selma march had galvanized political support behind voting rights. On August 6, 1965, President Johnson signed the Voting Rights Act into law (**6.9**).

6.1 Guyot on Mississippi in the early 1960s

SNCC worker Lawrence Guyot discusses, with Howell Raines, early 1960s voter registration efforts in Mississippi. Of note are the importance of the activists' relationship with the churches, the role of women and youth in the Movement, and the efforts to promote local leadership.

... I became involved late in '61. Late '61, early '62, I began becoming more and more involved in traveling with them around the state. Now the people ... there was Charles McLaurin, Colia Ladelle, James Jones, Lafayette Surney, Hollis Watkins, Curtis Hayes, myself, Luvaughn Brown, Diane Bevel, Rev. Bevel, Chuck McDew, Marion Barry, who is now a city councilman in Washington, and Bob Moses, who was later to become a legend in Mississippi. While it was clear that Moses was the leader of this group, his style of leadership was by example and directional discussion.

We met in Jackson at 714 Rose Street, and from there we had begun to conduct small workshops, speak in small meetings, attempt to get people to register to vote. And then the decision was made that what we needed was to go to the Delta where there were harsher conditions, where there was a large black population, where there were some counties with no black registration. We needed a person to provide contacts on a local basis, to provide an entree for us into the counties, and that person was Amzie Moore.

We met at his house, we stayed at his house. He had a hell of a network of individuals throughout the state and had had it for years ... Whenever anyone was threatened, Amzie Moore was sort of an individual protection agency. He had successfully fought against the Klan, both politically and physically, [was] a noted Bible scholar, a very good stump speaker ...

Now, Greenwood at the time we entered ... there was a war going on, and the war was a very simple one – surviving and just walkin' around talkin' to [black] people about what *they're* interested in. And it didn't make any difference. If it was fishing, how do you turn that conversation into when are you gonna register to vote? If it was religion, that was an easier one to turn into registering. If it was cotton acreage – our basic verbal mien was that there's nothin' that's not involved with politics ...

You learned very quickly that if you got that door slammed in your face, it just takes a day or two of talking to people to find out whose face the door won't be slammed in ... I mean, there are some towns you go into, and you find a man who has none of the characteristics of leadership as we identify them. He is the leader [of the black community] and has been and is unquestioned, and mess with him wrong – forgit it. Don't speed him up too much, dialogue with him, find out what his tempo is, what his objectives are. Then you might alter them a little bit, but don't, don't, don't – be careful. We learned over and over and over again how to find potential leadership, how to groom it, and the most painful lesson for some of us was how to let it go once you've set it into motion. See, I *loved* it, because it was dealing with people, what they could do against large tasks ...

It's no secret that young people and women led organizationally. When you talk about community mobilization, we not only did community mobilization in Greenwood, but the sociologists, when they were talking about community mobilization, would talk about 'like what SNCC is doing in Greenwood.' ...

I guess the reason we got away with what we did in Greenw[ood] a couple of reasons. One, we were soundly based in the churche[s] objectives were very clear. It was not to desegregate the two or [three] local white restaurants. It was simply to register people to vote ...

See, you have to understand the climate that we were dealing w[ith] people received a welfare check, there was a letter – a classic letter [I] forget – stating that people should be very concerned about regi[stering to] vote at the request of 'radicals' because this may terminate the ...

Howell Raines, *My Soul Is Rested: The Story of the Civil Rights M[ovement] in the Deep South* (New York: Penguin Books, 1983), pp. 238–241[.]

6.2 Dennis on Freedom Summer

In an interview with Howell Raines, Dave Dennis recounts his [and] Bob Moses's thinking concerning the strategic value of recrui[ting] White college students for Freedom Summer.

... We knew that if we had brought in a thousand blacks, the countr[y] would have watched them slaughtered without doing anything about [it.] Bring a thousand whites and the country is going to react to that in [two] ways. First of all is to protect. We made sure that we had the children, [sons] and daughters, of some very powerful people in this country over th[ere,] including Jerry Brown, who's now governor of California, for instanc[e –] we made sure of that ... The idea was not only to begin to organize fo[r the] Democratic Convention, but also to get the country to begin to res[pond] to what was going on there. They were not gonna respond to a thou[sand] blacks working in that area. They would respond to a thousand y[oung] white college students, and white college females who were down ther[e,] right? And that's the reason why, and if there were gonna take some d[ying] to do it, the death of a white college student would bring on more atte[ntion] to what was going on than for a black college student getting it. That'[s sad,] but that was also in another sense speaking the language of this co[untry.] What we were trying to do was get a message over to the country, [we] spoke their language. And that had more to do with that decision to [bring] 'em in by the two of us at the top than anything else ...

Raines, *My Soul Is Rested*, pp. 274–275.

6.3 Nonviolence questioned

White students recruited for Freedom Summer participated in training for the realities of Mississippi. Contrasting the message of Jim Lawson with that of Stokely Carmichael, one recruit questions nonviolence, foretelling a split in the Movement.

Dear Folks:

Yesterday was nonviolence day here. In the morning we heard Jim Lawson of Nashville, who gave us the word on nonviolence as a way of life. Lawson speaks of a moral confrontation with one's enemies, catching the other guy's eye, speaking to him with love, if possible, and so on ... 'Violence always brings more harm to the people who use it; economic and political forces have no place in the Movement ... etc.' These are the things Lawson came up with ... I feel very strongly that he does NOT represent the Movement.

Stokely Carmichael of SNCC rebutted him in the afternoon session: Nonviolence used to work because (1) it was new; (2) the newspapers gave it top coverage week after week, and most important (3) the demands were minor and the resistance to change was not hard-core. Now the North is tired of demonstrations, a very vigorous backlash has emerged, and the papers will only report major violence. Now we are responsible for what we do, and have to explain the stall-in instead of having it welcomed on the front pages of the press. Again most important, the movement has grown up, and is now aiming at the places where the white society really feels threatened – at jobs and at voting.

There comes a point when you get tired of being beaten and going back the next day for your beating for 5 days in a row. You get tired of being asked whether you are a Negro or a nigger, and ending up on the floor of the police station screaming at the top of your lungs that yes, you are a nigger, boss. You get tired of seeing young women smashed in the face right in front of your eyes. Stokely does not advocate violence. No SNCC workers are armed, nor are there guns in any SNCC office. What he is saying is that love and moral confrontations have no place in front of a brute who beats you till you cry nigger.

My feelings, and I think these are common, is that nonviolence is a perverted way of life, but a necessary tactic and technique. It is harmful to the human person to feel that he must love a man who has a foot in his face. The *only* reason that I will not hit back is because then I will be in the hospital two weeks instead of one, and will be useless to the movement during that extra week when I can only read Gandhi's latest book on how to win friends and influence people ...

Bill

Elizabeth Martinez, ed., *Letters from Mississippi* (Brookline, Mass: Zephyr Press, 2007), pp. 34–35.

6.4 Canvassing in Mississippi

Excerpts drawn from letters written by Freedom Summer volunteers give us a sense of the issues related to voter registration and the techniques pursued by volunteers.

Greenwood, July 15

We are trying to get people to go down to the courthouse to register. In Mississippi there are no deputy registrars, the only place that people can register is at the Courthouse at the County Seat. The county seat for Leflore County is Greenwood. This in itself restrains Negroes from voting because they don't like to go to the courthouse, which has bad connotations for them. Behind the courthouse is the Yazoo River. The river also has bad connotations; as Albert Darner said, it's 'Dat river where dey floats them bodies in.'

Gulfport, July 8

Canvassing, the main technique in voter registration, is an art ...

Techniques and approaches vary. Mine is often like this:

Hi. My name is Steve M. (shake hands, having gotten name, address, from a mailbox). I'm with COFO. There are a lot of us working in this area, going from house to house trying to encourage people to go down and register to vote. (Pause) Are you a registered voter? (This is the direct technique. Often people, being afraid, will lie and say yes, but you can usually tell, because they will be very proud.) Are you planning on going down soon? (This makes them declare themselves. Usually they say 'yes' or 'I hadn't thought about it much.' The other answer is 'No, I ain't going down at all.') 'Well, I have a sample of the registration form.' (Take it out and hand it to them.) 'You know, some people are a little afraid to go down because they don't quite know what they're getting into. It's something new and different, and they're not sure about it.'

Then I go on, 'You know, it is so important that everyone get the vote. As it stands now, that man downtown in charge of roads doesn't have to listen to the Negroes. They can't put him out of office. He should be working for you.' (Much gossip, chatter, mutual questions through all this).

Then pull out the Freedom Democratic Party application.

'This is a protest party. Anyone can join to protest the laws about voter

134

registration and the way elections are carried out.'

You get the picture. It goes on, 10 hours a day, 6 days a week. On Sundays we rest by working at other things. We go to church. Since all visitors are allotted time to speak, I relate voter registration to God. I have become a pretty good preacher ...

Martinez, ed., *Letters from Mississippi*, pp. 80–81.

6.5 Freedom School

Entries in the diary of a Freedom Summer volunteer reveal the essence of the Freedom School project.

Monday, July 20. The first day of school – 14 students, ages 12 to 47. A student was assigned to report on civil rights news for the next few days ... We gathered on benches under the trees. I asked one of the students to read an excerpt from a speech by Frederick Douglass. Asked three others to read aloud poems by Langston Hughes. When we finished, Arthur asked if he could take the Langston Hughes book home overnight.

Tuesday, July 21. Six students took turns standing and reading a play called 'Protest,' about a Japanese family confronted with change in the form of an alien, a chair. They seemed to enjoy it and three of them were quite good. Several of the boys went off by themselves and read Hughes' poetry aloud. I spoke to Mrs. _____ about the possibility of building book shelves so the building could be used as a permanent library for the community (a library that could be increased by books solicited after I go home) . I asked if she would be willing to act as librarian. She said she would think it over.

Wednesday, July 22. Discussed origin of slavery in America – slave revolts – Negroes in the American Revolution – mutiny on the *Amistad*. It would be fine if we had a Pictorial History of The Negro for every student – less lecturing and more discussion. Two students and I read 3 of James Thurber's *Fables For Our Time*. Well received. Summaries written. Books signed out. Mrs. _____ said she would act as librarian if we could get permission to use the building.

Thursday, July 23. Reviewed some myths about Negroes, asking students to give reasons why each was false. Some tried to defend them! Indoctrination has been well done ... Walter reported on 'The Harlem Rent Strike' – without using notes. Summaries of the day's work or essays on any subject were written.

Friday, July 24. 'Lectured' on the Reconstruction period. Discussed the

Civil Rights Act of 1875. The big hit of the week was the poetry of Langston Hughes. There was hardly a time during the day when some one wasn't reading our one copy of Selected Poems.

Sunday, July 26. At church today the congregation agreed to have the library. Everyone seemed pleased at the idea because there has never been any library available to the Negroes here.

So it went for another week. More plans for the library. Poetry, plays, oral reports, written reports, study of political and power structure of Mississippi, classes in typing, Spanish, French, Drawing, History. Students driving themselves on in a hot, faded wooden building. 'I didn't do so good on that report (an oral report). Could you give me another one?' (Ernest, age 18)

Tuesday, August 11. Gluckstadt Freedom School burned to the ground late last night. There is little doubt of the cause of the fire. There have been too many others like it in Mississippi. We start tomorrow to raise money to rebuild the building.

Martinez, ed., *Letters from Mississippi*, pp. 125–126.

6.6 Fannie Lou Hamer

Fannie Lou Hamer was an outstanding example of local leadership that SNCC and COFO identified and fostered. Hamer garnered national attention as a delegate of the MFDP at the 1964 Democratic convention. Unwilling to accept the 'compromise' concocted by Lyndon Johnson – one that would seat only two at-large delegates from the MFDP – she was also the target of Johnson's fury. This passage recounts her early involvement with SNCC and her disappointment at the Democratic convention.

… My parents were sharecroppers and they had a big family. Twenty children. Fourteen boys and six girls. I'm the twentieth child. All of us worked in the fields, of course, but we never did get anything out of sharecropping.

My life has been almost like my mother's was, because I married a man who sharecropped. We didn't have it easy and the only way we could ever make it through the winter was because Pap had a little juke joint and we made liquor. That was the only way we made it. I married in 1944 and stayed on the plantation until 1962 when I went down to the courthouse in Indianola to register to vote. That happened because I went to a mass meeting one night.

Until then I'd never heard of no mass meeting and I didn't know that a Negro could register and vote. Bob Moses, Reggie Robinson, Jim Bevel and James Forman were some of the SNCC workers who ran that meeting. When they asked for those to raise their hands who'd go down to the courthouse the next day, I raised mine. Had it up as high as I could get it. I guess if I'd had any sense I'd a-been a little scared, but what was the point of being scared? The only thing they could do to me was kill me and it seemed like they'd been trying to do that a little bit at a time ever since I could remember.

Well, there was eighteen of us who went down to the courthouse that day and all of us were arrested. Police said the bus was painted the wrong color – said it was too yellow. After I got bailed out I went back to the plantation where Pap and I had lived for eighteen years. My oldest girl met me and told me that Mr. Marlow, the plantation owner, was mad and raising sand. He had heard that I had tried to register. That night he called on us and said, 'We're not going to have this in Mississippi and you will have to withdraw. I am looking for your answer, yea or nay?' I just looked. He said, 'I will give you until tomorrow morning. And if you don't withdraw you will have to leave. If you do go withdraw, it's only how I feel, you might still have to leave.' So I left that same night. Pap had to stay on till work on the plantation was through. Ten days later they fired into Mrs. Tucker's house where I was staying. They also shot two girls at Mr. Sissel's ...

I've worked on voter registration here ever since I went to that first mass meeting. In 1964 we registered 63,000 black people from Mississippi into the Freedom Democratic Party. We formed our own party because the whites wouldn't even let us register. We decided to challenge the white Mississippi Democratic Party at the National Convention. We followed all the laws that the white people themselves made. We tried to attend the precinct meetings and they locked the doors on us or moved the meeting and that's against the laws they made for their ownselves. So we were the ones that held the real precinct meetings. At all these meetings across the state we elected our representatives to go to the National Democratic Convention in Atlantic City. But we learned the hard way that even though we had all the law and all the righteousness on our side – that white man is not going to give up his power to us.

We have to build our own power. We have to win every single political office we can, where we have a majority of black people.

The question for black people is not, when is the white man going to give us our rights, or when is he going to give us good education for our children, or when is he going to give us jobs – if the white man gives you anything just remember when he gets ready he will take it right back. We have to take for ourselves.

From Fannie Lou Hamer, *To Praise Our Bridges: An Autobiography* (Jackson, Miss.: KIPCO, 1967), reproduced in Clayborne Carson, David J.

Garrow, Gerald Gill, Vincent Harding, and Darlene Clark Hine, eds., *The Eyes on the Prize Civil Rights Reader* (New York: Penguin Books, 1991), pp. 176–179.

6.7 'The American Promise,' March 15, 1965

The following passages are excerpts from President Johnson's nationally broadcast special message to Congress, delivered in response to the violent developments in Selma.

... THE RIGHT TO VOTE

Our fathers believed that if this [nation's] noble view of the rights of man was to flourish, it must be rooted in democracy. The most basic right of all was the right to choose your own leaders. The history of this country, in large measure, is the history of the expansion of that right to all of our people ...

Yet the harsh fact is that in many places in this country men and women are kept from voting simply because they are Negroes.

Every device of which human ingenuity is capable has been used to deny this right. The Negro citizen may go to register only to be told that the day is wrong, or the hour is late, or the official in charge is absent. And if he persists, and if he manages to present himself to the registrar, he may be disqualified because he did not spell out his middle name or because he abbreviated a word on the application.

And if he manages to fill out an application he is given a test. The registrar is the sole judge of whether he passes this test. He may be asked to recite the entire Constitution, or explain the most complex provisions of State law. And even a college degree cannot be used to prove that he can read and write.

For the fact is that the only way to pass these barriers is to show a white skin ...

The Constitution says that no person shall be kept from voting because of his race or his color. We have all sworn an oath before God to support and to defend that Constitution. We must now act in obedience to that oath.

GUARANTEEING THE RIGHT TO VOTE

Wednesday I will send to Congress a law designed to eliminate illegal barriers to the right to vote ...

This bill will strike down restrictions to voting in all elections ... which

Figure 12 Bloody Sunday at the Edmund Pettus Bridge, Selma.

have been used to deny Negroes the right to vote.

This bill will establish a simple, uniform standard which cannot be used, however ingenious the effort, to flout our Constitution.

It will provide for citizens to be registered by officials of the United States Government if the State officials refuse to register them.

It will eliminate tedious, unnecessary lawsuits which delay the right to vote ...

To those who seek to avoid action by their National Government in their own communities, who want to and who seek to maintain purely local control over elections, the answer is simple:

Open your polling places to all your people ...

THE NEED FOR ACTION

There is no constitutional issue here. The command of the Constitution is plain.

There is no moral issue. It is wrong – deadly wrong – to deny any of your fellow Americans the right to vote in this country.

There is no issue of States rights or national rights. There is only the struggle for human rights ...

WE SHALL OVERCOME

But even if we pass this bill, the battle will not be over. What happened in Selma is part of a far larger movement which reaches into every section and

State of America. It is the effort of American Negroes to secure for themselves the full blessings of American life.

Their cause must be our cause too. Because it is not just Negroes, but really it is all of us, who must overcome the crippling legacy of bigotry and injustice.

And we shall overcome ...

A century has passed, more than a hundred years, since equality was promised. And yet the Negro is not equal.

A century has passed since the day of promise. And the promise is unkept.

The time of justice has now come. I tell you that I believe sincerely that no force can hold it back. It is right in the eyes of man and God that it should come. And when it does, I think that day will brighten the lives of every American ...

This great, rich, restless country can offer opportunity and education and hope to all: black and white, North and South, sharecropper and city dweller. These are the enemies: poverty, ignorance, disease. They are the enemies and not our fellow man, not our neighbor. And these enemies too, poverty, disease and ignorance, we shall overcome.

AN AMERICAN PROBLEM

Now let none of us in any sections look with prideful righteousness on the troubles in another section, or on the problems of our neighbors. There is really no part of America where the promise of equality has been fully kept. In Buffalo as well as in Birmingham, in Philadelphia as well as in Selma, Americans are struggling for the fruits of freedom.

This is one Nation. What happens in Selma or in Cincinnati is a matter of legitimate concern to every American. But let each of us look within our own hearts and our own communities, and let each of us put our shoulder to the wheel to root out injustice wherever it exists ...

PROGRESS THROUGH THE DEMOCRATIC PROCESS

The real hero of this struggle is the American Negro. His actions and protests, his courage to risk safety and even to risk his life, have awakened the conscience of this Nation. His demonstrations have been designed to call attention to injustice, designed to provoke change, designed to stir reform.

He has called upon us to make good the promise of America. And who among us can say that we would have made the same progress were it not for his persistent bravery, and his faith in American democracy.

For at the real heart of battle for equality is a deep-seated belief in the democratic process. Equality depends not on the force of arms or tear gas but upon the force of moral right; not on recourse to violence but on respect for law and order ...

In Selma as elsewhere we seek and pray for peace. We seek order. We seek unity. But we will not accept the peace of stifled rights, or the order imposed by fear, or the unity that stifles protest. For peace cannot be purchased at the cost of liberty ...

RIGHTS MUST BE OPPORTUNITIES

... All Americans must have the privileges of citizenship regardless of race. And they are going to have those privileges of citizenship regardless of race.

But I would like to caution you and remind you that to exercise these privileges takes much more than just legal right. It requires a trained mind and a healthy body. It requires a decent home, and the chance to find a job, and the opportunity to escape from the clutches of poverty.

Of course, people cannot contribute to the Nation if they are never taught to read or write, if their bodies are stunted from hunger, if their sickness goes untended, if their life is spent in hopeless poverty just drawing a welfare check.

So we want to open the gates to opportunity. But we are also going to give all our people, black and white, the help that they need to walk through those gates ...

Public Papers of the Presidents of the United States: Lyndon B. Johnson, 1965 (Washington, DC: Government Printing Office, 1966), entry 107, pp. 281–287.

6.8 Judge Johnson allows march

After the events of 'Bloody Sunday,' a number of the Black activists sought a federal district court injunction preventing Governor Wallace, Al Lingo (Alabama Director of Public Safety and commander of state troopers), and Sheriff Jim Clark from interfering with the planned march to Montgomery. Activists argued that such a march was protected by their constitutional right to assemble, demonstrate peaceably, and petition the Governor and state for redress of grievances. The following passages are excerpts from Judge Frank W. Johnson's decision, on March 17, 1965, granting the injunction and providing a descriptive narrative of the events.

Figure 13 The Selma to Montgomery voting rights march.

... Under Alabama law, registration is prerequisite to voting in any election. In several counties in central Alabama, including Dallas County wherein Selma, Alabama, is located, fewer than 10% of the Negroes of voting age are registered to vote. For the purpose of obtaining better political representation for Negro citizens in these counties, the Negro communities, through local and national organizations, have conducted voter registration drives in recent years. These voter registration drives in Dallas and other central Alabama counties have been intensified since September, 1964. Public demonstrations have been held in these several counties, particularly in Dallas County, for the purpose of encouraging Negroes to attempt to register to vote and also for the purpose of protesting discriminatory voter registration practices in Alabama. The demonstrations have been peaceful ...

The efforts of these Negro citizens to secure this right to register to vote in some of these counties, have accomplished very little. For instance, in Dallas County, as of November, 1964, where Negro citizens of voting age outnumber white citizens of voting age, only 2.2% of the Negroes were registered to vote ... The evidence in this case reflects that, particularly as to Selma, Dallas County, Alabama, an almost continuous pattern of conduct has existed on the part of defendant Sheriff Clark, his deputies, and his auxiliary deputies known as 'possemen' of harassment, intimidation, coercion, threatening conduct, and, sometimes, brutal mistreatment toward these plaintiffs and other members of their class ... This harassment, intimidation and brutal treatment has ranged from mass arrests without just cause to forced marches for several miles into the countryside, with the sheriff's deputies and members of his posse herding the Negro demonstrators at a rapid pace through the use of electrical shocking devices (designed for use on cattle) and night sticks to prod them along. The Alabama State Troopers, under the command of the defendant Lingo, have, upon several occasions, assisted the defendant Sheriff Clark in these activities, and the State troopers, along with Sheriff Clark as an 'invited guest,' have extended the harassment and intimidating activities into Perry County, where, on February 18, 1965, when approximately 300 Negroes were engaged in a peaceful demonstration by marching from a Negro church to the Perry County Courthouse for the purpose of publicly protesting racially discriminatory voter registration practices in Perry County, Alabama, Negro demonstrators were stopped by the State troopers under the command of the defendant Lingo, and the Negro demonstrators were at that time pushed, prodded, struck, beaten and knocked down. This action resulted in the injury of several Negroes, one of whom was shot by an Alabama State Trooper and subsequently died.

In Dallas County, Alabama, the harassment and brutal treatment on the part of defendants Lingo and Clark, together with their troopers, deputies and 'possemen,' and while acting under instructions from Governor Wallace, reached a climax on Sunday, March 7, 1965. Upon this occasion approximately 650 Negroes left the church in Selma, Alabama, for the purpose of walking to Montgomery, Alabama, to present to the defendant Governor Wallace their grievances ... These Negroes proceeded in an orderly and peaceful manner to a bridge near the south edge of the City of Selma on U.S. Highway 80 that leads to Montgomery, Alabama, which is located approximately 45 miles east of Selma. They proceeded on a sidewalk across the bridge and then continued walking on the grassy portion of the highway toward Montgomery until confronted by a detachment of between 60 to 70 State troopers headed by the defendant Colonel Lingo, by a detachment of several Dallas County deputy sheriffs, and numerous Dallas County 'possemen' on horses, who were headed by Sheriff Clark. Up to this point the Negroes had observed all traffic laws and regulations ... They were ordered to disperse and were given two minutes to do so by Major Cloud ... The Negroes failed to disperse, and within approximately one minute (one minute of the allotted time not having passed), the State troopers and the members of the Dallas County sheriff's office and 'possemen' moved against the Negroes. The general plan as followed by the State troopers in this instance had been discussed with and was known to Governor Wallace ... Approximately 20 canisters of tear gas, nausea gas, and canisters of smoke were rolled into the Negroes by these state officers. The Negroes were then prodded, struck, beaten and knocked down by members of the Alabama State Troopers. The mounted 'possemen' ... moved in and chased and beat the fleeing Negroes. Approximately 75 to 80 of the Negroes were injured, with a large number being hospitalized.

The acts and conduct of these defendants, together with the members of their respective enforcement agencies, as outlined above, have not been directed toward enforcing any valid law of the State of Alabama ... The attempted march alongside U. S. Highway 80 from Selma, Alabama, to Montgomery, Alabama, on March 7, 1965, involved nothing more than a peaceful effort on the part of Negro citizens to exercise a classic constitutional right ...

The law is clear that the right to petition one's government for the redress of grievances may be exercised in large groups. Indeed, where, as here, minorities have been harassed, coerced and intimidated, group association may be the only realistic way of exercising such rights ...

These rights may also be exercised by marching, even along public highways, as long as it is done in an orderly and peaceful manner; and these rights to assemble, demonstrate and march are not to by abridged by arrest or other interference so long as the rights are asserted within the limits of not unreasonably interfering with the exercise of the rights by other citizens to use the sidewalks, streets and highways, and where the protestors and demonstrators are conducting their activities in such a manner as not to deprive the other citizenry of their police protection ... [T]here must be in cases like the one now presented, a 'constitutional boundary line' drawn between the competing interests of society. This Court has the duty and responsibility in this case of drawing the 'constitutional boundary line.' In doing so, it seems basic to our constitutional principles that the extent of the right to assemble, demonstrate and march peaceably along the highways and streets in an orderly manner should be commensurate with the enormity of the wrongs that are being protested and petitioned against. In this case, the wrongs are enormous. The extent of the right to demonstrate against these wrongs should be determined accordingly ...

This Court finds the plaintiffs' proposed plan to the extent that it relates to a march along U.S. Highway 80 from Selma to Montgomery, Alabama, to be a reasonable one to be used and followed in the exercise of a constitutional right of assembly and free movement within the State of Alabama for the purpose of petitioning their State government for redress of their grievances ...

Williams v. Wallace, 240 F. Supp. 100, 106 (M.D. Ala. 1965).

6.9 Voting Rights Act (1965)

The Voting Rights Act of 1965 enforced the Fifteenth Amendment to the Constitution by suspending or providing remedies to practices that had traditionally served to disfranchise minorities in identified states. The following passages are excerpted from a bulletin published by the US Commission on Civil Rights.

• Suspends literacy tests and other devices (found to be discriminatory) as qualifications for voting in any Federal, State, local, general or primary election in the States of Alabama, Alaska, Georgia, Louisiana, Mississippi, South Carolina, Virginia and at least 26 counties in North Carolina.

• Provides for the assignment of Federal examiners to conduct registration and observe voting in States and/or counties covered by the Act.

• Directs the U.S. Attorney General to initiate suits immediately to test the constitutionality of poll taxes because the U.S. Congress found that the payment of such tax has been used in some areas to abridge the right to vote.

• Extends civil and criminal protection to qualified persons seeking to vote and to those who urge or aid others to vote ...

The 1965 Act provides new tools to assure the right to vote and supplements the previous authority granted by the Civil Rights Acts of 1957, 1960 and 1964. It is intended primarily to enforce the Fifteenth Amendment to the Constitution of the United States which provides in Section 1:

'The right of citizens of the United States to vote shall not be denied or abridged by the United States or by any State on account of race, color, or previous condition of servitude.'

The law has two central features:

1. Provision for suspending a variety of tests and devices that have been used to deny citizens the right to vote because of their race or color.

2. Provision for the appointment of Federal examiners to list voters in those areas where tests and devices have been suspended.

In this Act, the term 'voting' includes all action necessary – from the time of registration to the actual counting of the votes – to make a vote for public or party office effective.

VOTER REQUIREMENTS OUTLAWED BY THIS ACT

No State or political subdivision (counties, municipalities and parishes) covered by the Voting Rights Act may require the use of any test or device as a prerequisite for registration or voting ...

COVERAGE

The Voting Rights Act of 1965 states that no person shall be denied the right to vote in any Federal, State or local election (including primaries) for failure to pass a test if he lives in a State or political subdivision which:

1. Maintained a test or device as a prerequisite to registration or voting as of November 1, 1964 and
2. Had a total voting age population of which less than 50 percent were registered or actually voted in the 1964 Presidential election ...

States covered by the Act include Alabama, Alaska, Georgia, Louisiana, Mississippi, South Carolina, Virginia, and approximately 26 counties in North Carolina.

Cessation of Coverage

A State or political subdivision may be removed from coverage by filing a suit in a three-judge District Court for the District of Columbia. The State or political subdivision must convince the court that no test or device has been used for the purpose or with the effect of denying the right to vote because of race or color during the five years preceding the filing of the suit ...

FEDERAL EXAMINERS

Once it is determined that a political subdivision is covered by the Act, the U.S. Attorney General may direct the U.S. Civil Service Commission to appoint Federal examiners to list voters ...

POLL TAXES

The Act contains a Congressional finding that the right to vote has been denied or abridged by the requirement of the payment of a poll tax as a condition to voting.

The U.S. Attorney General is directed to institute suits against Alabama, Mississippi, Texas and Virginia which require the payment of poll taxes in order to determine if such taxes violate the Constitution ...

LANGUAGE LITERACY

If a person residing in a State where tests or devices have not been suspended has completed at least six grades in an 'American-flag' school (a school in the United States or its territories), his inability to speak the English language shall not be the basis for denying him the right to vote ...

CRIMINAL AND CIVIL PENALTIES

Public officials or private individuals who deny persons the right to vote guaranteed by the Voting Rights Act of 1965 or anyone who attempts to or intimidates, threatens, or coerces a person from voting are subject to criminal penalties ...

U.S. Commission on Civil Rights, *The Voting Rights Act of 1965*, Special Publication No. 4 (August, 1965).

Note

1 R. Weisbrot, *Freedom Bound: A History of America's Civil Rights Movement* (New York: Penguin, 1991), p. 127.

7

'We'll soon be free':
Northern efforts, Black Power,
legal endorsements

Only five days after the signing of the Voting Rights Act, Watts, the Black ghetto of Los Angeles, erupted into flame, sparked by an altercation between White police and Blacks and fueled by Black frustration. Such an event was not unanticipated. Whitney Young, in 1963 (7.1), had described the problems facing Northern Blacks, cautioning that violence could erupt and calling for a massive compensatory effort (a domestic Marshall Plan) to address the effects of historical discrimination in housing and jobs. While Johnson's War on Poverty targeted issues of concern, disenchantment with the slow pace of progress fueled a movement calling for Black self-reliance, Black Power.

Northern Ghettoes

Young's warning had not fallen on deaf ears, as President Johnson, in his State of the Union Address of January, 1964 called for 'an unconditional war on poverty.' Johnson avoided associating the War on Poverty specifically with race, but elements of the address promised to ameliorate the problems of urban Blacks. Those elements included the Economic Opportunity Act of 1964 (EOA), incorporating provisions for Head Start (a compensatory educational program for preschool children), the Job Corps (vocational and educational programs for disadvantaged youth), and other anti-poverty programs. The level of funding, however, was well below the level of rhetoric. Ultimately, Johnson's recognition of the need for affirmative action (7.2) held promise. The addition of Medicare (health insurance for the elderly), Medicaid (health insurance for the indigent), and expanded food stamp programs provided some measure of relief. With regard to the situation of Northern Blacks,

Roy Wilkins observed, 'There was no mystery to what was going on ... [W]e had reached into the worst corners of oppression in the South ... but we had not even touched the misery and desperation of the urban ghettos outside the South.'[1]

The evident success of nonviolent, direct action in the South attracted the attention of Black community organizers in the North. For example, in 1966, King and the SCLC joined the Chicago Freedom Movement to get that city to respond to Blacks' issues (7.3). In Chicago, Black demonstrations generated White violence, and White political leaders often were intransigent. Unlike that in the South, however, racism in the North was not grounded in a legal system specifically designed to dominate Blacks but in a socio-economic system and in time-honored, institutional policies and practices that marginalized them. It was one thing to identify and eliminate a law that enforced segregated housing patterns or disfranchised Black voters in the South and another to untangle the web of social arrangements and practices that characterized the various forms of discrimination in the North – especially when, at some levels, the practices might not have had discriminatory intent (7.4) or, at least, were not perceived so by many Whites. The Chicago Freedom Movement did generate an agreement with the city to combat housing segregation, and some progress was made with regard to jobs, but it is unclear that nonviolent, direct action had the desired impact. Alternatively, home-grown efforts at economic self-help among Blacks in the North, such as those initiated by the Rev. Leon Sullivan of Philadelphia, showed promise (7.5).

Ghettoes in the North continued to erupt into violence in the mid- to late-1960s, peaking with the reaction to the assassination of Martin Luther King, Jr. in April 1968. After the particularly troublesome summer of 1967, during which over 100 cities reported disturbances highlighted by major outbreaks of rioting, violence and looting in Newark, New Jersey, and Detroit, Michigan, President Johnson appointed a commission to study the outbreaks and their causes, and to make recommendations (7.6). But by that time, urban violence had done great harm to the Movement. Older civil rights leaders were upstaged by younger spokespersons who rejected integration and emphasized Black nationalism, separatism, and 'Black Power,' thus fragmenting the Movement. The media's juxtaposition of urban violence and calls for Black Power alienated many Whites, fostering White backlash and contributing to an era of conservative retrenchment. Nonetheless, within the broad reach of Black nationalism, the seeds of Black cultural pride were sown.

Black nationalism and Black Power

The intractability of problems in the North and the continued, violent resistance of Whites in the South despite legislative and court victories led a number of disenchanted Black activists to consider alternatives to nonviolent, direct action, and integration, its central aim. Many were attracted to expressions of Black separatism and nationalism. One of the most visible proponents of Black separatism was Elijah Muhammad, leader of the Nation of Islam (NOI). The NOI identified Whites as devils and the source of Black misery, imposed on its membership a strict moral code fostering self-improvement, and called for the development of independent Black social institutions and businesses. Elijah Muhammad's most effective spokesman was Malcolm X (7.7).

Although the NOI was based in the urban North, the doctrine of Malcolm X began to appeal to southern Black activists disillusioned with the slow pace of change and their belief, encouraged by the experience of the Mississippi Freedom Democratic Party at the Democratic National Convention in 1964, that the White liberal establishment was unreliable. As Fannie Lou Hamer observed (see 6.6), '[W]e learned the hard way that even though we had all the law and all the righteousness on our side – that white man is not going to give up his power to us.' Some activists, led by Stokely Carmichael, called for 'Black Power.'

In his book *Where Do We Go from Here: Chaos or Community?*,[2] Martin Luther King, Jr. addressed the many manifestations of Black Power. On one level, he argued that the slogan was a reaction to the failure of White power, where 'the gap between promise and fulfillment is distressingly wide.' Second, it was a 'call to black people to amass the political and economic strength to achieve their legitimate goals.' That call was clearly reflected by Stokely Carmichael (7.8); however, more radical manifestations were found in the demands of an organization such as the Black Panther Party (7.9). Finally, argued King, Black Power was a call to reject the psychological indoctrination of inferiority imposed by slavery and segregation, a call 'to a new sense of manhood, to a deep feeling of racial pride

150

and to an audacious appreciation of [Black] heritage.' That call 'to glory in blackness and to resurrect joyously the African past' had a tremendous impact on Black culture, language, and literature (**7.10, 7.11**). At the personal level, some responded to the call by shedding their 'slave names' in favor of names that reflected their heritage. For example, Ronald McKinley Everett, the creator of Kwanzaa, shed his slave name for Maulana Karenga, Swahili for 'master teacher' and 'nationalist.'

We have noted that the Black Church was central to the life of African Americans. As more Blacks were attracted to the concept of Black Power, Black theologians faced a dilemma. On the one hand, positive elements of the concept resonated with the Black community. On the other, the emphasis on power and the frankly militant expression of that emphasis among many spokespersons was offered as an alternative to the nonviolence and Christian love espoused by King. As a result of the tension created within the church, a new synthesis was articulated, a Black Christian theology of liberation (**7.12**). James Cone, a major proponent of liberation theology, argued that it sought to 'analyze the black man's condition in the light of God's revelation in Jesus Christ with the purpose of creating a new understanding of black dignity among black people, and providing the necessary soul in that people to destroy white racism.'[3]

Legal endorsements

While activists continued to work 'in the trenches,' the NAACP and its allies in the Johnson administration won a series of legislative and court battles during the mid- to late 1960s that supported federal civil rights legislation or further restricted Jim Crow. While the Twenty-Fourth Amendment (**7.13**) prohibited the payment of a poll tax as a requirement for voting in federal elections, the Supreme Court endorsed the constitutionality of the Civil Rights Act (**7.14 and 7.15**) and Voting Rights Act (**7.16**) while endorsing federal action against anti-civil rights terrorists (**7.17**). The Court also found anti-miscegenation laws unconstitutional (**7.18**), rejected the delaying tactics of Southern school systems (**7.19**), approved laws prohibiting private acts of discrimination (**7.20**), and prohibited the use of literacy tests if their effect was to deny the right to vote on account of race (**7.21**). The last major piece of federal civil rights legislation of the period, the Civil Rights Act of 1968 (**7.22**), addressed discrimination in housing.

7.1 Whitney Young on Northern ghettoes

In late 1963, Whitney Young of the National Urban League pointed out the potential for violence in Northern, Black ghettoes. He called for a domestic Marshall Plan to foster equal opportunity for urban Blacks.

In teeming northern ghettos, hundreds of thousands of Negro citizens – unemployed, ill-housed, disillusioned – are nearing the breaking point. Disorders have already begun. Violence could erupt at any moment unless swift and realistic action is taken to prevent violence by eliminating its basic cause.

For 18.7 million American Negroes, already handicapped by discrimination in employment and inadequate training and now caught up in the quicksand of rapid technological change, the problem is immediate and desperate.

Federal action, however commendable, is still too little – and may well be too late. We believe the answer lies in effective action by responsible individuals and institutions – acting privately and in concert – who will undertake a massive program to close the intolerable economic, social, and educational gap that separates the vast majority of Negro citizens from other Americans.

After World War II, our country initiated a Marshall Plan to help the war-shattered countries of Western Europe function in full partnership with the United States. Our Negro citizens are asking for a similar chance to attain their rightful position as full partners of every other citizen of the United States.

This is a plea for a special effort, but it is *not* a plea for special privilege. The effects of generations of deprivation and denial have made it almost impossible for the American Negro to take advantage of any guarantee of equal opportunity. Unless he can do so, legal progress is an illusion; and the civil rights struggle will continue with unforeseeable consequences ...

In this sense, the National Urban League urges the responsible leadership of our country to undertake a domestic 'Marshall Plan' – a special effort to help the Negro help himself and, by so doing, reach the point at which he can compete on a realistic basis of equality within the nation's complex economy ...

A great many of the intense needs and problems evident in so many Negro communities are the result of exclusion based on racial discrimination. Apart from historical equity, a massive compensatory effort may well be the only means of overcoming all present results of past neglect ...

To correct these and many other problems, the Urban League believes that a 'crash' attack is required. A cooperative and deliberate effort on the part of agencies, unions, business and industry, institutions and individuals, both public and private, could, if sustained for a realistic period of time, reverse the widespread social deterioration of Negro families and their children and help develop the tools and understanding for progress to full and equal citizenship ...

American Child, 45 (Washington, DC: National Child Labor Committee, November, 1963), pp. 5–8.

---

7. 2 'To Fulfill These Rights'

Amplifying his 'War on Poverty' theme, President Johnson, in a commencement address at Howard University on June 4, 1965, recognized that centuries of racial discrimination and oppression could not be wiped out by the simple declaration of equality. Evoking the need for affirmative action, he championed 'equality as a result.'

... In far too many ways American Negroes have been another nation: deprived of freedom, crippled by hatred, the doors of opportunity closed to hope ...

The voting rights bill will be the latest, and among the most important, in a long series of victories. But this victory – as Winston Churchill said of another triumph for freedom – 'is not the end. It is not even the beginning of the end. But it is, perhaps, the end of the beginning.'

That beginning is freedom ...

But freedom is not enough. You do not wipe away the scars of centuries by saying: Now you are free to go where you want, and do as you desire, and choose the leaders you please.

You do not take a person who, for years, has been hobbled by chains and liberate him, bring him up to the starting line of a race and then say, 'you are free to compete with all the others,' and still justly believe that you have been completely fair.

Thus it is not enough just to open the gates of opportunity. All our citizens must have the ability to walk through those gates.

This is the next and the more profound stage of the battle for civil rights. We seek not just freedom but opportunity. We seek not just legal equity but human ability, not just equality as a right and a theory but equality as a fact and equality as a result.

For the task is to give 20 million Negroes the same chance as every other American to learn and grow, to work and share in society, to develop their abilities – physical, mental and spiritual, and to pursue their individual happiness ...

[F]or the great majority of Negro Americans – the poor, the unemployed, the uprooted, and the dispossessed – there is a much grimmer story. They still, as we meet here tonight, are another nation. Despite the court orders and the laws, despite the legislative victories and the speeches, for them the walls are rising and the gulf is widening ...

[T]he isolation of Negro from white communities is increasing, rather than decreasing as Negroes crowd into the central cities and become a city within a city.

Of course Negro Americans as well as white Americans have shared in our rising national abundance. But the harsh fact of the matter is that in the battle for true equality too many – far too many – are losing ground every day ...

Negro poverty is not white poverty. Many of its causes and many of its cures are the same. But there are differences – deep, corrosive, obstinate differences – radiating painful roots into the community, and into the family, and the nature of the individual.

These differences are not racial differences. They are solely and simply the consequence of ancient brutality, past injustice, and present prejudice ...

Nor can these differences be understood as isolated infirmities. They are a seamless web. They cause each other. They result from each other. They reinforce each other.

Much of the Negro community is buried under a blanket of history and circumstance. It is not a lasting solution to lift just one corner of that blanket. We must stand on all sides and we must raise the entire cover if we are to liberate our fellow citizens ...

TO FULFILL THESE RIGHTS

There is no single easy answer to all of these problems.

Jobs are part of the answer. They bring the income which permits a man to provide for his family.

Decent homes in decent surroundings and a chance to learn – an equal chance to learn – are part of the answer.

Welfare and social programs better designed to hold families together are part of the answer.

Care for the sick is part of the answer.

An understanding heart by all Americans is another big part of the answer ...

WHAT IS JUSTICE?

For what is justice?

It is to fulfill the fair expectations of man ...

So, it is the glorious opportunity of this generation to end the one huge wrong of the American Nation and, in so doing, to find America for ourselves, with the same immense thrill of discovery which gripped those who first began to realize that here, at last, was a home for freedom ...

Public Papers of the Presidents of the United States: Lyndon B. Johnson, 1965, II (Washington, DC: Government Printing Office, 1966), entry 301, pp. 635–640.

7.3 Chicago Freedom Movement, 1966

The Chicago Freedom Movement combined the SCLC and the Coordinating Council of Community Organizations, a coalition of Chicago civil rights and Negro community organizations in collaboration with religious organizations, social agencies, and neighborhood groups. This statement is reflective of issues in virtually every major Northern city.

Introduction: The Problems of Racism, Ghettoes, and Slums

... Racism in the large Northern cities has not featured lynchings, denial of the vote, or other clear injustices that could easily be removed as is the case in the South. Yet, racism in Chicago has been a stark reality, visible in many dimensions. It is reflected in the existence of the massive overcrowded ghetto that grows each year. It is reflected in the crime-infested slums where the living standards of the Negro poor often do not cover the bare necessities of urban living. It is reflected in the exploitation of Negroes by the dominant white society in higher rents and prices, lower wages and poorer schools ...

... In the maintenance of law and order Negroes are frequently the victims of police brutality and of stop and search methods of crime detection ...

The Chicago Freedom Movement

The Chicago Freedom Movement is a coalition of forces for the purpose of wiping out slums, ghettoes and racism ...

Many groups in the Chicago region share with Negroes common problems of slum housing, welfare dependency, inferior education, police brutality, and color discrimination ... Therefore, the Freedom Movement is making many proposals that provide for the improvement and upgrading of conditions of Latin Americans, other non-whites and some white minorities.

The Freedom Movement proposals and demands are designed to set the broad guidelines for a just and open city in which all men can live with dignity. Three interrelated goals set forth the direction to such a society:

1. To bring about equality of opportunity and of results.
2. To open up the major areas of metropolitan life of housing, employment, and education.
3. To provide power for the powerless ...

In order to generate the necessary power the movement will:

1. Organize a series of direct actions which will make the injustices so clear that the whole community will respond to the need to change.
2. Organize people in every sector of the ghettoes – in neighborhoods, in schools, in welfare unions, in public housing, in hospitals, to give the strength of numbers to the demands for change.
3. Strengthen the institutions which contribute to the goals of a just and open society and withdraw support from those institutions – banks, businesses, newspapers and professions – which drain the resources of the ghetto communities without contributing in return.
4. Demand representation of the organizations of the ghetto community (Chicago Freedom Movement) on decision-making bodies at every level of government, industry, labor, and church, affecting the lives of people in the ghetto.
5. Promote political education and participation so that the needs and aspirations of Negroes and other oppressed minorities are fully represented.

The Chicago Freedom Movement and its constituent organizations use many means to bring about change. Community organization, education, research, job development, legal redress and political education are all weapons in the arsenal of the Movement. But, its most distinctive and creative tool is that of non-violent direct action ...

An Open and Just City

To wipe out slums, ghettoes, and racism we must create an *open* city with equal opportunities and equal results. To this end we have drawn up program proposals for employment and income, housing and metropolitan planning, education, financial services, police and legal protection ...

In employment our program proposals call for fair employment by the elimination of all forms of job bias and of all measures which screen out minority groups ... We call for effective job training and retraining with the provision of a job at the successful completion of the program.

In housing our program calls for an open city in which no man is discriminated against. We call for adequate financing and programs for the redevelopment of slum and deteriorating housing and for the elimination of exploitation by slum lords. We call for humanization of the present public housing projects. We propose the development of a vastly increased supply of decent low and middle cost housing throughout the Chicago area.

In planning we call for the development of a metropolitan-wide land and transportation plan, including the City of Chicago, that will promote and facilitate access to jobs and housing for all men throughout the entire region ...

In welfare we call for the elimination of welfare dependency by a guaranteed adequate annual income as a matter of right with provision for payment in the most dignified manner possible. In the immediate future, pending the change in the manner of income distribution, we propose measures to humanize the welfare system and to strengthen the autonomy and rights of recipients.

In politics and governments we call for increased representation of Negroes, Latin Americans, and other exploited minorities.

We call for measures to equalize protection from police and the courts, including a citizen review board to monitor complaints of police brutality and arbitrary arrest ...

Program of the Chicago Freedom Movement, July, 1966, http://cfm40. middlebury.edu/node/43 (accessed December 2008).

7.4 Institutional racism

The following passage is excerpted from an analysis of institutional racism in the United States in the 1960s. The pervasiveness of this form of racism in American society was foundational to calls among some activists for Black separatism and nationalism and to criticisms of the basic socio-economic system, capitalism. 'We must destroy both racism and capitalism,' proclaimed Huey Newton. The radical nature of the criticisms by Newton and others, in turn, fueled backlash against the Movement.

... The discrepancy between unprecedented white affluence and black poverty is the result of the almost total exclusion of black Americans from entrepreneurial activity and the market. The vast majority of blacks have functioned only as menial workers and exploited consumers. The present division of the economy along racial lines is the result of both intentional and unintentional institutional racism ...

Ownership of capital and the right to invest it in profit-making enterprises has always been associated with the American concept of freedom. Yet the white business world has consistently denied to black people the opportunity to control substantial financial resources ...

There are many problems within the ghetto itself which limit the development of black enterprise. The educational background of most black people effectively cripples them for highly skilled positions. Years of experiencing white prejudice and personal failure have created a chasm of despair in the ghetto, which works against ambition and participation in business ventures. But major responsibility for the *de facto* racist situation continues to rest with the white business world.

The greatest difficulty the black would-be businessman faces is the lack of available credit. Aside from overt discrimination among financiers, the black entrepreneur is at a sharp disadvantage in the face of credit standards designed to measure the reliability of white applicants. A financial institution considering a loan application examines the credit history of the applicant, the collateral to be held against the loan, the prospects for business success, and other related criteria. The black man is more likely than the white man to have a poor credit record due to the loan sharks and exploitative merchants that feed off ghetto residents. Black people usually have no property or investments that could be used as collateral. And the black businessman who wishes to locate in his own community, where the income level is at or near the poverty line, will have poorer prospects for success than the white merchant in the white middle-class community. *The present standards, when applied without regard to race, will lead to more white ownership of enterprises and less black participation in the economy.*

There are strong indications that the standards for assessing credit risk are not good measures of a black man's reliability. During the years 1954–1963, the Federal Small Business Administration made a total of 432 loans. Of this number only seven loans went to black businesses despite the fact that the organization was ostensibly following nondiscriminatory policies. Then, in 1964, the Small Business Administration launched its 6 × 6 plan:

$6,000 for six years. The SBA evaluated applicants for this program on criteria other than credit history or collateral. Of 219 loans made, 98 went to black people. Only eight of the 219 were delinquent and none were liquidated. These statistics cast doubt on the idea that black businesses are a high credit risk.

The black businessman is also plagued by insurance costs which are as much as three times higher than those that most whites pay. Insurance companies are hesitant to cover ghetto property due to the danger of possible damage in civil disturbances; only very high premiums will draw them back into the black community ...

Louis L. Knowles and Kenneth Prewitt, eds., *Institutional Racism in America* (Englewood Cliffs, NJ: Prentice-Hall, 1969), pp. 15–18.

7.5 Leon Sullivan on Black economic development

Minister and civil rights activist Leon Sullivan advocated self-help in the Black community. The creator of Opportunities Industrialization Centers (OIC), he promoted, through his various programs, capital investment, job training, and consumer education. In the early 1960s, Sullivan's use of 'selective buying' – that is, boycotts against White businesses that wouldn't hire Blacks – attracted the attention of Martin Luther King, Jr., and influenced the development of the SCLC's Operation Breadbasket. In the following passage, Rev. Sullivan describes aspects of his thinking regarding Black economic development.

I firmly believe that Black people must be integrated into the mainstream of American life. Black economic development has to be accomplished in terms of integration! There is no such thing as Black capitalism! There is no such thing as Black capital! ...

[The Black man's] paramount need is to get inside the door in terms of management, in terms of knowing what the economic structure is, in terms of development and control of capital. Then he will be able to move step by step through the process of building economic strength. In the final analysis the country, in fact the world, is run on money. Although people run on spirit, the nation is run on money, enterprise is developed on money, communities are built on money. Communities are built to help the people utilize money.

Unfortunately, Blacks have not had the financial capital that they have needed to develop enterprises ...

... [W]e have to utilize the resources we have in order to be economically emancipated. Before we started the OIC, we began a program that would generate capital for Blacks so that they could develop businesses, enterprises, and housing programs of their own. I looked in the Bible one Saturday night and I was reading about the feeding of the five thousand (Mark 6: 34–44). If Jesus himself could multiply a few loaves and fishes and feed five thousand people and have a few loaves left over, even that supernatural act would not have been as remarkable as the miracle of sharing that I believe really happened that day ...

So I went to my church and after preaching a sermon on gathering the fragments of life, I asked fifty members to invest ten dollars a month. The money could be used in two ways, one for nonprofit purposes in which there would be no immediate return, such as to build health facilities, to finance nonprofit housing developments, to develop educational scholarship funds, and to provide care for the sick and the infirm. The other portion would go into a profit venture. Initially not fifty, but two hundred people responded. Their response formed the base for the 10-36 Plan ...

Here we were with two hundred people pooling their money to build a million-dollar apartment complex, the first built by Blacks in Philadelphia. Soon we had some six hundred people participating in the program, and we built a two million-dollar shopping center – the first shopping center built by Blacks in America, perhaps the largest in the world built by Blacks. Then we opened the plan to five thousand people and as a result we built the first and largest aerospace company in the world owned by Blacks. Later we opened supermarkets where the Whites and the Blacks shopped together. We sought to develop a chain so that our food markets would be throughout Philadelphia and one day throughout America.

In this way we began to generate new capital. We began to buy office buildings. We worked the income from some of these into a charitable trust so that the income ultimately can improve education and provide scholarships. I call this money 'Community Capital.'

This effort began to move like a snowball so that by the time the Securities and Exchange Commission registered the '10-36 Plan' we could claim that this was the first time in history that stock issues which were both nonprofit and profit in nature had ever been registered by the federal government. Here is the plan:

Twenty thousand issues were placed on sale initially all over the country. We will have twenty thousand people giving ten dollars per month for thirty-six months. Our plan is to add up to as many as a half million shareholders all over the country, so that the kind of programs we developed in Philadelphia can be developed in up to one hundred cities ...

160

I particularly want church people to participate in the efforts to uplift the community as well as themselves. In this way we can change the mentality of Blacks from the 'hand out' to the 'put in' philosophy.

We have a training program for everything we do. People will be trained in what this plan is all about, wherever we have OIC and other institutional programs. In this way the people can be informed about this type of program and the benefits from it. This type of program can be used to build so much in our communities: shopping centers, housing developments, factories, investment houses, banks, and most of all, pride in ownership, and confidence ...

Another aspect of Black economic development is what I call AAE (Adult Armchair Education). This is a very interesting program on consumer education. I got the name when I was in a parsonage of a Baptist church in Springfield, Massachusetts. I was sitting in a big chair and the pastor was talking with me about a big problem that his people were facing. They were living in a community and being cheated by people who kept them in debt. At the same time they did not know how to stretch their money ...

In this program of Adult Armchair Education (AAE), consumer education is built around the way people are being cheated by stores in the communities. This happens in big and little stores wherever foodstuff is sold. For example, the large supermarkets will take the leftovers from the suburban areas where the food has become old and overripe, and they shine it off and square it up so that it looks good and ship it down to the Black community. The AAE program will contribute to public health by helping people to know what they are getting (whether it's fresh fruit) and also whether they are getting what they are paying for.

Blacks have to pay 10 percent more just to live in the ghettos. When corn is 27 cents in the suburbs, it is often 30 cents in the ghetto. Blacks have to pay 10 percent more, and often more than that, for rent for quarters comparable to those for Whites, 10 percent more for insurance (when they can get it at all), and even 10 percent more for funerals – caskets are often 10 percent higher in price. Consequently, an average Black family with an income of $7,000 pays $700 in overcharges and higher prices. Considering that one of every four Black families lives in the ghetto in America, Black families are being exploited in an amount of one billion dollars. Not only this, Blacks even die 10 percent faster, partly because pollution is so much worse in *the slums than* in the suburbs. AAE helps people to cope with these problems. Scales in many markets are adjusted to cheat the people. Many people do not realize that weights have to be inspected and that there should be an inspection notice indicating that the weights have been inspected. The AAE program reminds the people that the stores must be inspected and that at least a minimal standard of sanitation should prevail. AAE teaches people how to buy and what to buy. This kind of training is what we call consumer education.

This education was extended to include knowledge about living in houses, about public and private landlords ...

These programs became an exciting part of the development of the whole OIC program. We were able to pull support from the total religious community. In Philadelphia we were able to draw a considerable amount of support from the Catholic leadership as well as from Protestant churches of all denominations. Many of these churches sponsored armchair groups. In the Jewish community, many groups have formed educational forums, providing an opportunity to talk with Black leaders in their homes.

We have exchange meetings of individuals in Black communities and White communities, Jewish communities, and Catholic communities. People can begin to understand other communities and start working out the problems that usually affect everyone. It is my desire to see AAE groups increase the community's role in the OIC network until they blanket America ...

Throughout the program of consumer education the emphasis is on human relations. It is the best way we have found to place instructional relations on a really fruitful level. When people are in a common setting, they are able to discus human problems that affect everyone. That is the curriculum.

I'm doing these things to Americanize America. I see these projects as an extension of my ministry because I'm trying to prove that God is no respecter of persons and that God is father of us all. Instead of doing it all in the church, we are doing some of it in the homes, because the home is still the most important unit in the development of society.

Leon H. Sullivan, 'Black Economic Development,' in *Alternatives to Despair* (Valley Forge, Pa.: Judson Press, 1972), chap. 3, pp. 88–102.

7.6 Kerner Commission report, 1968

In the aftermath of the explosive riots in the summer of 1967, President Johnson appointed a commission to study urban unrest. The commission, chaired by Governor Otto Kerner of Illinois, hence 'the Kerner Commission,' issued a voluminous report describing what happened, why, and what might be done to prevent its recurrence. The commission's basic conclusion: 'Our nation is moving toward two societies, one black, one white – separate and unequal.' The following excerpt from the report's summary provides an overview of the causes of unrest.

In addressing the question 'Why did it happen?' we shift our focus ... to the factors within the society at large that created a mood of violence among many urban Negroes.

These factors are complex and interacting; they vary significantly in their effect from city to city and from year to year; and the consequences of one disorder, generating new grievances and new demands, become the causes of the next. Thus was created the 'thicket of tension, conflicting evidence and extreme opinions' cited by the President.

Despite these complexities, certain fundamental matters are clear. Of these, the most fundamental is the racial attitude and behavior of white Americans toward black Americans.

Race prejudice has shaped our history decisively; it now threatens to affect our future.

White racism is essentially responsible for the explosive mixture which has been accumulating in our cities since the end of World War II. Among the ingredients of this mixture are:

- Pervasive discrimination and segregation in employment, education and housing, which have resulted in the continuing exclusion of great numbers of Negroes from the benefits of economic progress.
- Black in-migration and white exodus, which have produced the massive and growing concentrations of impoverished Negroes in our major cities, creating a growing crisis of deteriorating facilities and services and unmet human needs.
- The black ghettos where segregation and poverty converge on the young to destroy opportunity and enforce failure. Crime, drug addiction, dependency on welfare, and bitterness and resentment against society in general and white society in particular are the result.

At the same time, most whites and some Negroes outside the ghetto have prospered to a degree unparalleled in the history of civilization. Through television and other media, this affluence has been flaunted before the eyes of the Negro poor and the jobless ghetto youth.

Yet these facts alone cannot be said to have caused the disorders. Recently, other powerful ingredients have begun to catalyze the mixture:

- Frustrated hopes are the residue of the unfulfilled expectations aroused by the great judicial and legislative victories of the Civil Rights Movement and the dramatic struggle for equal rights in the South.
- A climate that tends toward approval and encouragement of violence as a form of protest has been created by white terrorism directed against nonviolent protest; by the open defiance of law and federal authority by state and local officials resisting desegregation; and by some protest groups engaging in civil disobedience who turn their backs on nonviolence, go beyond the constitutionally protected rights of petition and free

assembly, and resort to violence to attempt to compel alteration of laws and policies with which they disagree.

- The frustrations of powerlessness have led some Negroes to the conviction that there is no effective alternative to violence as a means of achieving redress of grievances, and of 'moving the system.' These frustrations are reflected in alienation and hostility toward the institutions of law and government and the white society which controls them, and in the reach toward racial consciousness and solidarity reflected in the slogan 'Black Power.'

- A new mood has sprung up among Negroes, particularly among the young, in which self-esteem and enhanced racial pride are replacing apathy and submission to 'the system.'

- The police are not merely a 'spark' factor. To some Negroes police have come to symbolize white power, white racism and white repression. And the fact is that many police do reflect and express these white attitudes. The atmosphere of hostility and cynicism is reinforced by a widespread belief among Negroes in the existence of police brutality and in a 'double standard' of justice and protection – one for Negroes and one for whites.

National Advisory Commission on Civil Disorders, *Report of the National Advisory Commission on Civil Disorders* (New York: E.P. Dutton & Co., Inc., 1968), pp. 9–11.

7.7 Malcolm X at Abyssinian Baptist Church

In rousing invective, Malcolm X amplifies the theology of the NOI, providing stark contrast to the theology and Biblical interpretations propounded by the dominant leaders of the Civil Rights Movement.

Since the black masses here in America are now in open revolt against the American system of segregation, will these same black masses turn toward integration or will they turn toward complete separation? Will these awakened black masses demand integration into the white society that enslaved them or will they demand complete separation from that cruel white society that has enslaved them? Will the exploited and oppressed black masses seek integration with their white exploiters and white oppressors or will these awakened black masses truly revolt and separate themselves completely from this wicked race that has enslaved us?

Figure 14 Malcolm X addresses a rally in Harlem.

These are just some quick questions that I think will provoke some thoughts in your minds and my mind. How can the so-called Negroes who call themselves enlightened leaders expect the poor black sheep to integrate into a society of blood thirsty white wolves, white wolves who have already been sucking on our blood for over four hundred years here in America? Or will these black sheep also revolt against the 'false shepherd,' the handpicked Uncle Tom Negro leader, and seek complete separation ... The Honorable Elijah Muhammad teaches us that no people on earth fit the Bible's symbolic picture about the Lost Sheep more so than America's twenty million so-called Negroes ... The Honorable Elijah Muhammad, a godsent shepherd, has opened the eyes of our people. And the black masses can now see that we have all been here in this white doghouse long, too long. The black masses don't want segregation nor do we want integration. What we want is complete separation ... The Honorable Elijah Muhammad teaches us that this is the only intelligent and lasting solution to the present race problem ... [T]he Muslim followers of The Honorable Elijah Muhammad actually reject hypocritical promises of integration ...

The Honorable Elijah Muhammad teaches us that these same so-called American Negroes are God's long-lost people who are symbolically described in the Bible as the Lost Sheep or the Lost Tribe of Israel. We who are Muslims believe in God, we believe in his scriptures, we believe in

165

prophecy... Just as God destroyed the enslavers in the past, God is going to destroy this wicked white enslaver of our people here in America.

God wants us to separate ourselves from this wicked white race here in America because this American House of Bondage is number one on God's list for divine destruction today. I repeat: This American House of Bondage is number one on God's list for divine destruction today. He taught separation; Moses never taught integration, Moses taught separation. The innocent must always be given a chance to separate themselves from the guilty before the guilty are executed. No one is more innocent than the poor, blind, American so-called Negro who has been led astray by blind Negro leaders, and no one on earth is more guilty than the blue-eyed white man who has used his control and influence over the Negro leader to lead the rest of our people astray ...

... The Honorable Elijah Muhammad says that this problem can be solved and solved forever just by sending our people back to our own homeland or back to our own people, but that this government should provide the transportation plus everything else we need to get started again in our own country. This government should give us everything we need in the form of machinery, material, and finance-enough to last for twenty to twenty-five years until we can become an independent people and an independent nation in our own land ...

And in my conclusion I repeat: We want no part of integration with this wicked race that enslaved us. We want complete separation from this wicked race of devils.

Reprinted in Imam Benjamin Karim, ed., *The End of White World Supremacy: Four Speeches by Malcolm X* (New York: Seaver Books, 1971), pp. 67–74.

7.8 Stokely Carmichael on Black Power

Carmichael argues that Black Power promotes fundamental group solidarity founded on political reality and cultural integrity. Note that he rejects claims of reverse racism while also pointing out the shortcomings of nonviolence and integration.

The adoption of the concept of Black Power is one of the most legitimate and healthy developments in American politics and race relations in our time ... It is a call for black people in this country to unite, to recognize their heritage, to build a sense of community. It is a call for black people to begin to define their own goals, to lead their own organizations and to support those organizations. It is a call to reject the racist institutions and values of this society.

The concept of Black Power rests on a fundamental premise: *Before a group can enter the open society, it must first close ranks.* By this we mean that group solidarity is necessary before a group can operate effectively from a bargaining position of strength in a pluralistic society. Traditionally, each new ethnic group in this society has found the route to social and political viability through the organization of its own institutions with which to represent its needs within the larger society ...

The point is obvious: black people must lead and run their own organizations. Only black people can convey the revolutionary idea – and it is a revolutionary idea – that black people are able to do things themselves. Only they can help create in the community an aroused and continuing black consciousness that will provide the basis for political strength. In the past, white allies have often furthered white supremacy without the whites involved realizing it, or even wanting to do so. Black people must come together and do things for themselves. They must achieve self-identity and self-determination in order to have their daily needs met. Black Power means, for example, that in Lowndes County, Alabama, a black sheriff can end police brutality. A black tax assessor and tax collector and county board of revenue can lay, collect, and channel tax monies for the building

Figure 15 Stokely Carmichael addresses a rally in Berkeley, California.

of better roads and schools serving black people. In such areas as Lowndes, where black people have a majority, they will attempt to use power to exercise control. This is what they seek: control. When black people lack a majority, Black Power means proper representation and sharing of control. It means the creation of power bases, of strength, from which black people can press to change local or nation-wide patterns of oppression – instead of from weakness ...

Black Power recognizes – it must recognize – the ethnic basis of American politics as well as the power-oriented nature of American politics. Black Power therefore calls for black people to consolidate behind their own, so that they can bargain from a position of strength. But while we endorse the *procedure* of group solidarity and identity for the purpose of attaining certain goals in the body politic, this does not mean that black people should strive for the same kind of rewards (i.e., end results) obtained by the white society. The ultimate values and goals are not domination or exploitation of other groups, but rather an effective share in the total power of the society.

Nevertheless, some observers have labeled those who advocate Black Power as racists; they have said that the call for self-identification and self-determination is 'racism in reverse' or 'black supremacy.' This is a deliberate and absurd lie. There is no analogy – by any stretch of definition or imagination – between the advocates of Black Power and white racists. Racism is not merely exclusion on the basis of race but exclusion for the purpose of subjugating or maintaining subjugation. The goal of the racists is to keep black people on the bottom, arbitrarily and dictatorially, as they have done in this country for over three hundred years. The goal of black self-determination and black self-identity – Black Power – is full participation in the decision-making processes affecting the lives of black people, and recognition of the virtues in themselves as black people. The black people of this country have not lynched whites, bombed their churches, murdered their children and manipulated laws and institutions to maintain oppression. White racists have. Congressional laws, one after the other, have not been necessary to stop black people from oppressing others and denying others the full enjoyment of their rights. White racists have made such laws necessary. The goal of Black Power is positive and functional to a free and viable society. No white racist can make this claim ...

When the concept of Black Power is set forth, many people immediately conjure up notions of violence. The country's reaction to the Deacons for Defense and justice, which originated in Louisiana, is instructive. Here is a group which realized that the 'law' and law enforcement agencies would not protect people, so they had to do it themselves. If a nation fails to protect its citizens, then that nation cannot condemn those who take up the task themselves. The Deacons and all other blacks who resort to self-defense represent a simple answer to a simple question: what man would not defend his family and home from attack?

... Those of us who advocate Black Power are quite clear in our own minds that a 'non-violent' approach to civil rights is an approach black people cannot afford and a luxury white people do not deserve. It is crystal clear to us – and it must become so with the white society – that there can be no social order without social justice ...

'Integration' as a goal today speaks to the problem of blackness not only in an unrealistic way but also in a despicable way. It is based on complete acceptance of the fact that in order to have a decent house or education, black people must move into a white neighborhood or send their children to a white school. This reinforces, among both black and white, the idea that 'white' is automatically superior and 'black' is by definition inferior. For this reason, 'integration' is a subterfuge for the maintenance of white supremacy ...

The racial and cultural personality of the black community must be preserved and that community must win its freedom while preserving its cultural integrity. Integrity includes a pride – in the sense of self-acceptance, not chauvinism – in being black, in the historical attainments and contributions of black people. No person can be healthy, complete and mature if he must deny a part of himself; this is what 'integration' has required thus far. This is the essential difference between integration as it is currently practiced and the concept of Black Power ...

Stokely Carmichael and Charles V. Hamilton, *Black Power: The Politics of Liberation in America* (New York: Random House, 1967), pp. 44–55.

7.9 Black Panther Party manifesto (1966)

Along with traditional grievances in the areas of employment, housing, education, health care, and police brutality, the Black Panthers targeted capitalism and what they described as US aggression against oppressed peoples of the world. While reflecting the radicalization of elements of the Movement, such rhetoric offended many Whites and contributed to backlash against the Movement. An excerpt from the manifesto follows.

... We want an end to the robbery by the CAPITALISTS of our Black and Oppressed Communities. We believe that this racist government has robbed us and now we are demanding the overdue debt of forty acres and two mules. Forty acres and two mules were promised 100 years ago as restitution for slave labor and mass murder of Black people. We will accept the payment in currency which will be distributed to our many communities. The American racist has taken part in the slaughter of our fifty million Black people. Therefore, we feel this is a modest demand that we make.

For full text see www.blackpanther.org/TenPoint.htm (accessed December 2008).

7.10 Haki Madhubuti, 'Education'

Haki Madhubuti, formerly Don L. Lee, is a poet, essayist, publisher, advocate of independent Black institutions, and major figure in the Black Arts Movement of the 1960s. Lee's *Think Black*, from which the following poem was taken, was his first published book of poetry. As the title suggests, the poems reflected Madhubuti's rejection of assimilation into White culture and his celebration of Blackness. 'Black art will elevate and enlighten our people and lead them toward a awareness of self, i.e., their blackness,' he wrote in the book's introduction. 'It will show them mirrors. Beautiful symbols. And will aid in the destruction of anything nasty and detrimental to our advancement as a people.'

I had a good teacher,
He taught me everything I know;
how to lie,
> cheat,
> and how to strike the softest blow.

My teacher thought himself to be wise and right
He taught me things most people consider nice;
> such as to pray,
> > smile,
> > and how not to fight.

My teacher taught me other things too,
Things that I will be forever looking at;
> how to berate.
> > segregate,
> > and how to be inferior without hate.

My teacher's wisdom forever grows,
He taught me things every child will know;

how to steal,
   appeal,
   and accept most things against my will.
All these acts take as facts,
The mistake was made in teaching me
How not to be BLACK.

Haki R. Madhubuti (Don L. Lee), *Think Black* (Detroit, Mich.: Broadside
Press, 1969), p. 11.

7.11 Amiri Baraka, 'Soul Food'

Poet, author, playwright, and activist Amiri Baraka, formerly LeRoi
Jones, founded the Black Arts Repertory Theatre in Harlem in the
mid-1960s and was prominent in the Black Arts Movement. His
study of African American music, *Blues People* (1963), and play,
Dutchman (1963), are credited with initiating 'the cultural corollary
to black nationalism.' In the following piece from a collection of social
essays, Baraka celebrates elements of African American culture.

Recently, a young Negro novelist writing in *Esquire* about the beauties of
America mentioned that one of the things wrong with Negroes was that,
unlike the Chinese, boots have neither a language of their own nor a characteristic cuisine. And this to me is the deepest stroke, the unkindest cut, of
oppression, especially as it has distorted Black Americans. America, where
the suppliant, far from rebelling or even disagreeing with the forces that
have caused him to suffer, readily backs them up and finally tries to become
an honorary oppressor himself.
    No language? No characteristic food? Oh, man, come on.
    Maws are things ofays seldom get to peck, nor are you likely ever to hear
about Charlie eating a chitterling. Sweet potato pies, a good friend of mine
asked recently, 'Do they taste anything like pumpkin?' Negative. They taste
more like memory, if you're not uptown.
    All those different kinds of greens (now quick frozen for anyone) once
were all Sam got to eat. (Plus the potlikker, into which one slipped some
throwed away meat.) Collards and turnips and kale and mustards were not
fit for anybody but the woogies. So they found a way to make them taste
like something somebody would want to freeze and sell to a Negro going to
Harvard as exotic European spinach.

171

The watermelon, friend, was imported from Africa (by whom?) where it had been growing many centuries before it was necessary for some people to deny that they had ever tasted one.

Did you ever hear of a black-eyed pea? (Whitey used it for forage, but some folks couldn't.) And all those weird parts of the hog? (After the pig was stripped of its choicest parts, the feet, snout, tail, intestines, stomach, etc., were all left for the 'members,' who treated them mercilessly.) Is it mere myth that shades are death on chickens? (Deep fat frying, the Dutch found out in 17th century New Amsterdam was an African speciality: and if you can get hold of a fried chicken leg, or a fried porgie, you can find out what happened to that tradition.)

I had to go to Rutgers before I found people who thought grits were meant to be eaten with milk and sugar, instead of gravy and pork sausage … and that's one of the reasons I left.

Away from home, you must make the trip uptown to get really straight as far as a good grease is concerned. People kill chickens all over the world, but chasing them through the dark on somebody else's property would probably insure, once they went in the big bag, that you'd find some really beautiful way to eat them. I mean, after all the risk involved. The fruit of that tradition unfolds everywhere above 100th Street. There are probably more restaurants in Harlem whose staple is fried chicken, or chicken in the basket, than any other place in the world. Ditto, barbecued ribs – also straight out of the South with the West Indians, i.e., Africans from farther south in the West, having developed the best sauce for roasting whole oxen and hogs, spicy and extremely hot.

Hoppin' John (black-eyed peas and rice), hushpuppies (crusty cornmeal bread cooked in fish grease and best with fried fish, especially fried salt fish, which ought to soak overnight unless you're over fifty and can take all that salt), hoecake (pan bread), buttermilk biscuits and pancakes, fatback, i.e., streak'alean-streak'afat, dumplings, neck bones, knuckles (both good for seasoning limas or string beans), okra (another African importation, other name gumbo), pork chops – some more staples of the Harlem cuisine. Most of the food came North when the people did.

There are hundreds of tiny restaurants, food shops, rib joints, shrimp shacks, chicken shacks, 'rotisseries' throughout Harlem that serve 'soul food' – say, a breakfast of grits, eggs and sausage, pancakes and Alaga syrup – and even tiny booths where it's at least possible to get a good piece of barbecue, hot enough to make you whistle, or a chicken wing on a piece of greasy bread. You can *always* find a fish sandwich: a fish sandwich is something you walk with, or 'Two of those small sweet potato pies to go.' The Muslim temple serves bean pies which are really separate. It is never necessary to go to some big expensive place to get a good filling grease. You can go to the Red Rooster, or Wells, or Joch's, and get a good meal, but Jennylin's, a little place on 135th near Lenox, is more filling, or some place like the A&A food shop in a basement up in the 140's, and you can really get away. I guess a square is somebody who's in Harlem and eats at Nedicks.

LeRoi Jones (Amiri Baraka), 'Soul Food,' in *Home: Social Essays* (New York: William Morrow & Co., 1966), pp. 101–104.

7.12 Black Theology

While also clinging to the value and utility of Christianity, attacked in some quarters as the 'religion of the oppressor,' Black Christian theologians explicated and legitimated the distinctiveness of a Black Theology.

Why Black Theology?

Black people affirm their being. This affirmation is made in the whole experience of being black in the hostile American society. Black Theology is not a gift of the Christian gospel dispensed to slaves; rather it is an *appropriation* which black slaves made of the gospel given by their white oppressors. Black Theology has been nurtured, sustained and passed on in the black churches in their various ways of expression. Black Theology has dealt with all the ultimate and violent issues of life and death for a people despised and degraded.

The black church has not only nurtured black people but enabled them to survive brutalities that ought not to have been inflicted on any community of men. Black Theology is the product of black Christian experience and reflection. It comes out of the past. It is strong in the present. And we believe it is redemptive for the future.

This indigenous theological formation of faith emerged from the stark need of the fragmented black community to affirm itself as a part of the Kingdom of God. White theology sustained the American slave system and negated the humanity of blacks. This indigenous Black Theology, based on the imaginative black experience, was the best hope for the survival of black people. This is a way of saying that Black Theology was already present in the spirituals and slave songs and exhortations of slave preachers and their descendants.

All theologies arise out of communal experience with God. At this moment in time, the black community seeks to express its theology in language that speaks to the contemporary mood of black people.

What Is Black Theology?

Black Theology is a theology of black liberation. It seeks to plumb the black condition in the light of God's revelation in Jesus Christ, so that the black community can see that the gospel is commensurate with the achievement of black humanity. Black Theology is a theology of 'blackness.' It is the affirmation of black humanity that emancipates black people from white racism, thus providing authentic freedom for both white and black people. It affirms the humanity of white people in that it says No to the encroachment of white oppression.

The message of liberation is the revelation of God as revealed in the incarnation of Jesus Christ. Freedom is the gospel. Jesus is the Liberator! ... The demand that Christ the Liberator imposes on all men *requires* all blacks to affirm their full dignity as persons and all whites to surrender their presumptions of superiority and abuses of power.

What Does This Mean?

It means that Black Theology must confront the issues which are a part of the reality of black oppression. We cannot ignore the powerlessness of the black community. Despite the *repeated requests* for significant programs of social change, the American people have refused to appropriate adequate sums of money for social reconstruction. White church bodies have often made promises only to follow with default. We must, therefore, once again call the attention of the nation and the church to the need for providing adequate resources of power (reparation).

Reparation is a part of the Gospel message ... While reparation cannot remove the guilt created by the despicable deed of slavery, it is, nonetheless, a positive response to the need for power in the black community. This nation, and, a people who have always related the value of the person to his possession of property, must recognize the necessity of restoring property in order to reconstitute personhood.

What Is the Cost?

Living is risk. We take it in confidence. The black community has been brutalized and victimized over the centuries. The recognition that comes from seeing Jesus as Liberator and the Gospel as freedom empowers black men to risk themselves for freedom and for faith. This faith we affirm in the midst of a hostile, disbelieving society. We intend to exist by this faith at all times and in all places.

In spite of brutal deprivation and denial the black community has appropriated the spurious form of Christianity imposed upon it and made it into an instrument for resisting the extreme demands of oppression. It has enabled the black community to live through unfulfilled promises, unnecessary risks, and inhuman relationships.

As black theologians address *themselves to the issues* of *the* black revolution, it is incumbent upon them to say that the black community will not be turned from its course, but will seek complete fulfillment of the promises of the Gospel. Black people have survived the terror. We now commit ourselves to the risks of affirming the dignity of black personhood. We do this as men and as black Christians. This is the message of Black Theology. In the words of Eldridge Cleaver:

We shall have our manhood. We shall have it or the earth will be leveled by our efforts to gain it.

This statement, produced by the Committee on Theological Prospectus, National Conference of Black Churchmen (NCBC), was issued at the Inter-denominational Theological Center, Atlanta, Georgia. It was adopted at the NCBC 1969 annual convocation in Oakland, California. Reprinted in Gayraud S. Wilmore and James H. Cone, *Black Theology: A Documentary History*, I: *1966–1979* (Maryknoll, NY, Orbis Books, 1993) pp. 37–39.

7.13 Twenty-Fourth Amendment (1964)

This amendment prohibited the use of poll taxes to disfranchise voters in federal elections. The Supreme Court ruling in *Harper* v. *Virginia Board of Elections* (1966) extended the principle to state and local elections.

The right of citizens of the United States to vote in any primary or other election for President or Vice President, for electors for President or Vice President, or for Senator or Representative in Congress shall not be denied or abridged by the United States or any State by reason of failure to pay any poll tax or other tax.

Passed by Congress Auguest 27, 1962. Ratified January 23, 1964.

7.14 *Heart of Atlanta Motel* v. *United States* (1964)

Title II of the Civil Rights Act, banning discrimination in public accommodations, was challenged on the grounds that Congress exceeded its constitutional authority by attempting to regulate exclusively local business. The Supreme Court upheld Congress's authority.

... [T]he power of Congress to promote interstate commerce also includes the power to regulate the local incidents thereof, including local activities in both the States of origin and destination, which might have a substantial and harmful effect upon that commerce. One need only examine the evidence ... to see that Congress may – as it has – prohibit racial discrimination by motels serving travelers, however 'local' their operations may appear ...

379 U.S. 241 (1964).

7.15 *Katzenbach* v. *McClung* (1964)

The Court applied similar reasoning to that in *Heart of Atlanta* in this companion case, finding that local restaurants also fell under Congress's authority.

... [T]here was an impressive array of testimony that discrimination in restaurants had a direct and highly restrictive effect upon interstate travel by Negroes ... because discrimination practices prevent Negroes from buying prepared food served on the premises while on a trip, except in isolated and unkempt restaurants and under most unsatisfactory and often unpleasant conditions. This obviously discourages travel and obstructs interstate commerce, for one can hardly travel without eating. Likewise ... discrimination deterred professional, as well as skilled, people from moving into areas where such practices occurred and thereby caused industry to be reluctant to establish there ...

Confronted as we are with the facts laid before Congress, we must conclude that it had a rational basis for finding that racial discrimination in restaurants had a direct and adverse effect on the free flow of interstate commerce.

379 U.S. 294 (1964).

7.16 *South Carolina* v. *Katzenbach* (1966)

In the following decision, the Court found the 1965 Voting Rights Act an appropriate Congressional action enforcing the Fifteenth Amendment.

... We here hold that the portions of the Voting Rights Act properly before us are a valid means for carrying out the commands of the Fifteenth Amendment. Hopefully, millions of nonwhite Americans will now be able to participate for the first time on an equal basis in the government under which they live. We may finally look forward to the day when truly 'the right of citizens of the United States to vote shall not be denied or abridged by the United States or by any State on account of race, color, or previous condition of servitude.' ...

383 U.S. 301 (1966).

7.17 *United States* v. *Guest* (1966)

Clearly frustrating to civil rights activists was the federal deference to local and state authorities in cases of terrorist violence against activists. Federal authorities contended that they were powerless to arrest and prosecute those who interfered with Blacks exercising their constitutional rights (see 3.10). In *United States* v. *Price* and *United States* v. *Guest*, the Court broadened its understanding of Sections 241 and 242 of the United States Code, statutes that originally had been intended to provide punishment for deprivation of rights or conspiracy to deprive someone of rights secured by the Fourteenth Amendment. These decisions provided Congress as well as federal, executive authorities a means to strike at both state and private action that violated constitutional rights. *Price* upheld the arrests and convictions under conspiracy charges of the individuals involved in the murders of Schwerner, Chaney, and Goodman. *Guest* upheld similar charges against those involved in the murder of Lemuel Penn, a US Army Reserve lieutenant colonel who was attacked and murdered by Klansmen near Athens, Georgia, in July 1964. In sum, the Court affirmed Congress's authority to address terrorist actions. The concurring opinion of Justice William Brennan reflected the thinking of two-thirds of the Justices.

... A majority of the members of the Court expresses the view today that Section 5 [of the Fourteenth Amendment] empowers Congress to enact laws punishing all conspiracies to interfere with the exercise of Fourteenth Amendment rights, whether or not state officers or others acting under the color of state law are implicated in the conspiracy. Although the Fourteenth Amendment itself, according to established doctrine, 'speaks to the State or to those acting under the color of its authority,' legislation protecting rights created by that Amendment, such as the right to equal utilization of state facilities, need not be confined to punishing conspiracies in which state officers participate. Rather, Section 5 authorizes Congress to make laws that it concludes are reasonably necessary to protect a right created by and arising under that Amendment; and Congress is thus fully empowered to determine that punishment of private conspiracies interfering with the exercise of such a right is necessary to its full protection ...

383 U.S. 745.

7.18 *Loving* v. *Virginia* (1967)

Anti-miscegenation laws (see 1.1.C) were found by the Court to be in violation of the Fourteenth Amendment.

There can be no question but that Virginia's miscegenation statutes rest solely upon distinctions drawn according to race ... Over the years, this Court has consistently repudiated 'distinctions between citizens solely because of their ancestry' as being 'odious to a free people whose institutions are founded upon the doctrine of equality.' If they are ever to be upheld, they must be shown to be necessary to the accomplishment of some permissible state objective, independent of the racial discrimination which it was the object of the Fourteenth Amendment to eliminate.

There is patently no legitimate overriding purpose independent of invidious racial discrimination which justified this classification ...

388 U.S. 1 (1967).

7.19 *Green* v. *School Board of New Kent County* (1968)

The Supreme Court's relief decree in Brown required school systems to begin immediately to desegregate; however, recognizing that full implementation might take time, allowed the schools to pursue 'all deliberate speed.' School systems in the South, in fact, pursued a variety of delaying measures such as the imposition of complex administrative procedures that stymied the transfer of minority students to White schools and 'freedom of choice' plans under which little change occurred. By the mid- to late 60s, minimal desegregation had taken place. In 1968, the Court, in throwing out freedom of choice plans, indicated that it had tired of delay. Substantial desegregation followed.

The pattern of separate 'white' and 'Negro' schools in the New Kent County school system established under compulsion of state laws is precisely the pattern of segregation to which *Brown I* and *Brown II* were particularly addressed, and which *Brown I* declared unconstitutionally denied Negro school children equal protection of the laws …

In determining whether respondent School Board met the command by adopting its 'freedom-of-choice' plan, it is relevant that this first step did not come until some 10 years after *Brown* II directed the making of 'a prompt and reasonable start.' This deliberate perpetuation of the unconstitutional dual system can only have compounded the harm of such a system. Such delays are no longer tolerable … Moreover, a plan that at this late date fails to provide meaningful assurance of prompt and effective disestablishment of a dual system is also intolerable… .The burden on a school board today is to come forward with a plan that promises realistically to work, and promises realistically to work *now* …

… The Board must be required to formulate a new plan and, in light of other courses which appear open to the Board, such as zoning, fashion steps which promise realistically to convert promptly to a system without a 'white' school and a 'Negro' school, but just schools.

391 U.S. 430 (1968).

7.20 *Jones* v. *Mayer* (1968)

Housing discrimination received a double-barreled blow in 1968 with the passage of the Civil Rights Act of 1968 and the Supreme Court's decision in *Jones* v. *Mayer*. The Court found that statutes prohibiting private acts of discrimination in housing were a legitimate expression of Congressional power under the Thirteenth Amendment.

Surely Congress has the power under the Thirteenth Amendment rationally to determine what are the badges and the incidents of slavery, and the authority to translate that determination into effective legislation ... And when racial discrimination herds men into ghettoes and makes their ability to buy property turn on the color of their skin, then it ... is a relic of slavery.

Negro citizens North and South, who saw in the Thirteenth Amendment a promise of freedom – freedom to 'go and come at pleasure' and to 'buy and sell when they please' – would be left with 'a mere paper guarantee' if Congress were powerless to assure that a dollar in the hands of a Negro will purchase the same thing as a dollar in the hands of a white man. At the very least, the freedom that Congress is empowered to secure under the Thirteenth Amendment includes the freedom to buy whatever a white man can buy, the right to live wherever a white man can live. If Congress cannot say that being a free man means at least this much, then the Thirteenth Amendment made a promise the Nation cannot keep ...

392 U.S. 409 (1968).

7.21 *Gaston County* v. *United States* (1969)

Given the record that literacy tests had been used to disfranchise Black voters, the Court prohibited their use, even when administered 'impartially.'

We conclude that in an action brought under ... the Voting Rights Act of 1965 it is appropriate for a court to consider whether a literacy or educational requirement has the 'effect of denying the right to vote on account of race or color' because the state or subdivision which seeks to impose the requirement has maintained separate and inferior schools for its Negro residents who are now of age ...

Appellant urges that it administered the 1962 re-registration in a fair and impartial manner, and that in recent years it has made significant strides toward equalizing and integrating its school system. Although we accept these claims as true, they fall wide of the mark. Affording today's Negro youth equal educational opportunities will doubtless prepare them to meet, on equal terms, whatever standards of literacy are required when they reach voting age. It does nothing for their parents, however. From this record, we cannot escape the sad truth that throughout the years, Gaston County systematically deprived its black citizens of the educational opportunities it granted to its white citizens. 'Impartial' administration of the literacy test today would serve only to perpetuate these inequities in a different form ...

395 U.S. 285 (1969).

7.22 Civil Rights Act of 1968

Racially discriminatory practices in housing were a concern of Black activists in the North. The 1968 Civil Rights Act was addressed to that concern.

SEC 801. It is the policy of the United States to provide, within constitutional limitations, for fair housing throughout the United States ...

DISCRIMINATION IN THE SALE OR RENTAL OF HOUSING

SEC 804 ... [I]t shall be unlawful

(a) To refuse to sell or rent after the making of a bona fide offer, or to refuse to negotiate for the sale or rental of, or otherwise make unavailable or deny, a dwelling to any person because of race, color, religion, or national origin.

(b) To discriminate against any person in the terms, conditions, or privileges of sale or rental of a dwelling, or in the provision of services or facilities in connection therewith, because of race, color, religion, or national origin.

(c) To make, print, or publish, or cause to be made printed, or published any notice, statement, or advertisement, with respect to the sale or rental of a dwelling that indicates any preference, limitation, or discrimination based on race, color, religion or national origin or an intention to make any such preference, limitation, or discrimination.

(d)   To represent to any person because of race, color, religion, or national origin that any dwelling is not available for inspection, sale, or rental when such dwelling is in fact so available.

(e)   For profit, to induce or attempt to induce any person to sell or rent, any dwelling by representations regarding the entry or prospective entry into the neighborhood of a person or persons of a particular race, color, religion, or national origin.

DISCRIMINATION IN THE FINANCING OF HOUSING

SEC. 805. After December 31, 1968, it shall be unlawful for any bank, building and loan association, insurance company or other corporation, association, firm or enterprise whose business consists in whole or in part in the making of commercial real estate loans, to deny loans or other financial assistance to a person applying therefor for the purpose of purchasing, constructing, improving, repairing, or maintaining a dwelling, or to discriminate against him in the fixing of the amount, interest rate duration, or other terms or conditions of such loan or other financial assistance, because of the race, color, religion, or national origin of such person ...

82 U.S. *Statutes at Large*, p. 81.

Notes

1 R. Wilkins with T. Mathews, *Standing Fast: The Autobiography of Roy Wilkins* (New York: Viking Press, 1982), p. 313.
2 M. L. King, Jr., *Where Do We Go from Here: Chaos or Community?* (New York: Bantam, 1968), pp. 38–46.
3 J. H. Cone, *Black Theology & Black Power* (New York: Seabury Press, 1969), p. 117.

8

'Oh, freedom':
contemporary expressions

Some observers of the modern US civil rights movement argue that it now lacks the tempo, focus, and impact that attended its genesis; of greater importance, they observe, is that no single, charismatic leader fills the void left by the assassination of Dr. King. On the basis of such observations, many proclaim that 'the movement is dead.' While many issues that spawned the movement remain alive and unresolved, the Movement continues to function through multiple organizations and in multiple venues. It is clear that many individuals and organizations comprised the Movement in the 1950s and 60s, and it is equally clear that today, with the resurgence and emergence of numerous collectives and individuals, as well as the work of traditional civil rights organizations, civil rights issues have been reframed, and renewed effort has been committed to their resolution.

Despite some claims that inertia characterizes the Movement, progress is being sustained on many civil rights fronts, including formerly 'segregation now, segregation forever' strongholds. Nearly half a century after Little Rock, Birmingham, and Selma, African Americans occupy a majority of the seats on the Little Rock Board of Education, and Birmingham and Selma have elected African American mayors. In fact, between the years 1970 and 2000, the number of Black officials elected nationwide increased from 1,469 to 9,040.[1] This development has made possible Barack Obama's emergence and ultimate election to office of President of the United States. Yet, as reflected in his 'A More Perfect Union' speech, critical work remains (8.1). And, of course, the civil rights arena has broadened. For the first time in US legislative history, a woman is Speaker of the House of Representatives, and, notably, headlines regarding civil rights groups are followed often by text reporting activities of the National Council of La Raza, speaking for the 'nation's largest minority population,' or by various organizations representing the

183

human rights petitions of gay and lesbian citizens and other marginalized groups.

Nor has death claimed oppositional activities of the states rights advocates and other 'night riders.' Although it is neither frequently nor publicly that 'lips drip with interposition and nullification,' considerable opposition to full citizenship enjoys a vigorous life in America as witnessed by Mississippi senator Trent Lott lamenting the nation's failure to elect the arch-segregationist and South Carolina senator J. Strom Thurmond to the US presidency when Thurmond ran as a Dixiecrat in 1948. This was also demonstrated by Senator Joseph Biden in his run-up to the 2008 election, when he reminded an audience in Columbia, South Carolina, that Delaware, his state, was a slave state that would have fought on the side of the Confederacy had it not been for geographic constraints posed by states between Delaware and the Confederacy and, further, when he reveled with the audience in the fact that they were meeting in a facility where they also could view the original copy of the Articles of Secession.[2] Such attitudes lead some civil rights activists to conclude that the battle has been joined and fought with courage and dedication and with some notable successes, but that civil rights opponents have also succeeded in installing new and more sophisticated obstructions and impediments – legal and extralegal. In short, they note that raw, unabashed, historic Jim Crow has emerged as James Crow, Esquire.[3]

Voting rights

The new civil rights agenda is in many ways a continuation of the earlier Movement's effort 'to secure these rights.' Central among these is the franchise. Although the Voting Rights Act of 1965 (**6.9**) and various Constitutional Amendments and Supreme Court decisions (**7.13**, **7.16**, **7.21**) closed the door on certain aspects of the abridgement of the right of franchise, the intervening decades have ushered in new practices intended to reinstate impediments to full suffrage for some voters. Contemporary conventions and practices that range from enacting state statutes that disfranchise convicted felons, to deliberate publicizing of misinformation, to outright intimidation of targeted, prospective voters have all served to undermine the federal law. Document 8.2 addresses such issues.

Affirmative action

Reflecting his commitment to meaningful equality of opportunity (7.2), President Lyndon Johnson issued Executive Order 11246 in September 1965, requiring firms doing business with the federal government to pursue 'affirmative action' to address the effects of past discriminatory hiring practices. The Labor Department was given responsibility for enforcement, and under its auspices, policies designed to increase the numbers of minorities and women in the workplace were pursued. These policies were expanded during the Nixon administration to cover all employers, not just those doing business with the federal government. Effectively, companies employing disproportionately few minorities were required to establish and implement plans for achieving minority numbers reflective of their proportion of the workforce. To that end, qualified minorities were accorded preference during a company's hiring decisions. Opponents of these measures argued that 'preference' was simply 'reverse discrimination,' which was equally offensive to the constitutional principle of equal protection under law. Since the 1970s, the concept has been a hot political issue, and its application has been constrained by the Supreme Court. Likely no federal policy enjoys a more complex, even tortuous, history than does affirmative action. Easily and, some charge, intentionally, misunderstood based on opponents' appeals to 'meritocracy' and racism, it is a policy that arguably has as many opponents as proponents, with each cohort professing no malice but only principled interest in fairness. Document **8.3** explores elements of the debate.

Residential segregation

Race assuredly has a significant presence in the matter of inequities in housing. Much of the literature addressing suburban residential segregation demonstrates that the numerical incidence of Blacks and other racial minorities decreases precipitously as family income increases. That economically disadvantaged Blacks and minorities are left behind in the nation's inner city has been copiously documented, especially in the literature addressing 'white flight.'

Demographer Roderick Harrison notes that home ownership is a coveted American dream that in the last century has been eroded by overt discrimination achieved and sustained through such practices as restrictive covenants, red-lining, and block-busting. Emphasizing the monumental consequences of racial segregation, he acknowledges a decline in its incidence between 1920 and 2000, although this has been less pronounced in the latest decade.[4] Barack Obama, also addressing home ownership and the related economic realities, suggests that 'More minorities may be living the American dream, but their hold on that dream remains tenuous.'[5] He calls for concerted efforts to increase enforcement of nondiscrimination laws and to devise strategies to achieve the unfinished business of closing the housing inequality gap.

Red-lining and related 'containment' practices have been ruled illegal discrimination in the nation's highest courts. Still, it is simplistic to conclude that racism alone accounts for the existing lag in Black home ownership, as researchers have also concluded that the postwar boom economy and the disparities in wage earnings between Whites and Blacks figured significantly into Whites' out-migration and Blacks' in-migration. While racism, individual personal preference, and economic status are critical factors in housing inequities, also deeply implicated in the gap and its maintenance in the twenty-first century are zoning, land use ordinances and laws, and what Angotti (**8.4**) terms 'environmental racism.'

Schooling resegregation

The Supreme Court's decision in *Green* v. *School Board of New Kent County* (**7.19**) was followed by its decision in *Swann* v. *Charlotte-Mecklenburg Board of Education* (1971) endorsing busing, the redrawing of attendance zones, and racial ratios as tools for desegregation, and a series of decisions extending these tools to *de facto* manifestations of segregation in school systems in the North and West. Busing became a political issue contributing to White flight and the isolation of racial minorities in inner cities throughout the country, a phenomenon for which an increasingly conservative Supreme Court reasoned there was no judicial remedy. Orfield (**8.5**) discusses the role of the conservative Court in abetting resegregation.

Health disparities

The National Institute of Environmental Health Sciences argues, 'affluent citizens of this Nation enjoy better health than do its minority and poorer citizens. The most striking health disparities involve shorter life expectancy among the poor, as well as higher rates of cancer, birth defects, infant mortality, asthma, diabetes, and cardiovascular disease.'[6] Where unemployment or underemployment prevail they are accompanied by varying indices of substandard housing, public schooling facilities and personnel, and by health care facilities that are generally substandard, if they are accessible. Williams and Johnson (8.6), while addressing health disparities, assert the notion that 'Health is the place where all the social forces converge.'

CBC alternative budget

Residual civil rights issues that we have addressed include political, social, and economic equity and justice as pursued in behalf of all people both by individuals and collectives. A stalwart in this effort to conserve and extend the gains of the civil rights movement is the Congressional Black Caucus (CBC). As enunciated in its mission statement, a major role of the CBC is to sponsor and shepherd legislation that secures, preserves, and advances the interests of Black and all citizens. Of note, regarding CBC's monitoring of public policy, is the annual alternative budget that focuses priorities that would better serve the interests of the disfranchised (8.7).

Global nature of oppression

African Americans and other people of color endure social and economic disparities despite the considerable progress of the modern Civil Rights Movement. Underemployment or unemployment is a predictor of residence, which in turn is a predictor of schooling and of quality and access to health care. Marable (8.8), amplifying the unyielding 'color line' posited by W. E. B. Dubois, asserts that the matter is even more complicated by the onset of global capitalism, which fosters international stratification of resources – again disadvantaging people of color. His notion is that the earlier version of 'apartheid' or separation of the races has been extended beyond our national borders to become an international phenomenon.

8.1 Barack Obama, 'A More Perfect Union'

During the presidential primaries of the Democratic Party in early 2008, candidate Barack Obama was criticized for his long-time association with an African American minister whose sermons were grounded in elements of Black Theology. In response, Obama articulated a view of race relations in the United States that recognized both Black and White grievances. In closing, he outlined a path for both African Americans and Whites toward 'a more perfect union.'

... For the African-American community, that path means embracing the burdens of our past without becoming victims of our past. It means continuing to insist on a full measure of justice in every aspect of American life. But it also means binding our particular grievances – for better health care, and better schools, and better jobs – to the larger aspirations of all Americans – the white woman struggling to break the glass ceiling, the white man who's been laid off, the immigrant trying to feed his family. And it means taking full responsibility for our own lives – by demanding more from our fathers, and spending more time with our children, and reading to them, and teaching them that while they may face challenges and discrimination in their own lives, they must never succumb to despair or cynicism; they must always believe that they can write their own destiny ...

In the white community, the path to a more perfect union means acknowledging that what ails the African-American community does not just exist in the minds of black people; that the legacy of discrimination – and current incidents of discrimination, while less overt than in the past – are real and must be addressed. Not just with words, but with deeds – by investing in our schools and our communities; by enforcing our civil rights laws and ensuring fairness in our criminal justice system; by providing this generation with ladders of opportunity that were unavailable for previous generations. It requires all Americans to realize that your dreams do not have to come at the expense of my dreams; that investing in the health, welfare, and education of black and brown and white children will ultimately help all of America prosper ...

B. Obama, 'A More Perfect Union,' Philadelphia, Pa., March 18, 2008. For
the full speech see http://my.barackobama.com/page/content/hisownwords
(accessed December 2008).

8.2 Voting Rights Act: call for renewal

David Bositis provides insights regarding tactics and strategies used
to deny or abridge individuals' and communities' exercise of the
franchise as provided for in the Fifteenth Amendment and Voting
Rights Act (VRA) of 1965. To address such practices, Bositis advocates strengthening the VRA upon its renewal.

It has been 40 years since the passage of the Voting Rights Act in 1965,
and it has fundamentally transformed southern – and American – politics. The South was, and continues to be, the focus of the black voting
rights movement both because a majority of black people live in the South
and because it was predominantly in these states that they were denied
the right to vote. Many of the changes in southern politics are astonishing
when compared with the political landscape in the South prior to 1965. A
majority of African Americans are now registered to vote and make up a
significant share of actual voters in many of these states. Across the country,
the number of black elected officials has grown more than tenfold since
1965, an increase that includes a leap in the number of African Americans
in the U.S. Congress from six U.S. House members in 1965 to 40 U.S. House
members, one U.S. senator, and two non-voting delegates in 2005.

Despite these gains, significant challenges remain. An unintended consequence of the Voting Rights Act was the birth of racially polarized voting
in the South. After 1965, as the Democratic party embraced the goals of
the civil rights movement, southern white voters shifted to align themselves
with the Republican party. A new southern politics emerged: Democrats
appealed to black voters, while Republicans attracted white voters with
appeals to traditional white southern culture and political positions. The
result has been racially polarized voting – whites overwhelmingly vote for
Republican candidates, while blacks do not

Since the shift in white voters' partisanship, southern Democratic
candidates have fared poorly despite the fact that they often could win
with a comparatively modest share of the southern white vote. At least for
the near future, the interracial coalitional politics of southern Democrats
looks endangered, as racial polarization of the vote in the South continues
to increase.

The racially polarized voting that defines much of southern politics at this time is, in certain ways, recreating the segregated system of the old South – although it is a de facto system with minimal violence, rather than a de jure system. A racially polarized party system will inevitably affect the voting rights of African Americans, and if the political parties in the South are now a substitute for racial labels, then black aspirations there will continue to be limited.

Efforts to Keep Blacks from Voting in the South

The Voting Rights Act of 1965 ended a system in which southern African Americans had been effectively disenfranchised since Reconstruction. Yet resistance to the new system has never entirely ended. Over time, as the Republican party has become the party of southern whites, and the Democratic party has become the party of blacks, Republican campaigns and political operatives have developed strategies to diminish the black vote in the South. Many of the tactics that have been employed are subtle – and often legal – rather than blunt. Tactics reported in the press include: moving polling places in black precincts after each election, including primary elections; stationing state police cars near black polling places; locating polling places in venues that make some African Americans nervous, including venues near reputed hang-outs of Ku Klux Klan members.

One of the most important strategies that southern Republicans use to diminish the voting rights of African Americans is felony disenfranchisement laws, which bar ex-felons from voting. The U.S. prison population more than doubled between 1980 and 2000, with black men accounting for about half of that growth. Tougher drug laws and mandatory minimum sentences spurred the growth in inmates, and Republicans can fairly take credit for these changes. Accompanying the growth in the prison population was a rise in the number of ex-felons, as well as parolees and probationers. As a result, the number of disenfranchised persons has increased. In Alabama and Florida, 31 percent of all black men are permanently disenfranchised; in Mississippi, one in four black men is permanently disenfranchised; and in Texas, one in five is currently disenfranchised.

If southern politics were not so racially polarized, felony disenfranchisement would perhaps be a less partisan matter. However, southern politics is, in fact, racially polarized. In the state legislatures in the South, Republicans have effectively blocked changes to these laws because such changes would increase the number of black, and presumedly Democratic, voters. In Florida, Governor Jeb Bush and his appointed election commissioners have actively sought to purge ex-felons from the registration rolls—mainly in black areas of the state. In Virginia, when Governor Mark Warner restored voting rights to several ex-felons, which is within his legal power, one Republican state legislator called for an investigation.

A second strategy that southern Republicans use to diminish the black vote, and one of questionable legality, is what they call 'ballot security' programs. Laughlin McDonald of the American Civil Liberties Union refers to them as 'the new poll tax.' Ballot security programs are inherently partisan and racially prejudiced; they are invariably aimed only at minority populations and they are used only in elections where the outcomes are believed to be very close. The 1986 U.S. Senate election between Democrat John Breaux and Republican Henson Moore in Louisiana illustrates ballot security programs in action. The Moore campaign arranged to have letters sent to all registered voters in parishes where Walter Mondale received more votes than Ronald Reagan in the 1984 presidential election. All of those parishes were black since Reagan overwhelmingly won the white vote in Louisiana that year. The letters contained intimidating language suggesting that if all of the information on the recipient's registration form was not completely accurate, and the voter attempted to cast a ballot, he or she would be guilty of a serious crime and would be prosecuted. The Moore campaign challenged the registrations of those living at addresses where the letters were returned to the sender. Before the runoff between Breaux and Moore, documents were revealed showing that a Republican National Committee official said the ballot security program would eliminate 60,000 to 80,000 names from the rolls and could keep the black vote down considerably. In the civil case that followed, GOP [Grand Old Party: the Republican Party] officials entered into a consent decree, stating that they did nothing wrong, but promised not to do it again.

The Need to Strengthen the Voting Rights Act

The organized campaigns to keep African Americans from voting continue to cast a shadow on the legacy of the Voting Rights Act and raise legitimate doubts about whether a majority of southern whites have ever genuinely accepted the 1965 legislation. They also point to the need to strengthen the VRA when it comes up for renewal in 2007.

Genuine improvement to the VRA would take the form of new provisions to the Act forbidding the kind of practices, typified by ballot security programs, that are intended to discourage African Americans from exercising the franchise. Those changes would be welcome, signaling a re-commitment to upholding the right of all Americans to cast a ballot ...

D. Bositis, 'African Americans and the Voting Rights Act: 1965–2005,' *Focus*, 33/6 (November–December, 2005), pp. 5–6.

8.3 The affirmative action debate

From its origin, affirmative action – the concept and the practice – has endured a suspect rather than respected and principled life. Friend and foe have struggled for decades to define and implement policy that at once preserves societal balance and order and serves the disfranchised in their pursuit of the nation's credo of 'liberty and justice for all.' Randall Kennedy's essay, excerpted below, frames some essential elements of the debate that still resonate today as the Supreme Court continues to restrict use of affirmative action policies.

The controversy over affirmative action constitutes the most salient current battlefront in the ongoing conflict over the status of the Negro in American life ... [Ironically] the affirmative action controversy has contributed significantly to splintering the coalition principally responsible for the civil rights revolution ...

... [T]he affirmative action debate cannot be understood without acknowledging simultaneously the force of the openly stated arguments for and against preferential treatment and the submerged intuitions that disguise themselves with these arguments. To disregard either of these features of the debate is to ignore an essential aspect of the controversy. To appreciate both is to recognize the frustrating complexity of our racial situation ...

The Case for Affirmative Action

Affirmative action has strikingly benefited blacks as a group and the nation as a whole ... These breakthroughs engender self-perpetuating benefits: the accumulation of valuable experience, the expansion of a professional class able to pass its material advantages and elevated aspirations to subsequent generations, the eradication of debilitating stereotypes, and the inclusion of black participants in the making of consequential decisions affecting black interests. Without affirmative action, continued access for black applicants to college and professional education would be drastically narrowed ...

Furthermore, the benefits of affirmative action redound not only to blacks but to the nation as a whole ... Positive externalities have accompanied affirmative action programs ... most importantly by teaching whites that blacks, too, are capable of handling responsibility, dispensing knowledge, and applying valued skills.

The Claim That Affirmative Action Hurts Blacks

In the face of arguments in favor of affirmative action, opponents of the policy frequently reply that it actually harms its ostensible beneficiaries ... The most weighty claim is that preferential treatment exacerbates racial resentments ... Given the apparent inevitability of white resistance and the uncertain efficacy of containment, proponents of racial justice should be wary of allowing fear of white backlash to limit the range of reforms pursued ... A second part of the argument that affirmative action hurts blacks is the claim that it stigmatizes them by implying that they simply cannot compete on an equal basis with whites ... It is unrealistic to think, however, that affirmative action causes most white disparagement of the abilities of blacks. Such disparagement, buttressed for decades by the rigid exclusion of blacks from educational and employment opportunities, is precisely what engendered the explosive crisis to which affirmative action is a response ... In the end, the uncertain extent to which affirmative action diminishes the accomplishments of blacks must be balanced against the stigmatization that occurs when blacks are virtually absent from important institutions in the society. The presence of blacks across the broad spectrum of institutional settings upsets conventional stereotypes about the place of the Negro and acculturates the public to the idea that blacks can and must participate in all areas of our national life. This positive result of affirmative action outweighs any stigma that the policy causes.

A third part of the argument against affirmative action is the claim that it saps the internal morale of blacks. It renders them vulnerable to a dispiriting anxiety that they have not truly earned whatever positions or honors they have attained. Moreover, it causes some blacks to lower their own expectations of themselves ...

Although I am unaware of any systematic evidence on the self-image of beneficiaries of affirmative action, my own strong impression is that black beneficiaries do not see their attainments as tainted or underserved – and for good reason. First, they correctly view affirmative action as rather modest compensation for the long period of racial subordination suffered by blacks as a group. Thus they do not feel that they have been merely given a preference; rather, they see affirmative discrimination as a form of social justice. Second ... many black beneficiaries of affirmative action view claims of meritocracy with skepticism. They recognize that in many instances the objection that affirmative action represents a deviation from meritocratic standards is little more than disappointed nostalgia for a golden age that never really existed ...

... Inasmuch as the elevation of blacks addresses pressing social needs, they rightly insist that considering a black's race as part of the bundle of traits that constitute 'merit' is entirely appropriate ...

... One thing that proponents of affirmative action have neglected to emphasize strongly enough is that affirmative discrimination is but part – indeed a rather small part – of the needed response to the appalling crisis besetting black communities. What is so remarkable – and ominous – about the affirmative action debate is that so modest a reform calls forth such powerful resistance.

Does Affirmative Action Violate the Constitution?

The constitutional argument against affirmative action proceeds as follows: *All* governmental distinctions based on race are presumed to be illegal and can only escape that presumption by meeting the exacting requirements of 'strict scrutiny.' Because the typical affirmative action program cannot meet these requirements, most such programs are unconstitutional ...

... To opponents of affirmative action, the lesson ... is that, except in the narrowest, most exigent circumstances, race can play no legitimate role in government decision-making ...

Prior to *Brown*, the Supreme Court's validation of segregation statutes rested upon the premise that they did not unequally burden the Negro ... The Court finally recognized in *Brown* that racial subjugation constituted the social meaning of segregation laws. To determine that social meaning, the Court had to look past form into substance and judge the legitimacy of segregation laws given their intended and actual effects. Just as the 'neutrality' of the segregation laws obfuscated racial subjugation, so, too, may the formal neutrality of race-blind policies also obfuscate the perpetuation of racial subjugation ...

The Need for Motive Analysis

... Whether racism is partly responsible for the growing opposition to affirmative action is a question that is virtually absent from many of the leading articles on the subject. These articles typically portray the conflict over affirmative action as occurring in the context of an overriding commitment to racial fairness and equality shared by all the important participants in the debate ... This portrait, however, of conflict-within-consensus, is all too genial ... It ignores those who believe that much of the campaign against affirmative action is merely the latest in a long series of white reactions against efforts to elevate the status of blacks in American society ... They perceive ostensibly nonracist objections to affirmative action as rationalizations of white supremacy ...

The Importance of Motive Inquiry: The Case of the Reagan Administration

A good way to begin setting the record straight is by assessing the motives of those in high public office ...

President Reagan now declares himself 'heart and soul in favor of the things that have been done in the name of civil rights and desegregation ...'
This commitment, he maintains, accounts for his opposition to affirmative discrimination ...

... But President Reagan has provided ... reasons for distrusting his explanation of his racial policies. Repeatedly his Administration has shown callous disregard for the particular interests of blacks and resisted measures designed to erode racial hierarchy. These actions include the administration's opposition (1) to the amendments that strengthened and extended the Voting Rights Act, (2) to anything more than the most cramped reading of the Civil Rights Act of 1964, (3) to creating a national holiday honoring Dr. Martin Luther King, Jr., (4) to maintaining the integrity of agencies involved in federal enforcement of civil rights, and (5) to imposing sanctions on South Africa for its policy of apartheid ...

... The Reagan Administration's policies reflect, reinforce, and capitalize on widespread feelings that blacks have received an undeserved amount of the nation's attention. Unburdened by the inhibitions imposed by public office, ordinary white citizens have expressed quite openly the feelings that color their analysis of the affirmative action issue. The Reagan Administration has expertly tapped these feelings for political gain by dint of arguments for race-blindness that are, in fact, exquisitely attuned to the racial sensitivities of the dominant white majority ...

R. Kennedy, 'Persuasion and Distrust: A Comment on the Affirmative Action Debate,' *Harvard Law Review*, 99/6 (April, 1986), pp. 1327–1346.

8.4 Contemporary residential segregation

The manifest patterns of segregation in New York City are a reflection of policies and practices that spawn and perpetuate segregation in urban centers nationally. Angotti points out how zoning as an element of land use policy, regarded as simple, informed self-interest, results in segregation of neighborhoods and schools and related public facilities.

Thanks to the fiftieth anniversary of the Supreme Court ruling in *Brown v. Board of Education*, talk this month is about segregation in the schools.
Our education administrators could easily brush off the fact that city schools remain separate and unequal by blaming residential segregation – and with some justification. After all, most students go to their neighborhood

schools, particularly students whose parents have limited resources and can't afford long school commutes. Still, our educators should acknowledge that educational apartheid is both a product of residential apartheid and a stimulus for it. Whites protect their exclusive residential enclaves to protect their privileged schools.

In 'Separate and Unequal: Racial and Ethnic Neighborhoods in the Twenty first Century,' the Lewis Mumford Center found that the income disparity between black and white neighborhoods is gaping – black incomes are 55 percent of white incomes. The disparity between Hispanics and whites is even greater.

Today the ethnic division of the city is complex. Over one third of the city's population is foreign born. The city's newest immigrant groups are much more diverse than in the past. They come from many more countries and their incomes vary more widely. They don't easily fit into the historic black/white racial categories that have dominated the U.S. since the early days of slavery. Yet they are segregated.

There are of course many reasons for residential segregation, there is no agreed upon strategy for eliminating it, and it's not obvious what integration really means. But it is incredible that in this city where those formerly dubbed 'minorities' are now the majority there is no public discussion about how the city's policies may be responsible for segregation and the inequalities that go along with it. The political establishment seems to think everyone is color blind.

One set of city policies that appears to be immune from scrutiny relates to land use and zoning.

Zoning and the City of Enclaves

The main government mechanism for exercising land use policy is zoning. In principle, zoning separates industrial, commercial and residential functions, and controls the form and density of new development. In practice, zoning has been used to separate people by income and race. Zoning by itself isn't the cause of segregation, but it codifies and reinforces segregation patterns created by discrimination in real estate, and makes it difficult to change them.

There are at least two main ways that zoning codifies segregation and inequality: by encouraging gentrification and by maintaining environmental racism.

When the city's planners propose zoning changes in diverse neighborhoods that would spur massive new housing development, as they have done in Greenpoint and Williamsburg (Brooklyn), for example, they encourage the displacement of low-income working people and people of color, stimulating the conversion of the neighborhood to an all-white upscale enclave. As neighborhoods improve and property values go up, property owners put pressures on the city to change zoning rules and allow for new development. The city's planners normally applaud such trends as evidence of healthy development, and they then bestow on property owners windfall gains by 'upzoning' sections of the neighborhood. But this kind of zoning change has a ripple effect, jacks up property values in the surrounding areas, and makes the neighborhood unaffordable to the people who now live there. The end result is income segregation, and since blacks and Latinos disproportionately fall on the lower end of the income scale, the outcome is also racial segregation. Ironically, many of the working class tenants of European descent now living in Greenpoint will be forced to move from a relatively integrated neighborhood to a lily-white suburb.

There are tried and true zoning techniques that aim to prevent this gentrification from further segregating neighborhoods. One of these, inclusionary zoning, mandates that a portion of all new residential development be affordable to people with low incomes. Alas, the City Planning Department recently opposed a proposal for inclusionary zoning in Park Slope, Brooklyn and is resisting demands for inclusionary zoning in other parts of the city.

At the same time that relatively diverse central neighborhoods are turning into yuppie enclaves, the city's planners gleefully provide zoning protections for the less diverse lower density neighborhoods in the outer boroughs. Recently recommended zoning changes in Staten Island, for example, will provide further protections to white homeowner enclaves.

Environmental Racism

Another way that zoning reinforces segregation is by allowing most of the noxious, polluting infrastructure to be located only in the city's shrinking number of manufacturing districts. The people who live and work in and near these districts are disproportionately people with modest incomes and people of color. A fascinating but little-known study by Lehman College professor Juliana Maantay (Solid Waste and the Bronx: Who Pays the Price) showed how white neighborhoods have managed to get their industrial districts rezoned for new residential development much faster than low-income communities of color. Since 1961 the city's wealthiest borough, Manhattan, converted industrial zones to residential and commercial zones the fastest, while in the Bronx, the city's poorest borough, there have been the least conversions. Prof. Maantay looked more closely at waste-related facilities in the Bronx and found that 87% of people living within one-half mile of these noxious uses are people of color. These are neighborhoods with high rates of asthma and other diseases related to noxious uses.

Since the city has no long-range plan for retaining industry, it does very little to help clean up existing facilities so they will be compatible with residential neighborhoods and continue to provide industrial jobs in those areas. Instead, the city is basically telling neighborhoods the only way they can get rid of bad industrial neighbors is to become upscale, lily-white bedroom enclaves.

What About the Suburbs?

To be fair, New York City must share the responsibility for discriminatory zoning with the suburbs. Many towns in upstate New York, Long Island, New Jersey and Connecticut require minimum lot sizes for homes of half-acre, one acre, and in some cases up to 20 acres. As a result, only the most expensive homes can be built. Since whites are disproportionately among the wealthiest homeowners, this effectively excludes blacks and other people of color. It's also no coincidence that NYC has the majority of the region's low-income public housing units.

While whites find opportunities for affordable housing in the suburbs, middle class blacks usually have a much harder time finding any housing. As reported in the Mumford Center's Separate and Unequal study: 'Findings indicate that even minorities who have achieved higher incomes and moved to the suburbs live in more disadvantaged conditions than their white peers.'

T. Angotti, 'Residential Segregation,' *Gotham Gazette* (May, 2004), www.gothamgazette.com/article/landuse/20040519/12/984 (accessed December, 2008).

8.5 School resegregation

From the mid-1970s to the mid-1990s, the Supreme Court slowly restricted the tools that district courts and school systems might use to foster integration. As a result, segregation was never fully addressed in Northern metropolitan areas, and resegregation occurred in Southern communities after court-ordered desegregation plans expired. At the same time, the Court also circumscribed affirmative action policies in language that had clear implications for the use of race as a factor in decision-making related to college admissions and pupil-placement policies in public schools. In June, 2007, with two new, conservative Justices, a sharply divided Court found unconstitutional diversity policies that used race as one of several factors in pupil-placement decisions.

The goal of integrated schools took another defeat in the Supreme Court's June 2007 decision in the Louisville and Seattle voluntary desegregation cases. A divided Court held that the goal of integrated schools remained important, but that most of the efforts now used by school districts are unconstitutional. This decision forces a revision in the plan that was a central part of Kentucky becoming the least segregated state in the nation for black students. Segregation nationally had already been increasing for black students since 1990, reversing a third of a century of substantial progress, particularly in the South, where most black students have always lived. Now segregation will increase more.

School segregation is a key part of a system of multidimensional inequality operating powerfully to undermine intergenerational mobility by black youth in an economy where higher education and the 'soft skills' of working effectively in relationships within complex organizations are decisively important in determining a student's future. Segregation by race almost always means segregation by poverty as well and it usually means segregation by teacher quality and experience, by curriculum, by level of classroom competition, by peer groups, and by differing networks of contacts and opportunities for higher education and good employment. When whites are segregated in schools, they are segregated into middle-class schools, with more qualified and experienced teachers. They are segregated into schools with high graduation rates, high college going rates, and stronger reputations with colleges and employers. Neighborhood schools mean something very different on the opposite side of the color line.

The Court's Historic Reversal

The Supreme Court has been transformed from the leading edge of civil rights work into the most hostile branch of the federal government. The basis of its recent decision is a reinterpretation of the Fourteenth Amendment's guarantee of 'equal protection of the laws.' The Amendment, the most important legal result of the Civil War, was designed to give African Americans a guarantee that they would have equal legal rights. It was not understood to prohibit positive help to blacks, such as the Freedman's Bureau, whose purpose during Reconstruction was to help make freedom real for the former slaves. When the civil rights revolution came in the 1960s, it became obvious that racial inequality and discrimination were so deeply institutionalized that treating only individual cases of discrimination would leave the status quo largely untouched. In the Voting Rights Act, in school desegregation, in college access, in affirmative action in employment, and in intensely concentrated efforts to integrate the military, it became apparent that real changes required intentional race-conscious efforts and that such efforts could work. For example, in just five years of such efforts, from 1965 to 1970, the South went from having 98 percent of black students in totally segregated schools to having more integrated schools than any other region. The Supreme Court at that time unanimously endorsed such practices.

The Reagan administration began a full-scale assault on civil rights law. The administration claimed that the Fourteenth Amendment meant that any positive action to help African Americans amounted to discrimination against whites and that the Constitution required equal treatment of individuals in a colorblind way even if that would perpetuate inequality and segregation. Under this theory, positive race-conscious efforts for integration were just as illegal as policies mandating segregation. Two of the lawyers in the Reagan Justice Department who fought for this theory were John Roberts and Samuel Alito, who recently became Chief Justice and Associate Justice, respectively, of the Supreme Court.

Why It Matters

Though it was often imperfectly implemented and sometimes poorly designed, school integration was, on average, a successful policy linked to a period of social mobility, declining gaps in achievement and school completion, and improved attitudes and understanding among the races. Before this year's Supreme Court decision, 553 researchers from 201 colleges and research centers signed a social science brief warning the Court that such a decision would compound educational inequality. An independent analysis by the National Academy of Education of the research evidence submitted by all participants in the cases concluded that the best scientific evidence supports the benefits of integration.

One critical problem of segregated schools is a low graduation rate. Almost half (46 percent) of the nation's black students and close to two-fifths of Latino students (39 percent) attend schools with high dropout rates, compared to only 11 percent of white students. Two-thirds of intensely segregated schools with zero to ten percent whites had low rates of high school completion, compared to only three percent of intensely segregated white schools. Students in these schools are exposed to a peer group environment where dropping out is the norm, while students in white suburban schools attend schools where the norm is to graduate and go to college. Measuring the likelihood that a ninth grader will complete high school in four years with a regular diploma, Christopher Swanson of *Education Week* found strong associations between the segregation level of districts and their graduation rates and between the poverty concentration in districts and their graduation rates. He found the largest racial disparities in graduation rates in the Northeast and Midwest, the areas with both the highest average graduation rates for white students and the highest level of school segregation. In the Northeast, 44 percent of black students were graduating on time from high school, compared to 79 percent of whites and 65 percent of Asians.

Regional Patterns of Resegregation

Resegregation is continuing to grow and is accelerating the most rapidly in the only region that had been highly desegregated – the South. In 2004, blacks made up 17 percent of U.S. students, but 27 percent of students in the South. African Americans were one-sixth of students in the Northeast and Midwest, and only about a twentieth in the West. The average black student in the 2004–05 school year attended a school that was 53 percent black, 14 percent Latino, and just 30 percent white – and millions were in far more segregated schools. In addition, black students often end up in schools with another educationally disadvantaged group. By 2004, they were increasingly likely to be in schools with Latinos, the only group with even larger educational problems. In the West, blacks in schools segregated from whites were typically not in all-black schools, but were in schools where, on average, there were twice as many Latinos as blacks. Thus, not only were black students segregated from most higher achieving schools, but the schools they attended had to work out the relationships and educational problems of two groups with a history of educational problems, sometimes in circumstances of community and gang conflict. The soaring Latino population of the South, now 20 percent, means that these problems will increasingly come into the heartland of African American education.

By contrast, whites are twice as likely to attend middle-class schools as blacks. The vast majority (82 percent) of white students attend schools where less than half of the student body is poor, compared to 42 percent of blacks. Resegregation will increase these differences.

While segregation declined to low points in the 1980s, it is now on the rise. Illinois, Michigan, New York, and New Jersey, whose big cities never desegregated, have consistently been among the very most segregated. However, California and Maryland have moved up dramatically. In 1968, there were no southern states among the ten most segregated, but now Alabama, Mississippi, Louisiana, and Georgia are high up on the list and all the southern states show rising segregation.

Recommendations

First, with school desegregation plans being reversed by courts, there must be an intensified attack on housing segregation, which is a powerful root of many aspects of racial inequality – including segregated and unequal schools. There has been little enforcement of the fair housing laws, and all recent studies have shown continuing discrimination in rental, sales, and financing of housing. Housing segregation is the fundamental reason why middle-class black families have their children in much weaker schools on average than middle-class whites or Asians. Serious enforcement would require increased monitoring of home sales, rentals, mortgage financing, exclusion of subsidized housing, employment discrimination by real estate firms, and racial steering by agents, as well as positive efforts to support existing integrated communities and to bring cooperation by school, housing, and municipal authorities into the balance against the forces of resegregation.

Second, communities still under court order should exercise the greatest caution in ending their court orders, since such moves could strip local authorities of any right to take actions they believe necessary to address racial separation and prepare their students for living and working in a multiracial community. Under the Supreme Court's new decision, actions to maintain integrated magnet schools that are fully permissible under a court order become illegal as soon as the order is lifted.

Third, where desegregation is forbidden by a court, local school authorities should do what they can to pursue diversity, using other measures such as geographic diversity, linguistic diversity, socioeconomic and test score diversity, and other methods. School authorities should consider that there is an overwhelming prevalence of low achievement, low graduation rates, and other serious problems in concentrated charter schools. Student transfer programs – including No Child Left Behind transfers from schools not achieving adequate yearly progress – should be run in ways that create genuine access to better schools for children in very low achieving schools, regardless of district lines. This would not necessarily produce substantial desegregation by race, but it would increase diversity on some dimensions and give real options to children trapped in failing schools.

Finally, very serious efforts must be made to equalize the most important resources, including qualified, experienced teachers and challenging coursework in segregated schools.

G. Orfield, 'The Supreme Court and the Resegregation of America's Schools,' *Focus*, 35/5 (September–October, 2007), pp. 1, 15–16.

8.6 Health care disparities

Healthcare issues are central to the quality of life, and disparities between Whites and African Americans remain marked. At issue in the following piece is the degree to which race as a socio-cultural rather than biological construct plays a role in those disparities.

The legacy of racial and ethnic health disparities suffered by African-Americans ... consistently reminds patients, health practitioners and policy-makers of the taint of America's 'slave health deficit.' Infamous health scandals like the Tuskegee Syphilis Study affect the healthcare choices of both Blacks and their providers, often against a backdrop of racist, classist and paternalist medical conduct.

Despite passage of the 1964 Civil Rights Act, numerous medical milestones, and the government's 'Healthy People' initiative to eliminate minority health disparities by 2010, African-Americans still suffer much higher disease and excess death rates than other racial groups. Infant mortality … is twice as common in Black communities … and occurs across all socioeconomic ranges …

… Blacks also report suffering from disparities in the care they receive. … [Eighty] percent of Blacks believe they receive different medical treatment and have different care options due to their race and ethnicity … The Kaiser Family Foundation's National Survey of Physicians corroborates Black patients' sentiments … Of the white physicians interviewed, 77% believed that disparities in how people are treated within the healthcare system "rarely' or 'never' happen based on factors such as income, fluency in English, educational status, or racial or ethnic background.' In the same survey 8 out of 10 Black physicians reported that the 'healthcare system at least 'somewhat often' treats people unfairly based on various characteristics, with differences particularly striking with regard to race and ethnicity.'

In … 'The Meanings of 'Race' in the New Genomics: Implications of Health Disparities Research,' investigators question: 'To what extent are health disparities the result of unequal distribution of resources, and thus a consequence of varied socioeconomic status (or racism), and to what extent are inequities in health status the result of inherent characteristics of individuals defined as ethnically or racially different?' The historic conflicts and passionate opinions surrounding this question necessitate a commitment to social justice by both patient and provider to ensure the rights, equity, access and participation of African-Americans in health care …

The confluence of race, genetics and disease in explaining African-American health status presents race as a central health culprit. The concept of 'race' has been found to be largely psychological and sociopolitical, rather than biological … False constructs of racial effects on health must be studied in order to eliminate health disparities that are largely psychosocially, historically and economically driven … Vernellia Randall … outlines nine factors through which the corolla of race affects healthcare training and delivery systems: (1) lack of economic access to health care; (2) barriers to hospitals and healthcare institutions; (3) barriers to physicians and other providers; (4) discriminatory policies and practices; (5) lack of language and culturally-competent care; (6) inadequate inclusion in healthcare research; (7) commercialization of healthcare; (8) disintegration of traditional medicine; and (9) disparities in medical treatment.

To combat such factors, accurate conceptions of race must first be academically redefined, as suggested by the American Anthropological Association (AAA) … The AAA states:

The 'racial' worldview was invented to assign some groups to perpetual low status, while others were permitted access to privilege, power and wealth. The tragedy in the U.S. has been that the policies and practices stemming from this worldview succeeded all too well in constructing unequal populations among Europeans, Native Americans, and peoples of African descent. Given what we know about the capacity of normal humans to achieve and function within any culture, we conclude that present-day inequalities between so-called 'racial' groups are not consequences of their biological inheritance, but products of historical and contemporary social, economic, educational and political circumstances.

Although many members of the medical community recognize these aspects of race, certain circles use race as a scientific variable in research, to explain disease, and as a proxy for socioeconomic class when it should be used for accurate distinctions between biomedical and sociocultural causes of illness, disease and death. If such distinctions are not made, health practitioners may continue to associate patient race and income with the practitioner's appraisal of the patient's intelligence, feelings of affiliation toward the patient, and beliefs about the patient's propensity to engage in risky behaviors and noncompliance ...

... Although dialogues of ... racial constructs may be inflammatory in some circles, a recent study by researchers at the University of Maryland-Baltimore ... assert that most contemporary, middle-class, white citizens believe that race is a biological construct and health status is negotiated by self-determination, choice, and individual responsibility – assumptions that can falsely substantiate and justify health disparities while intensifying racist medical practices and erroneous assumptions about Black health.

... Constructions detailed by ... James Jones ... suggest that: (1) racism and racist behavior toward the African-American are 'normal,' spontaneous phenomena borne of the human need to categorize things and people into de facto or de jure hierarchies of inferiority, superiority or mediocrity; (2) racism and racist behavior are sustained by pervasive, consensual, learned cultural mythologies that perpetuate strong stereotypes and influence perceptions, judgments and behaviors; (3) the majority of institutions and power brokers will tolerate or encourage strategies promoting piecemeal advancement of the African-American only if it serves majority self-interest; and (4) the daily subtleties of racism and racist behaviors are often ignored or unconsciously not 'seen' as racist because of both the aforementioned need to categorize, and a phenomenon termed 'unconscious' or 'unthinking' discrimination. Only by studying constructions of whiteness can health practitioners, administrators and policymakers understand how notions of white identity and privilege affect the health and medical arenas, often to the detriment of Black patients, their families and their communities.

K. Williams and V. Johnson, 'Eliminating African-American Health Disparity via History-based Policy,' *Harvard Health Policy Archives*, 3/2 (Fall, 2002), www.hcs.harvard.edu/~epihc/currentissue/fall2002/williams-johnson.php (accessed December, 2008).

8.7 Congressional Black Caucus alternative budget

The Congressional Black Caucus, a principal and confirmed champion of equitable distribution of the national wealth, analyzes and challenges the federal budget to bring focus to the critical importance of providing for the well being of all citizens and especially for those citizens who by socio-economic circumstances would be deprived of health, education, and welfare. Annually the CBC responds to the administration's proposed budget with one that distributes funds more beneficially for domestic programs and support while generally reducing spending.

The Congressional Black Caucus (CBC) ... recently stepped into the debate over federal budget priorities by issuing its own set of spending proposals. Guided by the theme of 'Investing in Our Future While Returning to Fiscal Discipline,' the CBC alternative budget targets a number of areas for increased spending, the cost of which would be offset by spending cuts in other areas. The CBC proposal incorporates a requirement that all tax cuts, new entitlement programs, or expansions of existing entitlement programs be budget-neutral – i.e., offset by new taxes or cuts in existing entitlement programs. According to the CBC's calculations, its budget proposal will save $10.5 billion more than the Republican budget in interest on the national debt over the next five years and will balance the budget by FY [Fiscal Year] 2011, while the GOP budget projects a deficit of $163 billion in FY 2011.

Proposals to Generate Savings

... [T]he CBC proposes to re-allocate $57.7 billion in non-defense spending. $24.5 billion would come from rescinding the tax cuts enacted in 2001 and 2003 for individuals whose adjusted gross income is in excess of $200,000 per year.

By eliminating corporate incentives for off-shoring jobs, the CBC proposes to save another $10 billion in FY 2007. According to the CBC, the tax code has a number of preferences that directly or indirectly induce American businesses to relocate operations and jobs overseas.

Closing corporate tax loopholes, abusive shelters, and methods of tax avoidance … would save another $2 billion in FY 2007. Various other provisions that close tax loopholes primarily affecting wealthy individuals and large oil companies would … [bring] the total savings for FY 2007 to $57.7 billion. By FY 2011, the annual savings that these changes would bring would grow to $63.4 billion. The total savings over the five-year period would amount to nearly $300 billion.

Programs Targeted for Increased Funding

More than half of the savings in FY 2007 – over $32 billion – would go to education. Among the key items proposed by the CBC are $15.41 billion to fully fund No Child Left Behind. Included in the full funding proposal are additional funds for Safe and Drug Free Schools, 21st Century Learning Centers, Teacher Quality Programs, Education Technology, English Language Acquisition, and Migrant Education.

Under the CBC proposal, funding for the Individuals with Disabilities Education Act would go up by $3.3 billion, school construction would receive an extra $2.5 billion, Head Start would receive $2.2 billion in new funds, and over $1.5 billion more would go toward financial aid for higher education, including more than $500 million for Historically Black Colleges and Universities (HBCUs) and Hispanic Serving Institutions. An additional $2 billion would be allocated for rebuilding and restoring public schools and colleges in the areas damaged by Hurricane Katrina.

Investments in health under the CBC plan would claim the second-largest share of the savings – more than $6 billion. This includes $1 billion to re-authorize and fully fund the Ryan White CARE Act, which focuses on preventing HIV/AIDS and caring for its victims, and $700 million for Medicare. More than $350 million in Medicaid cuts would be restored, Community Services Block Grants would receive an extra $630 million, Social Services Block Grants would get $500 million more, and programs focused on improving minority health outcomes and eliminating health disparities would gain over $300 million. Greater resources would be provided for programs that prevent violence against women, provide children with a 'Healthy Start,' support rural health activities, and assist with family planning activities. An additional $1 billion would be provided to rebuild the health infrastructure in the Gulf Coast region.

For the $3.1 billion in additional funds allocated for the administration of justice, priorities would include preventing juvenile crime and violence against women, assisting with prisoner re-entry and drug elimination programs, staffing of the Civil Rights Division of the Justice Department, and strengthening public safety and community policing programs. These increases would facilitate a greater focus on prevention and rehabilitation and an end to racial and ethnic profiling.

Spending for agriculture would grow by $2.6 billion, including additional funds for the Special Supplemental Nutrition Program for Women, Infants, and Children (WIC), HBCUs, the Department of Agriculture's Office of Civil Rights, and other agriculture programs that affect minorities and socially disadvantaged farmers. Other non-defense items in the CBC budget include increased funding for the Section 8 Housing Program, the Low-Income Home Energy Assistance Program (LIHEAP), Child Nutrition Programs, and housing programs for the elderly and the disabled.

On the international affairs front, an additional $2.3 billion would go toward foreign aid to Africa and the Western Hemisphere and toward global issues such as child survival and health, the AIDS initiative, development assistance, and family planning programs.

For defense, the CBC budget would reduce funding for Ballistic Missile Defense in FY 2007 by $9.4 billion and reallocate the entire amount to provide additional support for the troops in Iraq (e.g., protective gear) and other defense items necessary to maintain our military strength and meet our homeland security needs (e.g., port and rail security, federal air marshals, and local law enforcement and first responders) and to strengthen veterans' programs and benefits (e.g., health care and long-term care initiatives).

M. Wenger, 'CBC Offers Alternative Budget,' *Focus*, 34/4 (July–August, 2006), p. 9.

8.8 The global nature of modern oppression

'James Crow, Esquire' is a derisive reference to the contemporary countenance of Jim Crow as it functions nationally and internationally to constrain the choices and participation of the underclass. James Crow, Esquire enjoys a robust and more sophisticated life as conceived in modern laws and, as such, poses greater resistance to dismantling and ultimate extinction. In this essay, Manning Marable provides perspective on that sophistication while addressing the nature of modern oppression of people.

In 1900, the great African American scholar W. E. B. Du Bois predicted that the 'problem of the twentieth century' would be the … unequal relationship between the lighter versus darker races of humankind. Although Du Bois was primarily focused on the racial contradiction of the United States, he was fully aware that what we call 'racialization' today – the construction of racially unequal social hierarchies characterized by dominant and subordinate social relations between groups – was an international and global problem ...

Building on Du Bois's insights, we can therefore say that the problem of the twenty-first century is the problem of global apartheid: the racialized division and stratification of resources, wealth, and power that separates Europe, North America, and Japan from the billions of mostly black, brown, indigenous, undocumented immigrant and poor people across the planet.

Inside the United States, the processes of global apartheid are best represented by what I call the New Racial Domain. This New Racial Domain is different from other, earlier forms of racial domination, such as slavery, Jim Crow segregation, and ghettoization, or strict residential segregation, in several critical respects. These earlier racial formations or domains were grounded or based primarily, if not exclusively, in the political economy of US capitalism. Anti-racist or oppositional movements that blacks, other people of color and white anti-racists built were largely predicated upon the confines or realities of domestic markets and the policies of the US nation-state. Meaningful social reforms such as the Civil Rights Act of 1964 and the Voting Rights Act of 1965 were debated almost entirely within the context of America's expanding domestic economy and a background of Keynesian, welfare state public policies.

The political economy of the 'New Racial Domain,' by contrast, is driven and largely determined by the forces of transnational capitalism and the public policies of state neoliberalism. From the vantage point of the most oppressed US populations, the New Racial Domain rests on an unholy trinity, or deadly triad, of structural barriers to a decent life. These oppressive structures are mass unemployment, mass incarceration, and mass disfranchisement. Each factor directly feeds and accelerates the others, creating an ever-widening circle of social disadvantage, poverty, and civil death, touching the lives of tens of millions of US people ...

With the onset of global capitalism, the new jobs being generated for the most part lack the health benefits, pensions, and wages that manufacturing and industrial employment once offered. Neoliberal social policies, adopted and implemented by Democrats and Republicans alike, have compounded the problem ...

Not too far in the distance lies the social consequence of these policies: an unequal, two-tiered, uncivil society characterized by a governing hierarchy of middle- to upper-class 'citizens' who own nearly all private property and financial assets, and a vast subaltern class of quasi- or subcitizens encumbered beneath the cruel weight of permanent unemployment, discriminatory courts and sentencing procedures, dehumanized prisons, voting disfranchisement, residential segregation, and the elimination of most public services for the poor. Institutions that once provided space for upward mobility and resistance for working people, such as unions, have been largely dismantled. Integral to all of this is racism, sometimes openly vicious and unambiguous, but much more frequently presented in race-neutral, color-blind language.

The anti-globalization must confront this New Racial Domain with something more substantial than tired ruminations about 'black and white, unite and fight.' ...

The anti-globalization movement must be, first and foremost, a world-wide, pluralistic, anti-racist movement, with its absolutely central goal of destroying global apartheid and the reactionary residue of white supremacy and ethnic chauvinism. But to build such a dynamic movement, the social composition of the anti-globalization forces must change, especially here in the United States. The anti-globalization forces are still overwhelmingly upper middle-class, college-educated elites, who may politically sympathize with the plight of the poor and oppressed but who do not share their lives or experiences. In the Third World, the anti-globalization movement has been more successful in achieving a broader, more balanced social class composition, with millions of workers getting actively involved ...

The radical egalitarian tendency of global anti-racists speaks about inequality and power. It seeks the abolition of poverty, the realization of universal housing, health care and educational guarantees across the non-Western world. It is less concerned about abstract rights and more concerned about concrete results. It seeks not political assimilation in an old world order, but the construction of a new world from the bottom up. It has spoken a political language more in the tradition of national liberation than of the nation-state.

Scholars and activists alike must contribute to the construction of a broad front bringing together both the liberal democratic and radical egalitarian currents. New innovations in social protest movements will also require the development of new social theory and new ways of thinking about the relationship between structural racism and state power. Global apartheid is the great political and moral challenge of our time. It can be destroyed, but only through a collective, transnational struggle.

M. Marable, 'Globalization and Racialization,' *Synthesis/Regeneration*, 39 (Winter, 2006), www.greens.org/s-r/39-06.html (dated February 22, 2006).

Notes

1 Chandler Davidson, 'Renewing the Non-Permanent Features of the Voting Rights Act', *Focus*, 34/4 (July–August, 2006), pp. 1, 13–14.
2 *The Greenville News* (Nov. 29, 2006), p. 7B; (Dec.7 2006), p. 9A.

3 See Robert Hill, 'The Strength of Black Families' Revisited,' *The State of Black America 2003* (Washington, DC: National Urban League, 2003), pp. 107–150.

4 Roderick Harrison, 'The Status of Residential Segregation,' *Focus*, 29/7 (July–August 2001), pp. 3–4, 8.

5 Barack Obama, *The Audacity of Hope: Thoughts on Reclaiming the American Dream* (New York: Crown Publishers, 2006), p. 243.

6 www.niehs.nih.gov/oc/factsheets/disparity/ (accessed December 2008).

Chronology

1865 Thirteenth Amendment to the US Constitution ratified
  - slavery abolished
1868 Fourteenth Amendment to the US Constitution ratified
  - citizenship defined to include African Americans
  - equality under the law and due process protected from state actions
1870 The Fifteenth Amendment to the US Constitution ratified
  - right to vote cannot be denied based upon race, color, or previous condition of servitude
1896 *Plessy v. Ferguson*
  - Supreme Court recognizes principle of 'separate but equal,' allowing states to pass segregation laws
1909 The National Association for the Advancement of Colored People chartered
1911 National Urban League chartered
1925 A. Philip Randolph founds Brotherhood of Sleeping Car Porters
1936 *Brown v. Mississippi*
  - Supreme Court declares confessions extracted by violence inadmissible as evidence
1941 March on Washington organized by A. Philip Randolph, then called off
  Roosevelt issues Executive Order 8802 in response to threat of march on Washington
  - affirms nondiscrimination in defense and government employment and creates Fair Employment Practices Committee (FEPC) to oversee executive order
1942 Committee of Racial Equality (CORE) founded
  - advocates strategies for change based on nonviolence
1944 *Smith v. Allwright*
  - Supreme Court overturns use of all-White primary
1945 *Morgan v. Virginia*
  - Supreme Court finds Virginia state law enforcing segregation

in interstate travel a violation of the Interstate commerce clause of the Constitution

1947 Journey of Reconciliation, April 9
- sponsored by CORE, tests effect of *Morgan* decision in upper South
Committee on Civil Rights report, *To Secure These Rights*
- establishes legislative agenda for civil rights for next two decades

1948 President Truman issues Executive Order 9981, desegregating US armed forces, July 26

1950 *McLaurin v. Oklahoma State Regents*
- Supreme Court indicates that it will accept nothing less than truly equal facilities under principle of 'separate but equal'

1954 *Brown v. Board of Education of Topeka*
- Supreme Court rules that segregated public education is inherently unequal, thus violating equal protection clause of Fourteenth Amendment

1955 Emmett Till murdered in Money, Mississippi, August 28
Rosa Parks defies order to surrender her seat, sparking Montgomery Bus Boycott, December 1

1956 Southern Manifesto issued
- Southern Senators and Congressmen sign statement in opposition to Supreme Court decision in *Brown*, March

1957 Southern Christian Leadership Conference founded, January 10
Civil Rights Act passed, August 29
- first Civil Rights Act since Reconstruction
101st Airborne Division dispatched to Little Rock, Arkansas, to enforce federal court school desegregation decree, September 25

1958 *Cooper v. Aaron*
- Supreme Court applies supremacy clause of Constitution against Arkansas state attempts to block desegregation of schools

1960 Student protesters launch 'sit-in' in Greensboro, North Carolina, February 1
Student Nonviolent Coordinating Committee (SNCC) founded, April 15
Boynton v. Virginia
- Supreme Court extends *Morgan* ruling to bus terminals, finding segregated facilities for interstate passengers a violation of Interstate Commerce Act

1961 Freedom Rides initiated to test *Morgan* and *Boynton* decisions in deep South, May 4
Albany Movement launched in Albany, Georgia, November 17

1962 James Meredith enrolls at University of Mississippi, September 30

1963   Birmingham Movement, April
University of Alabama desegregated, June 11
President Kennedy delivers national address supporting civil rights, June 11
Medgar Evers assassinated, June 12
Dr. King delivers 'I Have a Dream' speech at March on Washington, August 28
Sixteenth Street Baptist Church, Birmingham, Alabama, bombed, September 15
President Kennedy assassinated, November 22

1964   Twenty-Fourth Amendment ratified, January
Freedom Summer launched, June
Civil rights workers Goodman, Schwerner, and Chaney murdered in Philadelphia, Mississippi, June 21
Civil Rights Act signed into law, July 2
Heart of Atlanta Motel v. *United States*
   – Supreme Court endorses Civil Rights Act of 1964 under commerce clause
Katzenbach v. *McClung*
   – Supreme Court endorses application of Civil Rights Act of 1964 under commerce clause even when restaurant is not directly involved in interstate commerce
Freedom Democratic Party rebuffed at Democratic National Convention, August

1965   Malcolm X assassinated, February 21
Bloody Sunday at Edmund Pettus Bridge in Selma, Alabama, March 7
Johnson delivers 'American Promise' speech in response to Selma, March 15
Selma to Montgomery march, March 21–5
Johnson delivers 'To Fulfill These Rights' speech at Howard University, June 4
Voting Rights Act signed into law, August 6
Watts section of Los Angeles, California, erupts in violence, August 11

1966   Dr. King joins Chicago Freedom Movement, January 22
South Carolina v. *Katzenbach*
   – Supreme Court endorses Voting Rights Act of 1965 under enforcement clause of Fifteenth Amendment
United States v. *Guest*
   – Supreme Court extends the protections of the Fourteenth Amendment to include conspiracies of private individuals that deprive individuals of constitutional rights, providing Congress with a tool to fight white Southern terrorism

'Black Power' introduced as a concept portraying Blacks' sense of self and self-reliance, June

Black Panther Party founded in Oakland, California, October

1967   *Loving* v. *Virginia*
- Supreme Court finds Virginia anti-miscegenation law unconstitutional under both equal protection and due process clauses of Fourteenth Amendment

Urban riots erupt in Newark, New Jersey, and Detroit, Michigan, July

Thurgood Marshall appointed to the US Supreme Court, September 1

1968   Martin Luther King assassinated in Memphis, Tennessee, April 4

Fair Housing Act signed into law, April 11

     Green v. *School Board of New Kent County*
- Supreme Court finds freedom of choice desegregation plans inadequate

     Jones v. *Mayer*
- Supreme Court finds that statutes prohibiting private acts of discrimination in housing are a legitimate expression of Congressional power under the Thirteenth Amendment

1969   *Gaston County* v. *United States*
- Supreme Court prohibits use of 'impartial' literacy tests that perpetuate Black disfranchisement

1971   The Congressional Black Caucus is formed with thirteen congressional members

Guide to further reading

Anderson, Terry H., *The Pursuit of Fairness: A History of Affirmative Action* (New York: Oxford University Press, 2004).

Arsenault, Raymond, *Freedom Riders: 1961 and the Struggle for Racial Justice* (New York: Oxford University Press, 2006).

Ball, Howard, Dale Krane, and Thomas P. Lauth, *Compromised Compliance: Implementation of the 1965 Voting Rights Act* (Westport, Conn.: Greenwood Press, 1982).

Beals, Melba Pattillo, *Warriors Don't Cry* (New York: Pocket Books, 1994).

Belfrage, Sally, *Freedom Summer* (Charlottesville: University Press of Virginia, 1990).

Belknap, Michael, *Federal Law and Southern Order: Racial Violence and Constitutional Conflict in the Post-Brown Era* (Athens: University of Georgia Press, 1987).

Berman, William C., *The Politics of Civil Rights in the Truman Administration* (Columbus: University of Ohio Press, 1970).

Biondi, Martha, *To Stand and Fight: The Struggle for Civil Rights in Postwar New York City* (Cambridge, Mass.: Harvard University Press, 2003).

Branch, Taylor, *Parting the Waters: America in the King Years, 1954-63* (New York: Simon & Schuster, 1988).

——, *Pillar of Fire: America in the King Years, 1963–1965* (New York: Simon & Schuster, 1998).

——, *At Canaan's Edge: America in the King Years, 1965–68* (New York: Simon & Schuster, 2006).

Brauer, Carl, *John F. Kennedy and the Second Reconstruction* (New York: Columbia University Press, 1977).

Brown, Cynthia Stokes, *Refusing Racism: White Allies and the Struggle for Civil Rights* (New York: Teachers College Press, 2002).

Carawan, Guy, and Candie Carawan, *Sing for Freedom: The Story of the Civil Rights Movement Through its Songs* (Montgomery, Ala.: NewSouth, 2007).

Carson, Claybrne, *In Struggle: SNCC and the Black Awakening of the 1960s* (Cambridge, Mass.: Harvard University Press, 1981).

Chafe, William H., *Civilities and Civil Rights: Greensboro, North Carolina, and the Black Freedom Struggle* (New York: Oxford University Press, 1981).

Chappell, David L., *A Stone of Hope: Prophetic Religion and the Death of Jim Crow* (Chapel Hill: University of North Carolina Press, 2004).

Cluster, Dick, *They Should Have Served That Cup of Coffee* (Boston: South End Press, 1979).

Colburn, David R., *Racial Change and Community Crisis: St. Augustine, Florida, 1877-1980* (New York: Columbia University Press, 1985).

Cone, James, *Martin and Malcolm and America: A Dream or a Nightmare?* (Maryknoll, NY: Orbis, 1991).

Countryman, Matthew J., *Up South: Civil Rights and Black Power in Philadelphia* (Philadelphia: University of Pennsylvania Press, 2005).

Crawford, Vicki L., Jacqueline Anne Rouse, and Barbara Woods, eds., *Women in the Civil Rights Movement: Trailblazers and Torchbearers, 1941-1965* (Bloomington: University of Indiana Press, 1993).

Curry, Constance, *Silver Rights* (Chapel Hill, NC: Algonquin Books, 1995).

D'Ernilio, John, *Lost Prophet: The Life and Times of Bayard Rustin* (New York: Free Press, 2003).

Dittmer, John, *Local People: The Struggle for Civil Rights in Mississippi* (Urbana: University of Illinois Press, 1994).

Durr, Virginia, *Outside the Magic Circle* (Tuscaloosa: University of Alabama Press, 1990).

Eskew, Glenn T, *But for Birmingham: The Local and National Movements in the Civil Rights Struggle* (Chapel Hill: University of North Carolina Press, 1997).

Evers, Myrlie B., *For Us, the Living* (New York: Doubleday, 1967).

Fairclough, Adam, *To Redeem the Soul of America: The Southern Christian Leadership Conference and Martin Luther King, Jr.* (Athens: University of Georgia Press, 1987).

——, *Race and Democracy: The Civil Rights Struggle in Louisiana, 1915-1972* (Athens: University of Georgia Press, 1995).

Floyd, Samuel A., Jr., *The Power of Black Music: Interpreting its History from Africa to the United States* (New York: Oxford University Press, 1995).

Garrow, David J., *Bearing the Cross: Martin Luther King, Jr., and the Southern Christian Leadership Conference* (New York: William Morrow, 1986).

Graham, Hugh Davis, *The Civil Rights Era: Origins and Development of National Policy, 1960-1972* (New York: Oxford University Press, 1998).

Grant, Joanne, *Ella Baker: Freedom Bound* (New York: John Wiley, 1998).

Griffin, Farah Jasmine, *'Who Set you Flowin'?' The African-American Migration Narrative* (New York: Oxford University Press, 1995).

Higginbotham, Evelyn Brooks, *Righteous Discontent: The Women's Movement in the Black Baptist Church,* 1880-1920 (Cambridge: Harvard University Press, 1993)

Jones, LeRoi, *Black Music* (New York: William Morrow, 1967).

Kasher, Steven, *The Civil Rights Movement: A Photographic History, 1954–1968* (New York: Abbeville Press, 1996).

King, Martin Luther, Jr., *A Testament of Hope: The Essential Writings and Speeches of Martin Luther King Jr.,* ed. James M. Washington (New York: Harper Collins, 1986).

King, Mary, *Freedom Song: A Personal Story of the 1960s Civil Rights Movement* (New York: William Morrow, 1987).

Klarman, Michael J., *From Jim Crow to Civil Rights: The Supreme Court and the Struggle for Racial Equality* (New York: Oxford University Press, 2004).

Kluger, Richard, *Simple Justice: The History of Brown v. Board of Education and Black America's Struggle for Equality* (New York: Vintage, 1975).

Kotz, Nick, *Judgment Days: Lyndon Baines Johnson, Martin Luther King, Jr., and the Laws that Changed America* (Boston:. Houghton Mifflin, 2005).

Lau, Peter, *Democracy Rising: South Carolina and the Fight for Black Equality in America Since 1865* (Lexington: University of Kentucky Press, 2006).

Lawson, Steven F., *Black Ballots: Voting Rights in the South, 1944-1969* (New York: Columbia University Press, 1976).

——, *Civil Rights Crossroads: Nation, Community, and the Black Freedom Struggle* (Lexington: University of Kentucky Press, 2003).

Litwack, Leon, *Trouble in Mind: Black Southerners in the Age of Jim Crow* (New York: Vintage Books, 1998).

Logan, Rayford, *The Betrayal of the Negro: From Rutherford B. Hayes to Woodrow Wilson* (New York: Da Capo Press, 1997).

Malcolm X, and Alex Haley, *Autobiography of Malcolm X* (New York: Ballantine Books, 1992).

Marable, Manning, *Beyond Black and White* (New York: Verso, 1995).

Meacham, John, *Voices in Our Blood: America's Best on the Civil Rights Movement* (New York: Random House, 2001).

McDonald, Laughlin, *A Voting Rights Odyssey: Black Enfranchisement in Georgia* (Cambridge: Cambridge University Press, 2003).

Meier, August, and Elliott Rudwick, *CORE: A Study of the Civil Rights Movement, 1942-1968* (New York: Oxford University Press, 1973).

Mills, Kay, *This Little Light of Mine: The Life of Fannie Lou Hamer* (New York: Dutton, 1993).

Moody, Anne, *Coming of Age in Mississippi* (New York: Dial, 1968).

Moore, Charles, *Powerful Days: The Civil Rights Photography of Charles Moore*, text by Michael Durham (New York: Stewart, Tabori, and Chang, 1991).

Nichols, David A., *A Matter of Justice: Eisenhower and the Beginning of the Civil Rights Revolution* (New York: Simon & Schuster, 2007).

Norrell, Robert Jefferson, *Reaping the Whirlwind: The Civil Rights Movement in Tuskegee* (New York: Vintage, 1986).

Olson, Lynn, *Freedom's Daughters: The Unsung Heroes of the Civil Rights Movement from 1830-1970* (New York: Scribner, 2001).

O'Reilly, Kenneth, *'Racial Matters': The FBI's Secret File on Black America, 1960-1972* (New York: Free Press, 1989).

Parker, Frank M., *Black Votes Count: Political Empowerment in Mississippi after 1965* (Chapel Hill: University of North Carolina Press, 1990).

Patterson, James T., *Brown v. Board of Education: A Civil Rights Milestone and its Troubled Legacy* (New York: Oxford University Press, 2001).

Payne, Charles M., *I've Got the Light of Freedom: The Organizing Tradition and the Mississippi Freedom Struggle* (Berkeley: University of California Press, 1995).

Powledge, Fred, *Free at Last? The Civil Rights Movement and the People Who Made it* (New York: Harper, 1991).

Robnett, Belinda, *How Long? How Long? African-American Women in the Struggle for Civil Rights* (New York: Oxford University Press, 1997).

Seeger, Pete and Bob Reiser, *Everybody Says Freedom* (New York: W. W. Norton, 1989).

Smethurst, James Edward, *The Black Arts Movement: Literary Nationalism in the 1960s and 1970s* (Chapel Hill: University of North Carolina Press, 2005).

Sokol, Jason, *There Goes my Everything: White Southerners in the Age of Civil Rights, 1945–1975* (New York: Alfred A. Knopf, 2006).

Theoharis, Jeanne, and Komozi Woodard, *Freedom North* (New York: Palgrave Macmillan, 2003).

Whelan, Charles, and Barbara Whelan, *The Longest Debate: A Legislative History of the 1964 Civil Rights Act* (New York: New American Library, 1986).

White, Deborah Gray, *Too Heavy a Load: Black Women in Defense of Themselves, 1894–1994* (New York: W. W. Norton, 1989).

Index

Note: Page numbers in *italics* refer to illustrations

Adult Armchair Education (AAE)
   161
affirmative action 185, 192–195,
   198, 199
Alabama 8, *59*, 61, *95*, 117–118,
   128–129, 145, 146, 190, 201
   see also Anniston, Alabama;
     Birmingham, Alabama;
     Montgomery, Alabama;
     Selma, Alabama
Alabama Christian Movement for
   Human Rights (ACMHR)
   104, 113–115
Alabama State College 29–30
Alabama, University of 105, 119
Alaska 145, 146
Albany Movement 102–103,
   107–109, 110–111
Alito, Samuel 200
all deliberate speed 50, *65*, 179
alternative budget 187, 205–207
American Anthropological
   Association 203
'American Promise, The' 138–141
Anderson, William G. 103,
   110–111
Anniston, Alabama 80, *93*
anti-desegregation statute 60
anti-globalization 209
anti-miscegenation 151, 178
   see also interracial marriage
apartheid 188, 195, 196, 208, 209

Arkansas 9, 36, 61
   see also Little Rock, Arkansas
Azbell, Joe 70–72

Baker, Ella 78–79, 89–91
Baldwin, James 6, 21–22
ballot security programs 191
Bankhead, John 37
Baraka, Amiri 171–173
Bardolph, Richard 3
Barnett, Ross 105
Barry, Marion 87, 130
Bates, Daisy 61–64, 66
Baton Rouge, Louisiana 51, 73
Bevel, James 87, 104, 115–116,
   130, 137
Biden, Joseph 184
Bilbo, Theodore 5, 11–12
Bill of Rights 109
Birmingham, Alabama 36,
   93–94, 103–105, 111–112,
   113–114, *116*, 183
Birmingham Manifesto 114–115
Black Church 25–26, 28–29,
   52–53, 70, 151, 173
Black nationalism 149–150, 171
Black Panther Party 150, 169–170
Black Power 148–151, 164,
   166–169
Black Theology 173–175, 188
Black Worker, The 32
block-busting 186

Bloody Sunday 129, *139*, 141
Boynton v. *Virginia* 80, 91–92
Brotherhood of Sleeping Car
    Porters (BSCP) 26, 30
Browder v. *Gayle* 72–73
Brown II 50, 179
Brown v. *Board of Education of*
    Topeka 49, 54–55, 67, 72,
    195
Brown v. *Mississippi* 43

Carmichael, Stokely 133, 150,
    166–169, *167*
Central High School 50, 61, 64
Chaney, James 127, *132*, 177
Chicago Freedom Movement 149,
    155–157
Christian love 53, 151
Citizens Steering Committee 30
civil disobedience 38, 87, 100, 163
Civil Rights Act
    1957 49, 75–77
    1964 106–107, 121–124, 195,
        208
    1968 152, 180, 181–182
Civil Rights Division 79, 206
Clark, Jim 128, 141, 142, 143
Clark, Kenneth B. 56–57
Clark, Septima 27, 40–42, *41*
Clark, Tom 11
Cold War 24, 79
Commission on Civil Rights 33,
    75, 121, 123, 124, 145
Committee on Civil Rights 33
Communist totalitarianism 24
Congress of Racial Equality
    (CORE) 27, 38, 79
Congress of Industrial
    Organizations (CIO) 12, 36
Congressional Black Caucus (CBC)
    187, 205–207
Connor, Eugene 'Bull' 104, 105
Cooper v. *Aaron* 67–68
Council of Federated Organizations
    (COFO) 126–127, 134, 136

de facto segregation 158, 186, 190
Deacons for Defense 168
debt slavery 6
Delaware 54, 184
Dennis, Dave 127, 131
detrimental effect 55
Dexter Avenue Baptist Church 51
direct action, nonviolent 28, 36, 37,
    47, 51, 53, 78, 79, 81, 104,
    149, 150
    see also mass action; mass
        movement
disfranchisement/
    disenfranchisement 3, 6, 7,
    11–14, 25, 190, 208
disparity/disparities 186, 187, 200,
    202–204, 206
Dixon, Frank M. 36, 37
Dubois, W. E. B. 187
Durr, Virginia 40, 41, 42

Eastland, James 81
Eberhardt, John Lee 20–21
Eckford, Elizabeth 61–64, *62*
Economic Opportunity Act (EOA)
    148
Edmund Pettus Bridge *139*
Eisenhower, Dwight D. 50, 54,
    64–65, 66, 76
Emancipation Proclamation 25
environmental racism 186, 196,
    197–198
Equal Employment Opportunity
    Commission (EEOC)
    123–124
Evers, Medgar 106
Executive Order 31, 33, 64, 185

Fair Employment Practice Act 34
Fair Employment Practices
    Committee (FEPC) 26, 36
fair housing 201
    see also Civil Rights Act of
        1968
Farmer, James 27, 38–40, 106
Faubus, Orval 50, 61

Fellowship of Reconciliation (FOR) 27, 38
felony disenfranchisement 190
Fifteenth Amendment 5, 27, 44, 145, 177, 189
Foreman, Clark 6, 20–21
Forman, James 102, 107–109, 110
Fourteenth Amendment 4, 7, 43, 47, 54, 55, 59, 68, 73, 177, 178, 199, 200
Freedmen's Bureau 25
Freedom Rides 36, 79–81, 98, 102
Freedom Schools 127, 135–136
Freedom Summer 126–127, 131–136
Freedom Train 41–42

Gandhi, M. K. 38, 39, 53, 87, 110, 133
Gaston County v. *United States* 180–181
gentrification 196–197
Georgia 20, 36, 145, 146, 177, 201
  see also Albany Movement
global apartheid 208–209
Goodman, Andrew 127, *132*, 177
gospel songs 26
Green v. *School Board of New Kent County* 179, 186
Greensboro, NC 78, 85–87
Grovey v. *Townshend* 44
Guyot, Lawrence 129–131

Hamer, Fannie Lou 127, 136–137
Hayes, Roland 36
Head Start 148, 206
Heart of Atlanta Motel v. *United States* 175–176
Henderson v. *U.S. Interstate Commerce Commission and Southern Railway* 45
Highlander Folk School 1, 26, 27, 40, 51
Holt Street Baptist Church 70
Horton, Myles 40
Howard University 153

income disparity 196
Individuals with Disabilities Education Act 206
inequality/inequity 49, 54, 185, 186, 196, 199, 200, 201, 209
infant mortality 187, 203
institutional racism 157–159
interposition 50, 51, 59, 117, 184
interracial marriage 8
  see also anti-miscegenation
Interstate Commerce Act 91–92, 98, 99
Interstate Commerce Commission 45, 81, 98–99

Jackson, Jimmy Lee 128
James Crow, Esquire 184, 207
Jim Crow 3
  see also James Crow, Esquire
Jim Crow laws
  cemeteries 11
  games 112
  interracial marriage 8, 10
  jails 8
  neighborhoods 9
  public entertainment 10, 112
  railway cars 8
  restaurants 111
  schools 8
  streetcars 9, 112
  taxicabs 112
  telephone booths 10
  textbooks 10
  voting 7
Job Corps 148
Johnson, Frank 129, 141–144
Johnson, Lyndon B. 106, 127, 128, 129, 136, 138–141, 148, 149, 153–155, 162, 185
Jones v. *Mayer* 180
Journal of Negro Education 76
Journey of Reconciliation 36, 47, 80
Justice, Department of 11, 33, 35, 79, 103, 104, 109, 200, 206

Karenga, Maulana 151
Katzenbach v. *McClung* 176
Kennedy, John F. 79, 105, 106, 119–121
Kennedy, Randall 192–195
Kennedy, Robert 95, 97, 98, 108, 109
Kentucky 10, 199
Kerner Commission, The 162–164
King, M.L., Jr. 1, 35, 52–53, 73, 79, 100, 103, 104, 106, 109–111, 128, 129, 149, 150–151
Ku Klux Klan 15, 66, 92, 99, 100, 101, 106, 190

Labor, Department of 185
LaFayette, Bernard 87, 128
law and order 50, 80, 99, 100, 101, 128, 141, 156
Lawson, Jim 79, 87, 88, 133
leadership styles 107
    group-centered 90, 102
    leader-centered 89, 90, 103
    charismatic 51, 183
League of White Supremacy 37
Lewis, John 79, 87–88, 95–98, 106, 129
Lewis, Rufus 30
Lingo, Al 141, 143
literacy requirement 5
Little Rock Nine 51
Little Rock, Arkansas 36, 50, 65
Liuzzo, Viola 129
Lott, Trent 184
Louisiana 4–5, 8, 10, 60, 145, 146, 191, 201
    see also Baton Rouge, Louisiana
Loving v. *Virginia* 178
Lowery, Joseph 26, 28–29
lynching 6, 14, 20–21, *20*, 155

McLaurin v. *Oklahoma State Regents* 45–47, 54
McNeil, Joe 85–86
Madhubuti, Haki 170–171

Malcolm X 150, 164–166, *165*
Marable, Manning 207–209
Marbury v. *Madison* 68
March on Washington 26, 31, 102, 106
marriage, interracial 8
    see also anti-miscegenation
Marshall Plan 152
    domestic 148, 152
Marshall, Burke 104
Marshall, John 68
Marshall, Thurgood 47, 49
Marxism 40
mass action 26, 32, 53, 104
    see also direct action, nonviolent
mass movement 51–52, 78, 103
    see also direct action, nonviolent
massive resistance 78
Medicaid 148, 206
Medicare 148, 206
Meredith, James 105
Mississippi 7, 10, 11, 36, 43, 66, 81, 105, 106, 126, 128, 129, 145, 146, 190, 201
Mississippi Freedom Democratic Party (MFDP) 127, 150
Mississippi Sovereignty Committee 85
Mississippi, University of 105
Montgomery Advertiser 70
Montgomery, Alabama 24, 26, 40, 113, *142*, 143, 144
Montgomery Bus Boycott 29, 49, 51, 53, 73
Montgomery Improvement Association (MIA) 51
Moore, Amzie 130
'More Perfect Union, A' 183, 188–89
Morgan v. *Virginia* 36, 45
Morris, Aldon D. 25, 27, 38, 51
Moses, Bob 127, 130, 131, 137
movement center 51–52, 103, 104
Muhammad, Elijah 150, 165, 166
Muste, A. J. 38

Nash, Diane 87
Nation of Islam (NOI) 150
National Association for the
    Advancement of Colored
    People (NAACP) 24, 30, 31,
    61, 100
Negro Spirituals 25–26
neoliberalism 208
New Deal 24
New Jersey 21, 149, 198
New Orleans, LA 4, 73, 80,84
New Racial Domain 208–209
Niebuhr, Reinhold 87
Nixon, E. D. 26, 30, 51
No Child Left Behind 202, 206
nonviolence 27, 37, 38–40, 87–88,
    89, 151
    criticism of 99–101, 133, 166
North Carolina 9, 11, 99, 145, 146
    see also Greensboro, North
    Carolina; Raleigh, North
    Carolina
North Carolina Agricultural and
    Technical College 85
nullification 50, 59, 117, 184

Obama, Barack H. 183, 186,
    188–189
Operation Breadbasket 159
Opportunities Industrialization
    Centers (OIC) 159

Parchman State Penitentiary 81
Parks, Rosa M. 1, 2, 24, 27, 40–42,
    41, 51, 68, 70
passive resistance 87, 100
    see also nonviolence
Patterson, John 80, *95*
Patterson, Robert 84
Peck, James 38
Penn, Lemuel 177
Plessy v. *Ferguson* 4–5, 7, 27, 54,
    55, 58, 73
Pointer, Ann 6, 18–19
police powers 4, 7, 45, 60, 73, 114
poll tax 5, 7, 12, 13–14, 34, 145,

146, 151, 175, 191
preferential treatment 192, 193
    see also reverse discrimination
Pritchett, Laurie 103, 107,
    109–110
Progressive Democratic Association
    30

racial awareness 56–57
racialization 207
Raines, Howell 109, 129, 131
Raleigh, North Carolina 78, 91
Randolph, A. Philip 26, 31–32, 53,
    106, 129
Rankin, John 37
Reagan, Ronald 195, 200
Reagon, Cordell 102, 107
Reconstruction 3, 54, 135, 190,
    199
red-lining 186
redemptive suffering 87–88
Reeb, James 129
resegregation of schools 186–187,
    198–202
restrictive covenant 35, 186
reverse discrimination 185
    see also preferential treatment
Roberts, John 200
Robinson, Jo Ann 26, 29–30, 51,
    68–70
Roosevelt, Franklin Delano 24, 26,
    31, 32, 33
Rowe, G. T., Jr. 92–95
Rustin, Bayard 27, 28, 35–38, 47,
    53, 73–74, 78, 81–85, 106,
    129

Schwerner, Michael 127, *132*, 177
segregation amendment 60
segregationists 2, 30, 50, 54, 67, 98
Seigenthaler, John 97
self-defense 99, 101, 168
Selma, Alabama 128–129, *139*,
    142–144, *142*, 183
separate but equal 27, 46, 49, 54,
    55, 58, 72, 73

separatism 149, 150, 157
sexual exploitation 18–19
sharecropping/sharecroppers 6, 14, 136
Sherrod, Charles 102, *108*
Shuttlesworth, Fred 53, 73, 74, 104
sit-ins 78, 85, 86, 90, 104, 108, 115
Sixteenth Street Baptist Church 106
Smiley, Glenn 53
Smith v. *Allwright* 11, 44
social activism 2
social conventions 6, 16–18
social gospel 40, 53
South Carolina 5, 54, 74, 145, 146
South Carolina v. *Katzenbach* 177–178
Southern Christian Leadership Conference (SCLC) 53, 73–74
Southern Manifesto, The 50, 57–58
Soviet Union 24
Steel, C. K. 53
Student Nonviolent Coordinating Committee (SNCC) 79, 80, 89, 102, 126, 128, 130
Sullivan, Leon 149, 159–162
Swann v. *Charlotte-Mecklenburg Board of Education* 186
Sweatt v. Painter (1950) 45

Talmadge, Eugene 36
Tennessee 3, 36
terror/terrorist 6, 20, 66, 73, 80, 101, 128, 151, 163, 175, 177–178
Texas 36, 44, 146, 190
theology of liberation 28, 151
Third World 24, 209
Thompson, Charles H. 54, 76–77
Thoreau, H. D. 87
Thurmond, J. Strom 184
Till, Emmitt 66
Tillman, Benjamin 5

'To Fulfill These Rights' 153–155
To Secure These Rights 26, 33–35
Truman, Harry S. 24, 26, 33
Tuskegee Institute 6
Twenty-Fourth Amendment 151, 175

United Nations 1, 41, 42, 65
United States v. *Guess* 177–178
United States v. *Price* 177

Virginia 9, 45, 54, 91, 145, 146, 178, 190
Voting Rights Act 129, 145–147, 151, 177, 180, 184, 189–191, 199, 208

Walker, Wyatt T. 25
Wallace, George 105, 117–118, 128, 129, 141, 143
War on Poverty 148, 153
Washington, Booker T. 27, 84
Watts, Los Angeles, California 148
White Citizen Council (WCC) 78, 81–85
White City Roller Skating Rink 39–40
White superiority/supremacy 3, 4, 5, 11, 12, 15, 28, 29, 66, 78, 81, 126, 167, 169, 194, 209
Wilkins, Roy 106, 129, 149
Williams v. *Wallace* 141–144
Williams, Robert F. 81, 99–101
Women's Political Council (WPC) 29, 51, 68, 69
World War II 11, 27, 36, 152, 163
Wright, Richard 14–15

Young, Whitney, Jr. 106, 129, 148, 152

zoning 186, 195–198
Zwerg, Jim 96, 97